SAMUEL PEPYS

NATIONAL MARITIME MUSEUM

SAMUEL PEPYS

PLAGUE, FIRE
REVOLUTION

Edited by Margarette Lincoln

Note on conventions

The information in the catalogue has been given as accurately as possible but some areas of uncertainty inevitably remain.

All in-text references to Pepys's diary refer to his diary of 1660–69, and quotations from it are as published in the standard edition by Latham and Matthews. Where Pepys's Tangier diary is meant, this is indicated in the text.

Dates in Pepys's diary are given in 'Old Style' but we have shown the year as beginning on 1 January. Until the Calendar Act of 1752, the year in England began officially on 25 March (Lady Day), not 1 January.

Catalogue entries have been compiled in the following order:

Title of the object is shown in red type.

Date of the object where known.

Inscriptions are given where they add to the meaning of the object.

Artist/maker/author and their dates or school or place of origin where appropriate or certain.

Media, and dimensions in mm, height × width, are given where known for paintings, miniatures and single-leaf prints.

Collection and reference number where documented. Full lender and picture credits are detailed on p. 280.

Literature. Up to four works are selected for some objects, listed in order of importance. The full reference appears in Sources and Further Reading on p. 278.

Each catalogue entry is followed by the initials of its author(s). The abbreviations are explained on p. 281.

Captions give titles of published prints, where known, in italics.

Contents

Foreword

Samuel Pepys has fascinated generations since 1825 when his diary was first published, in bowdlerized form. This exhibition brings fresh insights into Pepys's world. It underlines Pepys's career as a naval administrator and his connection with Greenwich at key moments of his life, which together make an exhibition at the National Maritime Museum eminently appropriate. It presents key objects from the material culture of seventeenth-century London and features many objects that Pepys himself owned or would have encountered.

Pepys was a remarkable man, the son of a tailor, whose rise to power owed something to circumstance but much more to his own tenacity, drive and personal charm. There could be no better guide to the remarkable events that took place in his lifetime – including some that continue to affect the way we are governed in Britain today.

Claire Tomalin has been a liberal source of knowledge and advice. Other contributors have also generously given their time and expertise to help scope the exhibition and this catalogue.

Many organizations and individuals have loaned to the exhibition and the Museum is grateful to them all, but I would particularly like to thank Her Majesty The Queen and the staff of the Royal Collection, the British Museum and the British Library, the National Portrait Gallery, and the Clothworkers' Company. We also extend our gratitude to other lenders who prefer to remain anonymous.

An exhibition on this scale is always a museum-wide effort. I wish to thank Robert Blyth, Senior Curator of World and Maritime History and Kristian Martin, Exhibitions Curator, who curated this exhibition; Matthew Lawrence, Senior Exhibitions Project Manager; our in-house design team: Vassiliki Holeva, Exhibitions Designer and Cathy Carr, Designer; and our conservation and collections management teams.

Thanks are also due to Margarette Lincoln, who edited the catalogue, to Pieter van der Merwe, the Museum's General Editor, and to the publishing team. Particular thanks go to Kara Green who skilfully project managed the publication, to Emma Lefley who sourced the images, and to the staff of the Museum's Photographic Studio who photographed many of the images for this book. The team at Thames & Hudson and Kit Shepherd, the copy editor, also deserve thanks for expertly steering the project through to completion.

Finally, the Trustees and staff of the Museum would like to record their gratitude to those who have helped with the exhibition and, in particular, the generous support of the City of London Corporation.

Dr Kevin Fewster, AM, FRSA
Director, Royal Museums Greenwich

Lenders to the Exhibition

Her Majesty The Queen
The Bodleian Libraries, University of Oxford
The Bowes Museum, Barnard Castle, Co. Durham
The British Library, London
The British Museum, London
The Burghley House Collection
His Grace the Archbishop of Canterbury and the Trustees
    of Lambeth Palace Library, London
Claydon House, The Verney Collection (The National Trust)
The Clothworkers' Company
The College of Optometrists (British Optical Association
    Museum), London
Dyrham Park, The Blathwayt Collection (The National Trust)
Trustees of the Goodwood Collection
Gordon Museum, GKT School of Medicine, King's College London
Government Art Collection
The Horniman Museum and Gardens, London
Knole, The Sackville Collection (The National Trust)
Mrs Diana MacMullen
Magdalene College, University of Cambridge
Manuscripts and Special Collections, University of Nottingham
Ministry of Defence Art Collection
Museum of London
The National Archives, London
National Portrait Gallery, London
Northampton Museums and Art Gallery
Parliamentary Archives, Houses of Parliament, London
Dean and Chapter of Portsmouth Cathedral
Board of the Trustees of the Royal Armouries
Royal College of Physicians
The Royal Institution of Cornwall
The Royal Society, London
St Olave Hart Street Parochial Church Council
The Science Museum, London
Scottish National Portrait Gallery, National Galleries
    of Scotland, Edinburgh
Vaughan Family Trust, by courtesy of the Fashion Museum,
    Bath and North East Somerset Council
Victoria and Albert Museum, London
The Wellcome Collection
Dean and Chapter of Westminster Abbey
Trustees of the Weston Park Foundation
The Worshipful Company of Glovers
Yale Center for British Art, New Haven, Connecticut

1659/60.

[shorthand] y. [shorthand]

[shorthand]

I q Axe-yard h₃ [shorthand] — ℰ Jane —

[shorthand] — 6 3 ..

[shorthand] 7 [shorthand]

[shorthand] yᵉ [shorthand]

[shorthand] ∴ [shorthand] a ¹³ 2 [shorthand]

[shorthand] Lamb. [shorthand] 2 [shorthand]

[shorthand] 2 yʸ ∴ Lawson [shorthand]

River — Monke [shorthand] q Scott:

[shorthand] Lamb.ᵗ [shorthand] 7 [shorthand] q 2 [shorthand]

[shorthand] ¹³ [shorthand] 2 [shorthand]

[shorthand]

Samuel Pepys's famous diary opens an astonishing window into the heart of the seventeenth century – that supremely interesting period of English history, when monarchy, lords and bishops were thrown out and then brought back again, when politics and religion were publicly and ferociously debated, when notable advances were made in science, when plague and fire devastated London, and when the Dutch humiliated and terrified the country by sailing up the Medway, burning part of the English fleet and carrying off the flagship, the *Royal Charles* – the most ignominious defeat ever suffered by the navy. Pepys devoted six fat notebooks containing one and a quarter million words written in shorthand to the years from 1660 to 1669, giving us a day-to-day account of what it was like for a well-educated, ambitious young Londoner with a keen eye and an appetite for knowledge, work and pleasure to live through these extraordinary times. His curiosity about the world around him was matched by a curiosity about himself: Samuel Pepys, he quickly realized, made a very good subject. And towards the end of his life he decided to make sure his diary was preserved for posterity.

The success of his arrangements for its preservation, its transcription from shorthand to longhand, and its publication – completed only in 1976 – means that anyone interested in sharing his world, his experiences and his feelings is free to do so. Pepys thought about the importance of leaving a legacy that kept your name alive after your death, and he succeeded beyond any expectations he may have had. Reading the diary, you feel he is holding his hand out to you. You become his friend.

Pepys was born in London in 1633, the son of a tailor living off Fleet Street; he lived through five reigns, from Charles I to Queen Anne, as well as the Interregnum or Commonwealth period, when Oliver Cromwell was in charge; and he died in 1703, having witnessed several regime changes and some large-scale disasters. As a child during the Civil War, he saw the citizens of London put up ramparts and forts around the whole city to keep off the Royalist army. He saw the

Claire Tomalin

Samuel Pepys,

Renaissance Man

Parliamentary soldiers deployed in the streets, and was an approving schoolboy at the execution of Charles I in 1649. A rich cousin, Edward Montagu, who was a close friend of Cromwell, fought at the battles of Marston Moor and Naseby and became a leading figure in Cromwell's government and a commander in the Commonwealth navy, helped and encouraged the young Pepys; and after school at St Paul's and college at Cambridge, he was given work by Montagu.

In 1655, Pepys married Elizabeth de St Michel, half French, not quite fifteen years old, and penniless. It was a love match, and a quarrelsome one, as both were jealous and stubborn. Pepys's health was giving trouble: he had suffered all through his childhood from a painful stone in his kidney, and when it moved into his bladder things became much worse. In 1658, he made the bold decision to have surgery to remove the stone. The operation was risky, but it was a success. Pepys could now look forward with confidence – this good outcome may have encouraged him to start on his diary. In the same year, Cromwell died and a period of political confusion followed. No one knew which direction the country was going in, whether there would be further fighting, a republic, a military government, or even a monarchy again.

Pepys's political journey had begun as a London boy who naturally supported Parliament and Cromwell, his cousin's friend and patron. The admiration for Cromwell remained – to the end of his life Pepys kept a large image of him in his album of royal portraits. In 1660, he belonged to a club that debated political subjects very freely. At the same time, Montagu, who feared that England was descending into chaos, decided he must support the restoration of Charles II. He sailed to Holland to fetch him, taking Pepys as his secretary, and promised they would rise together. He was as good as his word, and when the grateful king immediately rewarded him, making him Earl of Sandwich and a Privy Councillor, he secured a position for Pepys at the Navy Board. In this way, Pepys came to serve Charles II and his brother, James, Duke of York and Lord High Admiral. The diary makes plain that Pepys saw Charles and James as fallible men and was critical of

Edward Montagu
Oil on canvas, by Sir Peter Lely
(1618–80), c.1646.

Private collection.

their faults, but at the same time his career depended on their favour, and he served them well.

Pepys's quickness to master naval matters and his skills as an administrator meant he soon made his mark. He drew attention and praise particularly for addressing Parliament on naval matters during the wars with the Dutch. In 1673, he became Secretary to the Admiralty Board and, in the same year, a Member of Parliament. The diary records his rising prosperity, and as a man of substance he was made a governor of Christ's Hospital school in 1675, and of Bridewell prison; Master of Trinity House, the shipmasters' association in 1676; and Master of the Clothworkers' Company in 1677. But serving the Stuart kings could be a precarious business and the political upheavals of 1679 led to him being accused of 'Piracy, Popery and Treachery' and imprisoned in the Tower of London. He was forced to fight hard to save himself. After four years without employment he was dispatched by the king to Tangier to supervise the abandonment of the English colony there. This was in 1683: it was a grim trip, recorded in a much sparser diary.

The death of Charles II in 1685 brought James II to the throne. Pepys had become an MP through James's patronage and, as king, James allowed him to push through naval reforms and embark on a shipbuilding programme. But the king was increasingly distrusted as a Catholic and suspected of aiming to become an absolute monarch. In 1688, he was driven out of the country and replaced by his daughter Mary and her Dutch husband, William of Orange.

Pepys wanted no more changes: he refused to give his allegiance to William III. He withdrew from the Navy Office, lost any chance of being elected to Parliament again, and was twice imprisoned. After this he was left in peace. He was always a Londoner, with no wish to leave town; and, retired from public life, he devoted himself to his library, music and the company of learned friends. In 1694, Christopher Wren consulted with him about plans to build a naval hospital in Greenwich. In the same year the Bank of England was established, with one of his most intimate friends, James Houblon, on the board. In 1698, Whitehall Palace, which he knew so well, was destroyed by fire. In 1699, he was made a freeman of the City of London.

There was always much more to Pepys's life than naval matters. It was his good fortune to be elected to the Royal Society, a newly founded institution that brought together a set of men whose brilliance has rarely been equalled. Although not a scientist himself, he was alert to the scientific discoveries of his day, and his curiosity spurred him to acquire a telescope which he set up on his roof, and a microscope which he used in conjunction with his copy of Robert Hooke's *Micrographia*. His interest in anatomy led him to attend dissections, of dogs and of a man. He knew Hooke, Robert Boyle and the physician and naturalist Hans Sloane, who became his doctor and would perform the autopsy on him after his death. He enjoyed the conversation of the multi-talented William Petty, who proposed a national health service, education for women and decimal coinage among his many ideas, and John Wilkins (Cromwell's brother-in-law), who wrote of establishing a universal language. Christopher Wren and Isaac Newton were also well known to him. When the Royal Society published Newton's *Principia Mathematica* in 1687, Pepys's name was on the title page, as President. In old age, he set up Newton's optical experiment using prisms for himself, describing it to his friend and fellow diarist John Evelyn. To Evelyn, when he asked what Pepys was doing, he wrote one of his best remarks. 'Why, truly, nothing that will bear naming, and yet am not (I think) idle; for who can [be], that has so much … to think on as I have? *And thinking, I take it, is working*' (my italics).[1]

Pepys was a true Renaissance man, alert to every type of human activity he came across. He called himself a 'liberal genius', indicating that he would have devoted his life to the arts had he not been obliged to earn his living. Music was his greatest love, whether church music, theatre music, or music made at home: 'Music is the thing of the world that I love most', he wrote. As well as singing, he played several instruments, wind and string – flageolet, recorder, viol, violin and lute or theorbo – and composed a little. He gave musical parties and recommended that music should form part of every education.

He was also a keen and constant theatre-goer. He saw the first woman perform on the English stage, and the great actor-manager Thomas Betterton as Hamlet, 'the best part, I believe, that ever man acted'. He dismissed *Twelfth Night* as 'one of the weakest plays that ever I saw on the stage', and *A Midsummer Night's Dream* as 'an insipid ridiculous play', but probably saw botched adaptations. Nothing kept him from the theatre.

He loved paintings and commissioned many portraits. He read and collected books throughout his life, as well as prints of street songs, ballads and other ephemera. Interior decoration, the arrangement and furnishing of the houses he lived in, was another steady preoccupation: he was always improving, enlarging, knocking through, embellishing and redecorating. He had the first known loft extension set up on his roof, and the first moveable bookcases made for his library – they are now in the Pepys Library in his Cambridge college, Magdalene (see p. 247). When his wife died in 1669, he commissioned a memorial bust from the sculptor John Bushnell, who had learned from Bernini, and produced a wonderfully animated head of Elizabeth, caught as though in mid-conversation. Pepys had her installed high up in St Olave's Church, where she can still be seen.

As well as pursuing his friendships with scholars, Pepys spent his last years re-cataloguing and ensuring the preservation of his own library, in which the six volumes of his diary were placed. His household now consisted of Will Hewer, once his clerk, grown rich in his own right, and bound to Pepys by strong ties of affection; Mary Skinner, his mistress since 1670, accepted by his friends as his consort; and his nephew John Jackson. From 1701, they were all settled in Hewer's large house in Clapham, where Evelyn

helped to design the gardens – with a bowling green, ponds, walks, woods, and hedges of different heights – and Pepys's library was set out splendidly with gilded shelves, paintings on the walls, globes on pulleys, models of ships and volumes of prints and pamphlets.

All the books were to go to Magdalene, with conditions carefully laid down by Pepys that ensured no one but the Master of the college might remove any book. And there in Magdalene the diaries remained almost unnoticed until the nineteenth century, when they were transcribed and partially published. Some readers were shocked and some were snobbish in their reactions, but most were enthralled, and the historian Thomas Babington Macaulay saw their value at once.

What Macaulay seized on was the immediacy of the diary. As he put it, Pepys takes you with him so that you have the sensation you are actually walking through the streets of London at his side – whether in Whitehall and St James's Park where the king was often to be found, or through the City with its traders and apprentices, or in Piccadilly to gaze at Chancellor Clarendon's great new house being built, or to the theatres, shops and markets, or into a church to check if there were any pretty women to be seen. He takes us further, by boat on the Thames upstream to Barn Elms, or down to Rotherhithe for a family picnic, where on a spring day his wife and maid gathered cowslips, and to Greenwich and Deptford on naval business. To committee meetings, to funerals, to a wine house for lobster and sex with a girlfriend. Inside a captured Dutch East Indiaman, crammed with 'the greatest wealth in confusion': pepper, cloves and nutmegs you could walk in above the knees, silks in bales and boxes of copper plate. To Huntingdon, where cousin Montagu's great house of Hinchingbrooke looked out over the meadows, with his uncle's modest home nearby at Brampton. You can still follow the paths he took.

His account of an Arcadian walk with his father in the meadows tells us of 'seeing the country-maids milking their Cowes there (they being now at

Elizabeth Pepys
Plaster cast, after a 1672 marble original attributed to John Bushnell (c.1636–1701), 1970.

National Portrait Gallery, NPG 4824.

William Hewer Esqʳ.
Engraving, by Robert Cooper (d. 1828)
after Sir Godfrey Kneller, 1825.

National Maritime Museum, PBE9953/6.

grasse) and to see with what mirth they come all home together in pomp with their milk, and … have musique go before them'.[2]

Pepys gives us the look and feel of the world he lived in. He also gives us the people – through him we know more about men and women of many classes and conditions in the seventeenth century than we can find from any other source: from shepherds and sailors to statesmen and kings; from clerks, shop girls and servants to actresses and a countess. He does not draw formal portraits, but through single scenes and cumulative touches conveys a great deal about the people who interest him, or catch his passing fancy.

Pepys's cousin Edward Montagu is a central figure, who from the age of seventeen was Cromwell's supporter. From Montagu's decision to bring back Charles II, and take Pepys to Holland as his secretary when he fetched the king, followed Pepys's rise in life. Pepys was grateful of course. He also shrewdly observed the changes in Montagu as an earl and a courtier. From being a pious Puritan, he declared himself sceptical about all religion. He sent his sons to France to polish their manners, and spoke sharply to his wife when she remarked that she would like to marry their daughter to a good merchant – he told her that he would rather see her with a pedlar's pack at her back than marry a common citizen. And Pepys shows Montagu's pain when he was obliged to sit in judgment on old friends he had fought beside, sending them to be hanged, drawn and quartered as regicides.

Throughout the diary, 'My Lord' is praised and honoured by Pepys, but with reservations. But 'My Lady' – now the countess – was his ideal woman, gentle and good, known from boyhood when she welcomed him to Hinchingbrooke. He dined with her whenever he could, visited her when she was ill or had just given birth. She was kind to Elizabeth. She called on Pepys at his house, and he led her by the hand through the courtyard of the office so that his colleagues could see her, with the train of her dress held up by her page, and afterwards took her to Greenwich, where they rambled up the hill together. He helped her to organize her daughter's wedding in the absence of the earl. They laughed and chatted together: and she was 'My best Lady Sandwich' and 'the most excellent, good, discreet lady that ever was'.

His wife, Elizabeth, loved for her comely person, but difficult and dissatisfied, inspired him to give one of the most brilliant accounts of marriage ever written. Educated by nuns in Paris, she enjoyed reading, shopping and theatre-going. She cooked an excellent *boeuf en daube*. But she was prone to quarrel with her servants, and drove Pepys to mad jealousy by flirting with her dancing master. When angry with Pepys she said she would turn Catholic, or leave him, and once threatened him with red-hot tongs. She suffered from her periods and other pains and failed to get pregnant – Pepys sought advice about this from a group of women friends, in vain. And although he was unable to keep his hands off other women, he loved her.

Then there is Jane, their maid. She started working for the Pepyses at seventeen,[3] a country girl paid £2 a year, whose job was to do everything from cleaning grates to laundry, washing floors and clearing up meals. She sometimes shared a bed with her mistress, and Pepys records 'reading myself asleep while the wench sat mending my breeches by my bedside'.[4] He shows us a hardworking, merry, intelligent girl, who made him laugh by mimicking a neighbour, and by cutting off the long moustaches of an over-attentive carpenter working in the house. She could read, and she owned a book.

Jemima Montagu, Lady Sandwich
Oil on canvas, by Sir Peter Lely
(1618–80), c.1646.

Private collection.

When she gave notice, Pepys 'could hardly forbear weeping' and she cried, 'saying that it was not her fault that she went away'. Presently she was persuaded to return. 'This day my poor Jane, my little old Jane, came to see us again.' She was promoted to cook, taken for outings in a Navy Office boat and to the theatre. Jane saw the Great Fire first, because she was up working at midnight, preparing for a dinner party the next day. She was pretty enough to tempt Pepys – she combed his hair in the kitchen – and firm enough to keep him at bay. Will Hewer said no other maid served them so well as Jane, and years after the diary, when she was a widow, she worked for him and for Pepys again. Pepys sent her son Sam to Christ's Hospital, and by the time of Pepys's death Sam had risen to be a lieutenant in the navy.

Pepys maintained long relationships with the people who worked for him. He appointed his own clerks from the first, and they stayed with him. He took a risk with Will Hewer, whose uncle had lost his position for political reasons in 1660 and went to Pepys asking him to give the boy a chance. Hewer grew up in the Pepys household, was beaten and bullied by Pepys, fell in love with Elizabeth and became their surrogate son. He made himself a fortune and never married. Pepys appointed him his executor and in his will wrote of his 'more than filial affection and tenderness expressed towards me through all the occurrences of my life for forty years past'.

When Pepys closed his diary at the end of May 1669, believing he was in danger of losing his sight, he felt that giving it up was like a form of death, 'almost as much as to see myself go to the grave'. He was not in fact going blind but suffering from long sight and an astigmatism, then untreatable.

The diary remained unnoticed in Cambridge until 1819, when the publication of John Evelyn's diary the year before led to its discovery. The first transcription took three years, and a heavily cut version was published in 1825. It was seen at once to be of great historical interest. Further editions followed, and a second transcription was made in the 1870s. Pepys's frankness about sex was thought to make a complete edition out of the question, and only after the passing of the Obscene Publications Act in 1959 was an unexpurgated text considered possible. Two scholars, Robert Latham and William Matthews, were responsible for the definitive edition. Their heroic labours establish beyond any doubt its position as a masterpiece.

The first page of John Smith's transcription of Pepys's diary 1819.

Pepys Library, Magdalene College, Cambridge, Smith Transcription/1.

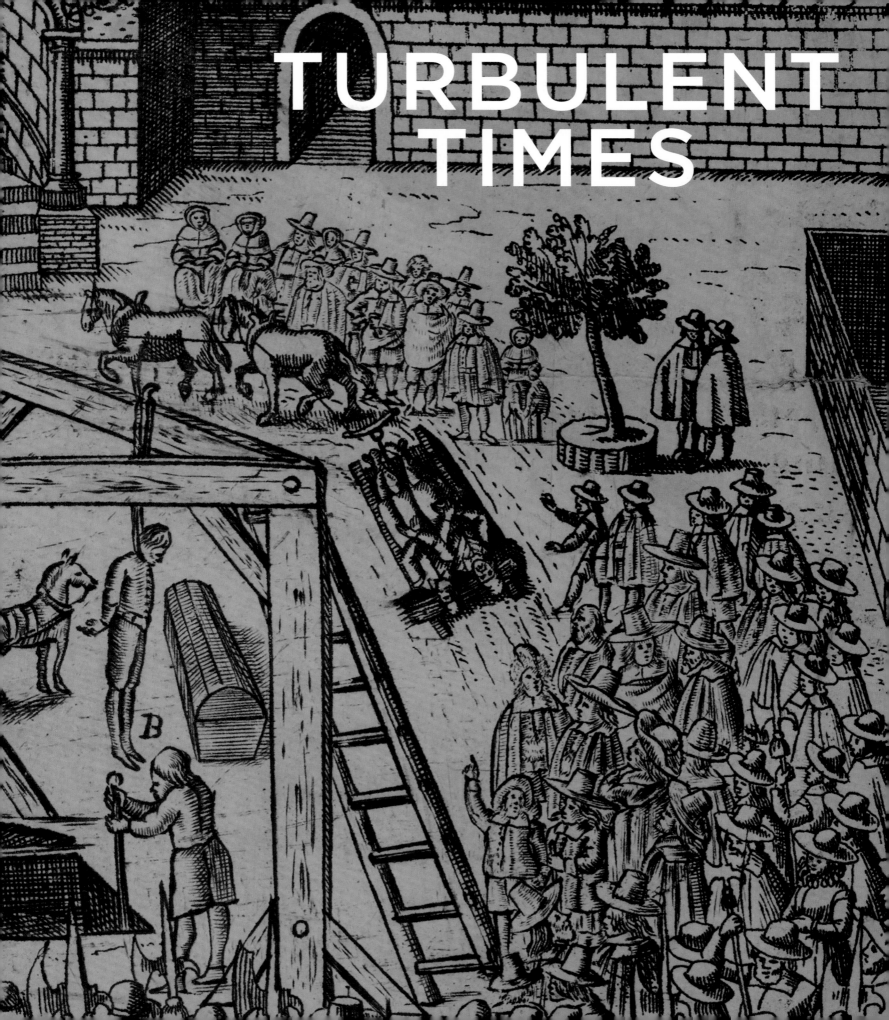

TURBULENT
TIMES

The drama of Pepys's life was in part due to his lively personality but also owed much to the extraordinary times he lived through. Pepys witnessed two revolutions, the first as a child, the second at the height of his adult career, and together these revolutions transformed English politics, religion, economics, foreign policy and public opinion. As a servant of the state, and sometimes as a focus of public attention, Pepys contributed to this larger history; but it also helped to shape his own individual story. This essay therefore sketches the wider context and times in which Pepys's life can be placed.

In January 1649, when he was fifteen, Pepys witnessed and rejoiced at the execution of King Charles I. The Civil Wars had begun in 1642 between supporters of the king (Royalists) and Parliament (Parliamentarians or 'Roundheads' as they were derisively called by their opponents). Initially the king's forces had seemed to have the upper hand; but the Parliamentarians regrouped and defeated them in 1646. A second civil war erupted in 1647 but ended, after the Battle of Preston the following year, in the capture and then trial of Charles. A 'great roundhead' at school, the young Samuel strongly took the Parliamentary side.

After the king's execution, Parliamentarians declared the creation of a republican 'free state' and 'commonwealth'. From 1649 until the restoration of the monarchy in 1660, Britain experimented with forms of republican government. Between 1649 and 1653, a 'rump' of Parliamentarians (purged of those who had hesitated to remove the king) held power, but were then briefly replaced by an assembly of the Puritan godly. That was forcibly dissolved and a Protectorate created, with Oliver Cromwell, the leading military figure, at its head. The Protectorate survived Oliver's death in 1658 when, in what was an almost monarchical succession, his son Richard temporarily followed him; but, in 1659, he was removed by the army, which restored the 'Rump' MPs. Yet relations between the Rump and the army were so poor that a military council again resumed control. Ironically, this created the conditions for the restoration of the monarchy. Early in

Mark Knights

Pepys's England: Revolutions and Transformations

1660, the general of the armed forces in Scotland, George Monck, marched south and reinstated the moderate MPs who had been excluded from Parliament, thereby paving the way for the election of a special Parliament, the Convention, that proclaimed Charles II as king.

Such an outline conveys the extraordinary shifts of political fortune and jockeying for power in and after a period of civil war, but it only goes a little way to explaining why the period 1642–60 amounted to a revolution. Identifying the factors in play is important, because they had an enduring effect for the rest of Pepys's life.

One important revolutionary force was religion – indeed, for many historians the Civil Wars are 'wars of religion'. Religious fractures had been a feature of Protestantism since the Reformation in the sixteenth century had thrown off Catholicism (or 'popery' as most Protestants dismissed it). But in the early seventeenth century, a rift had appeared within the nationally established Protestant church between different types of reformers. On the one hand, there were those, such as the Archbishop of Canterbury, William Laud, who sought to restore what he called the 'beauty of holiness' to religious worship, through an increased stress on ceremonies and an emphasis on the power of the individual to work for his or her own salvation rather than the Calvinist stress on the free grace of God. On the other hand, there were those who thought Laud's programme fell little short of an attempt to reintroduce 'popery', and they sought reform in a very different direction, by reducing the power of the church hierarchy, chiefly the bishops, and adopting a purist attitude to the Calvinism that had so influenced continental Europe's shift to Protestantism. The English Calvinists were called 'Puritans' by their enemies or 'Presbyterians' in Scotland, where the Reformation had been more vigorous than south of the border. When war erupted, the two sides split largely on religious grounds, hence the label 'Puritan revolution' that is often attached to the period. Yet the Puritans were themselves increasingly divided: between those who sought to remodel and reform the national church (and they successfully abolished the old state church in 1646),

and those who sought religious freedom outside a single, national church. In the late 1640s and 1650s, Protestant sects, as those groups which sought independent paths were called, proliferated: the Baptists, Congregationalists and Quakers, for example, flourished. By 1660, Britain's Protestantism had been fundamentally fractured.

Religious tensions remind us that it is right to talk of the mid-century revolution as a British one. Catholic Ireland and Presbyterian Scotland played key parts in triggering and shaping the war. Indeed, the revolution was the result of an almost constant interplay between the three kingdoms, which were not constitutionally united but shared the same monarch. English attempts to impose religious reforms on Scotland provoked war on the border in 1639 and the Scots defeated the English army at Newburn in Northumberland in 1640. Rebellion in Ireland in 1641, provoked again by English policies, sparked fears that Catholics would invade and ravage England, heightening anxiety about

The Execution of the Regicides
Etching, 1660–99.

British Museum, 1848,0911.405.

the 'popish' inclinations of the king and pushing the nation towards war. The revolutionary wars were thus 'the wars of the three kingdoms'. Once the monarchy had been abolished, pacification of the British Isles was enforced militarily in bloody massacres in Ireland and conquest in Scotland. Then a policy of political union could be pursued: when the Protectorate was created in late 1653, Scotland and Ireland were, for the first time, given representation at Westminster.

Other revolutionary forces also erupted to reshape the social and economic spheres. The political and religious turmoil provoked enormous public interest in 'news', and the first regular 'news papers' appeared in the 1640s. Even before the Civil Wars began, the government lost control of its ability to restrict the press, unleashing a flood of highly charged print that provided a forum for vituperative debate. Political and religious revolution led to heated ideological exchanges in print that created something like 'public opinion', or at least a very fractured and fractious version of it.

War also changed the state and its money-raising abilities. One of the problems that neither the Tudors nor the early Stuarts, James I and Charles I, had resolved was how to raise sufficient taxes to wage the expensive type of war that larger and more sophisticated armies and navies necessitated. The problem was cracked by Parliament in the 1640s, with the introduction of the excise tax and monthly assessments. The Commonwealth was thus associated with high taxes as well as with repeated purges of those who held office and the intrusion into government of men from outside the traditional ruling class. The expanded state also flexed its muscles. Whereas England had largely avoided continental war under the early Stuart kings, Cromwell sought a more expansive, even aggressive, foreign policy. Although the Dutch were fellow republicans and Protestants, war was declared in 1652 when Cromwell and his advisers felt the Dutch had ignored their overtures and threatened English trading interests: they were bad republicans and bad Protestants, who needed teaching a lesson. The First Anglo-Dutch War ended in 1654, but this was only the opening

round of a longer-lasting struggle. Cromwell then swung English military force against the Catholic Spanish, seizing Jamaica in 1655, thereby laying the foundations of British power in the West Indies. Britain increasingly had colonial ambitions.

When Pepys began his diary in January 1660, he was thus doing so at a highly charged moment of transition, from a republican back to a monarchical regime. The restoration of the monarchy was accompanied by an attempt to repress many of the disruptive revolutionary forces just outlined. A general election in 1661 returned a majority of MPs intent on revenge rather than reconciliation. Those held to be responsible for killing the king (the 'regicides') were tried and executed. A Sedition Act tightened definitions of treason and the Militia Act returned the sole right to raise armed forces to the king, who was also given back power over when Parliament sat. The national state church was restored, and not only were the Protestant sectarians, associated so closely with the forces of rebellion, excluded from it, but they were also penalized if they worshipped independently. In a series of repressive laws passed between 1662 and 1665, an attempt was made to restore religious unity by punishing 'dissenters' or 'nonconformists' who would not worship in the state church. Over 2,000 ministers, with thousands more followers (especially in urban areas), went underground, preaching in secret; and local office-holding was restricted to members of the re-established church.

There were other attempts to put the genie back in the bottle. The freedom of the press, which had poured print on to the streets during 1659–60, was again subjected to governmental supervision: officially, authors now needed a licence to publish their works, and the number of printing presses was restricted. Measures were also brought against mass petitioning, a weapon mobilizing public opinion that many Royalists believed had contributed to the outbreak of civil war in 1642. The House of Lords, abolished in 1649 with the king, was restored, and the union with Scotland and Ireland was dissolved.

Edoardus Hide [Edward Hyde,
1st Earl of Clarendon]
Engraving, by David Loggan, 1666.

National Maritime Museum, PBE9953/6.

Not everyone was happy with the attempt to turn the clock back to pre-1642: indeed, after the initial and genuinely popular enthusiasm for the Restoration, it sometimes seemed that few continued to support it. The republicans and dissenters, of course, were alienated, but that was to be expected. More worryingly, in 1662 the king himself attempted (unsuccessfully) to moderate the strict terms of the religious settlement. Many ex-Royalists were also disgruntled that their estates, sold to pay fines or confiscated by the Parliamentarian regime, were so difficult to recover, and that some who had complied or even collaborated with the Commonwealth had retained their offices, both locally and in London. A Second Anglo-Dutch War (1665–67), fought now as an ideological battle by a monarchical regime against a destabilizing republic on England's doorstep, went disastrously wrong. There was some success in North America, where New Amsterdam was captured in peacetime in 1664 and renamed New York after Charles II's brother, James, Duke of York, but the naval war was a humiliation, with the French joining the Dutch against England in 1666. The sense of disaster was heightened by plague in 1665 and the Great Fire of London in 1666. All this produced a coalition of critics that turned on Charles II's chief adviser, Edward Hyde, Earl of Clarendon, who was brought down in 1668 and fled the country to avoid Parliamentary prosecution. Pepys, too, was caught up in this maelstrom: as a rising navy official he had an uncomfortable time helping to explain why the naval war had gone so badly wrong (as well as avoiding embarrassing questions about how much money he had made out of his office).

The period between the end of Pepys's diary in 1669 and the revolution of 1688 showed not only how little the Restoration settlement had actually settled but also how closely Pepys's own career was now intertwined with larger national forces. These created another period of instability. A third war with the Dutch in 1672–74 was more successful militarily, but the Dutch fought a skilful propaganda campaign that undermined trust in Charles II's government. Although the king did find a minister in Thomas Osborne, Earl of Danby, who was able to appeal to those Royalists who were strong adherents of the restored Church of England and dominate Parliament between 1673 and 1678, the hold on power of the 'prime minister' (the first to be called as much) was always somewhat precarious. The revelation in late 1678 of the 'Popish Plot', an alleged conspiracy to re-introduce Catholicism, blew away his control (and also landed Pepys in prison, on suspicion of complicity in it).

Indeed, many observers thought that Britain again came close to civil war during the crisis of 1678–81 and feared that revolutionary ideologies were being recycled. Part of the agitation revolved around the heir to the throne, Charles II's brother James, who had converted to Catholicism, and there were attempts to exclude him from the succession; but the crisis was much wider, exposing deep ideological divisions over the constitution, religion, foreign policy and the nature of public debate. The closing years of Charles II's reign witnessed a clamp-down (in which Pepys played a part) on perceived radicalism and this had some

success. Although there was a popular rebellion in 1685 at the start of James II's reign, headed by Charles II's illegitimate son, the Duke of Monmouth, it was limited to the West Country and relatively easily suppressed. Yet three years later, James II lost his throne in what became known as the 'Glorious Revolution'.

Many of the factors underlying this period of turbulence were the same as those that had contributed to the earlier, mid-century revolution. The first of these was religion. From the late 1660s onwards, there was a series of attempts to relax the boundaries of the national church, so that moderate dissenters could worship within it, and to give freedom of worship to those who still could not conform. Defenders of the re-established church fought these proposals vigorously, and there were periods of tension, particularly during the early 1680s, when dissenters were prosecuted in large numbers.

The role of dissent had become more controversial because of the rise of anti-popery: as fears of resurgent Catholicism took hold at home and abroad, so desire for Protestant unity against the Catholic threat increased and prompted calls for the exclusive Restoration settlement to be unpicked. Ironically, it was the Catholic James II who came closest to achieving religious toleration. He threw a cat among the pigeons by trying to form an alliance between Catholics and Protestant dissenters, since both groups wanted freedom of worship.

The domestic concerns about 'popery' stemmed from Charles II's attempt in 1672 to give limited freedom of worship to Catholics as well as Protestant dissenters; from James II's conversion to Catholicism and subsequent refusal, in 1673, to conform to the established Protestant church; from the so-called Popish Plot; and from James II's explicitly catholicizing agenda as king. But they were also strengthened by the growing threat from the greatest Catholic force in Europe, Louis XIV's France. Contemporaries were alarmed that in the Third Anglo-Dutch War (1672–74) England had sided with Catholic France against Protestant Holland (French advances were only stemmed when the Dutch deliberately flooded their own country). Moreover, during

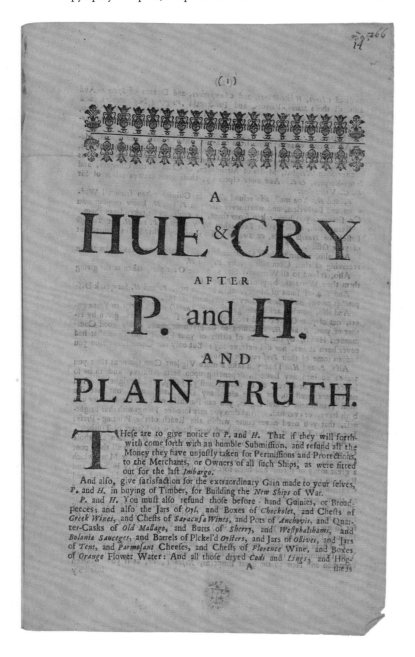

A Hue & Cry after P. and H. and Plain Truth
(London, 1679).
This attack on Pepys and his friend Will Hewer, accusing them of corruption, was published during the Popish Plot.

National Maritime Museum, PBE9983.

25

the 1670s, Parliament encouraged the king to break with Louis and even paid for forces to be raised against France; but Charles II failed to declare war, prompting suspicions that he too might be tainted with 'popery'. James II's continued adherence to Louis XIV, even when the latter began persecuting French Protestants (many of whom fled to London, bringing their silk-weaving skills with them), further heightened the alarm both in England and in Holland, where William of Orange, who had married James II's daughter Mary, was desperate for English support against what he thought was self-evidently a common enemy. William's invasion of England and seizure of James's throne in November 1688 was in large part an attempt to guarantee that English resources were finally turned against France.

Charles II's and James II's friendship with France led some to believe that they admired Louis XIV's authoritarian form of rule as well as his religion. 'Popery' thus became intrinsically linked to fears about the growth of 'arbitrary government', that is to say, government subject to the king's will rather than to the law. Critics pointed to Danby's deliberate manipulation of Parliament (buying MPs' loyalties in ways that dwarf current scandals about Parliamentary standards); to Charles II's ridding himself of Parliament in 1681 after it had sat just a week; to his revocation of charter rights that lay at the heart of local government in England and its colonies; and to James II's high-handed suspension of the religious legislation enacted at the Restoration in order to achieve his goal of toleration. Even more worryingly for the critics, James II was becoming increasingly financially independent of Parliament. Charles II had fought a constant battle with debt (in no way helped by the Anglo-Dutch Wars), and although there were important financial reforms towards the end of his reign, it was not until an economic boom in the mid-1680s that crown finances began to look healthy. But that raised the alarming question: if the king did not need Parliament for money, might he dispense with it altogether, or at least simply ignore its wishes?

Just as the mid-century revolution had highlighted the power of public opinion and the press, so too did the turbulent 1670s and 1680s. During the 1670s, Dutch propaganda and then illegally published English material debated the growth of popery and arbitrary government. In 1679, in the aftermath of the Popish Plot, the legislation restricting the press lapsed and another burst of energetic printed discussion took place, although the government regained some control in the mid-1680s. That printed debate, together with growing divisions among MPs over the constitutional, religious and foreign policy issues of the day, led to the emergence of two-party politics. In 1681 the names Whig and Tory were coined to denote the two parties. Each was a term of abuse. A Whig was a Scottish (and hence Puritan) rebel; a Tory was an Irish (and hence Catholic) thief. The application of the two labels reinforced the continuing destabilizing effect on England of the other two kingdoms. James II's build-up of a Catholic army, part of it stationed in Ireland, increased fears about his intentions, and James also used his Stuart ancestry to build up a power base in Scotland.

The Royall Orange Tree Or a thankfull remembrance of Gods mercifull Deliverance ... by the Prudent conduct of his Illustrious Highness the Prince of Orange now our Gracious King
Engraving, published by Randall Taylor, 1691.
This engraving celebrates William's martial prowess (each of the roundels depicts a victorious episode in the defeat of James II's forces).

British Museum, Y,1.125.

James II
Oil on canvas, by Nicolas de Largillière
(1656–1746), c.1686.

National Maritime Museum, BHC2798.

Pepys was very closely associated with James when the latter was Lord High Admiral during Charles II's reign and then when he succeeded to the throne. An efficient and strong navy was a key part of both Charles II's and James II's foreign policy. Moreover, as a loyal MP, Pepys supported James II's domestic policies, including the king's declarations of 1687 and 1688 signalling his commitment to freedom of worship. The revolution of 1688 was thus a personal as well as a national one. Pepys was once more arrested and never again held government office.

The second revolution did address a number of the destabilizing factors that had bedevilled Britain since Pepys's birth. The Toleration Act of 1689 introduced a measure of freedom of worship for Protestant dissenters, though it excluded Catholics, atheists and those who denied the Trinity from its provisions. The Corporation Act still officially restricted local office-holding to members of the Church of England, but its provisions were often evaded by dissenters taking communion once a year at their parish churches. The growth of popery was also contained by the war that William III launched against France and against James II's forces in Ireland and Scotland (William of Orange had taken the crown, jointly with his wife, in 1689). The depiction in Belfast murals of King Billy on his white charger is a legacy of the forcible suppression of the Catholic forces in Ireland, just as the contemporary debate about Scottish independence is a legacy of the 1707 Union that tied the countries together in order to provide security for a Protestant succession.

The revolution also enacted measures against arbitrary government. Parliamentary elections were, from 1694, mandatory every three years; and Parliamentary sessions were held every year from 1689 onwards, largely as a result of the need to raise Parliament-approved finance to wage a hugely expensive continental and naval war against France. In 1695, the licensing system for the press was finally allowed to lapse: thereafter, prosecutions for sedition and libel continued, but they could take place only after material had been published. As a result, press freedom became more routine (though far from complete) and periodicals and newspapers flourished: the first daily newspapers appeared, as did the first evening ones.

Yet the divisions signalled by the emergence of Whigs and Tories in the reign of Charles II failed to heal, and it would be a mistake to see the revolution of 1688 as resolving all the problems that had destabilized England during Pepys's lifetime. Religious divisions persisted: Tory adherents of the Church of England resented the Whig-inspired concessions made to the dissenters and feared that their institution was being allowed to wither by an indifferent government or actively undermined by republican-sympathizing dissenters. Two years before Pepys died, the firebrand cleric Henry Sacheverell preached a provocative sermon that set out what he saw as a sinister plot against the established church. The nature and direction of the war against France also provoked division. Tories wanted a primarily defensive, and hence cheaper, naval war rather than the extensive and horrendously expensive land war favoured by the Whigs. This was because they feared that Whig City financiers benefited from the war at the expense of the Tory country gentlemen who shouldered its burden. The creation of the Bank of England in 1694, largely a Whig project, was thus highly controversial for the social consequences of the shift away from landed towards monetary wealth that it set in train. Also, the cost of the

war was met by the creation of a national debt, with interest payments serviced by Parliamentary taxation; while this created a machine capable of sustained warfare (and was a very significant factor in Britain's rise as a European and transatlantic power after 1689), the fiscal–military state seemed to the Tories to be an endless pool of jobs and money for their Whig rivals. Some Tories (Pepys among them) had refused to sign up to the change of dynasty, and a smaller number actively plotted for the return of the exiled James II. In 1696, there was even an attempt to assassinate William. Some saw him as another Cromwell, waging merciless war on his enemies and ruling with cunning.

William's death, by natural causes, in 1702 made way for the accession of Queen Anne, who, as a daughter of James II, at least had Stuart blood in her veins. Yet her reign, which lasted until 1714, witnessed one of the bitterest periods of party conflict in British history, prompting a paper war in which Daniel Defoe and Jonathan Swift honed their literary talents. When Pepys died in 1703, he left a country still racked by conflict, though this conflict was one that had moved from the battlefield to the coffeehouses that had proliferated in London and many market towns.

The two revolutions through which Pepys lived transformed Britain. The England of his death in 1703 was very different from the nation of his birth in 1633. Britain was emerging as a 'great power' in European politics, with an expanding state, empire and commercial might. Safeguards against monarchical tyranny had been introduced (though in the second half of the eighteenth century the strength of these was severely questioned) and a measure of religious plurality had been established (again this would remain controversial for long afterwards). The public had emerged as an important voice, now institutionalized through frequent elections and petitions, as well as more informally through the press, street protest and the 'polite' culture of the coffeehouse. What had not changed in the half century since Pepys witnessed the beheading of the king was the highly charged nature of debate or the depth of ideological difference dividing the people of England.

The Embleme of Englands distractions as also of her attained, and further expected Freedome, & Happines
Engravings, 1658 and c.1690.
The left print depicts Cromwell; the one opposite, William III, on a reworked plate. The implication, despite the ostensibly positive iconography, is that William III might be a new Cromwell.

British Museum, 1935,0413.184 and 1932,1112.4.

Anno 1650.

Nem, eū prius admiss: Samuell Peapys filius Johannis Peapys civis Londinens̄
fuisse in Aulā Trin:
1. dis Junÿ ejusdm ā̄; ...annos natus   è Scholā Paulinā admissus est Sizato
t patet ex testif m̄i ...no Morland.
wells ibidem Socio, da

Nov: 12. 1650.

Max: 4. 165 0/1 , quo die
hā in ordinē transÿt   generosi
Pensionariorum apud nos,   Johannes Hobson filius Guilielmi Hobson, de Stamford
    Comitatu Lincolniæ annos septendecim natus è Scholā de ...
    bridge admissus est Comensalis, Tutore M̄ro Merryweather

Dec: 17. 1650.

Nem eū in ordinem Com
...saliū transÿsse Junÿ   Johannes Twells filius Guilielmi Twells Eliensis de
...ie 11o anni sequentis.   ...bich in Comitatu Cantabrigiæ annum agens decimum
...in: 1651.   tum è Scholā de Gormanchester in Comitatu Huntin
    miensi admissus est Pensionarius, Tutore M̄ro Tall...

Feb: 10. 1650.

Samuel Lincolne filius   Lincolne generō
de Thetford in Comitatu Norfolciensi annum agen
decimū septimū è Scholā de S̄ti Edmundi Burgo
Comitatu Suffolciensi admissus est Pensionarius, T
tore M̄ro Pallents.

Mar: 29. 1651.

Gulielmus Pell filius Guilielmi Pell de Sheffield
Comitatu Eboracensi Septendecim annos natus è sch
Rotheramensi admissus est Sizator, Tutore M̄ro H...

Apr: 5. 1651.

Ann: 1651.

Johes Hollins filius Johis Hollins de Medley
Comitatu Eboracensi annū agens decimū septimū

M. E. J. Hughes

Samuel Pepys: A Scholar and a Gentleman

In September 1618, Mrs Mary Robinson of Marck Lane, in the parish of St Olave in London, left to the Mercer's Company the sum of £500. This was to be invested in land in order to produce £25 a year to be paid to four poor students in Cambridge at the nomination of the company 'so as they should become students in divinity and preachers of the gospel'.[1] The late Mrs Robinson, who also left £200 to a church in Virginia to educate the Powhatan Indians in Christianity, was one of the benefactors who made Samuel Pepys's education possible. Such sponsors enabled greater social mobility than we might imagine, and their gifts actively encouraged poor children to achieve their potential.

The reasons for educational patronage were various. Piety and devotion were important, but there was also a pragmatic element. Society was in a state of transformation. The governance of towns and cities, the management of the professions such as law and medicine, the pursuit of science and the day-to-day functioning of the army and navy were all routinely placed in the hands of professional bureaucrats, often from the urban lower and middle classes. This created a real incentive to educate bright but poor city boys such as Pepys.

Literacy was key to social mobility, offering opportunities throughout the professions. It is likely that Pepys picked up the basics of reading and writing as a child in London, though there is no evidence that this was achieved in any formal or methodical way. Literacy was often of a practical nature, and it is plausible that the young Samuel was introduced to the written word in bills of sale and terms of agreement. Moreover, we know from the evidence of Pepys's own collection that access to the printing press was not reserved for an intellectual elite: advertisements, political squibs, ballads and other ephemera were everywhere. The written word was part of life for anyone in business, and we should not confuse a lack of familiarity with Homer or Virgil with illiteracy.

Pepys's first taste of formal learning appears to have been in Huntingdon, where he probably attended the grammar school while staying in the nearby village of Brampton. The fine Norman building

The record for Pepys's entry in Magdalene's admission register, 1 October 1650 (detail)

Magdalene College, Cambridge, Archives, B.422, f. 12b.

where Pepys (and Oliver Cromwell before him) would have been set to his books still exists. It has gone through architectural remodelling from its monastic origins as the Hospital of St John the Baptist[2] to its current role as a museum dedicated to the Lord Protector. In Pepys's day, the building was probably at its worst: the impressive, high-roofed, high-windowed, single chamber had been divided to provide a schoolmaster's lodgings on the first floor and what must have been a dark and inhospitable schoolroom below. Even worse, the Master of the school, Henry Cooke, was 'not interested in the job', employing a stand-in to take lessons and moving his family away from the town.[3] Money rather than pedagogy was his main interest.[4] Pepys mentioned his time here only once, and then to talk not of education but of friendship. In 1660, he met (after sixteen years) an old school chum, Thomas Alcock, perhaps related to the Thomas Alcock who was appointed in 1558 as Master of the Hospital of St John (by then a school). He was probably the Alcock whom Pepys later recommended as a ship's carpenter and who was accused of embezzlement (wrongfully it turned out, though Pepys seemed quick to believe it).

The practice of teaching in the time of the Civil War was somewhat hit-and-miss, but there was much interest in the theory. Pepys later owned several books about education,[5] and there were many essays published about its utility, notably an influential piece by John Milton.

Charles Hoole, the educational writer, published his account of the finest way to run a primary or 'petty' school (from the French petit) in 1660, about twenty years after Samuel Pepys first encountered Henry Cooke's locum, but some of Hoole's enlightened practices were visible in the best establishments even in Pepys's day. Later in life, Pepys took a personal and financial interest in the education of his nephews John and Sam Jackson, corresponding about their progress with their tutor, John Matthews.[6]

Learning to write was an important skill for boys, and technically little had changed since the Tudor copybooks with their woodblock illustrations of alphabets. In later life, Pepys included samples of these in his three stunning and carefully constructed calligraphy albums 'put together', as he declares on the title page, in 1700.[7] The copybooks would begin from the basics: how to hold the pen, how to prepare the nib, how to avoid schoolboy blots. There is a direct progression from such primitive squiggles and pen-trials to the elaborate calligraphy that so delighted Pepys. Legible writing was essential for many professions and trades – Pepys made his living by it; but at the 'high end' of the market, exquisite writing was an important art form.

The learning materials offered in schools give an insight into Pepys's practices: it is possible that he developed his love of scrapbooks and compilations from his school days. Commonplace books, in which the student recorded elegant, useful or morally uplifting passages, were highly recommended in educational handbooks. Milton and Francis Bacon, the politician and philosopher, both kept commonplace books. This process of the routine acquisition and recording of wisdom goes back to classical times, and it flourished throughout the Middle Ages in the form of florilegia, or anthologies: at the time of his death in 1703, Pepys owned several such collections, including a remarkable fifteenth-century manuscript that juxtaposes Latin devotional poetry with prognostications concerning the weather, and musical theory with maxims on physiology.[8]

Ludus Literarius: Or, the Grammar Schoole
John Brinsley (London, 1627).
This page shows a sample of penmanship.

Magdalene College, Cambridge, Old Library, F.6.27, p. 36.

From *A Guide to Pen-man-ship*
(London, 1673).
This page from one of the many copybooks dismantled and preserved in Pepys's albums of 1700 is an example of witty and elegant penmanship.

Pepys Library, Magdalene College, Cambridge, PL 2981, p. 117.

Pepys's attendance at Huntingdon Grammar School was a brief respite from the Civil War in London. His education at St Paul's, which he entered around 1644, influenced his life in two crucial ways. First, he met people who were to populate his world, from his schoolmate Thomas Gale (who became High Master of St Paul's from 1672 to 1697) to the Surmaster (deputy head), Samuel Cromleholme, whose personal library was the finest in England until its destruction in the Great Fire of 1666. Second, he followed the rich curriculum of the grammar school, which introduced him to poetry, theatre, languages and debate.

Pepys was gregarious by nature, but he also made close friends like Richard Cumberland. The fathers of both boys were tailors and neighbours, and indeed later on Pepys wanted Cumberland to marry his sister. Like Pepys, Cumberland was interested in science, engineering and mechanics: as a Cambridge student, Cumberland invented the first mechanical model of the planets and, when Pepys was President of the Royal Society, he dedicated his *Essay towards the Recovery of Jewish Weights and Measures* to Pepys in 1686.

Pepys's time at St Paul's gave him a taste for books, too. He was subsequently a benefactor to the school library, making gifts in 1662 (when he was not yet a rich man), and again thirteen years later. A list of books given to establish a new collection in the school begins with Pepys's donation of Strabo's *Geographia* (Paris, 1620).[9] Pepys returned to his school on many occasions, and in 1677 was Steward of the Feast, participating in this annual celebration which had been reinstated after the Restoration. He was to show an interest in old boys of the school throughout his life. For example, he recorded hearing a good sermon by his contemporary Richard Meggott on Christmas Day 1664.

Milton, an earlier old boy of St Paul's, defined education as 'that which fits a man to perform justly, skilfully and magnanimously all the offices both private and publicke of peace and war'.[10] The function of education as preparation for life complemented its role in encouraging inner spiritual growth: it did not replace the devotional agenda, but it directed the curriculum.

Languages were key. Hoole recommended that study of the Bible should be through the explication of the text 'according to its several languages: viz Hebrew, Chaldie, Samaritane, Syriack, Arabic, Persian, Aethiopike, Armenian, and Coptick'.[11] This was all part of theological practice, and the seventeenth century was the zenith of production of Polyglot Bibles, which intricately juxtapose the same text in several languages (Pepys had a finely bound one in six volumes).[12] An emphasis on acquiring languages, however, had applications beyond the theological. By adulthood, Pepys seems to have augmented the Latin and Greek of his schooling with Italian, French, Spanish, Dutch and German. He also collected books in Chinese and Russian, and he owned over a dozen volumes on philology. The many advantages of a linguistic education served Pepys well: Latin and Greek marked him as a scholar, modern languages as a man of the world; and a proficiency in learning new languages quickly made him a resourceful colleague in trade, diplomacy and politics.

It is worth remarking, too, on the deficiencies in the curriculum. The most significant in Pepys's education was the lack of mathematics. A seventeenth-century treatise on the formation of the 'generall scholar' by the controversial defender of humanist learning, Méric Casaubon, found 'noe great use; much less, necessitie' for the subject, though he certainly studied it himself.[13] Things were no better for Pepys, and we find him at the age of twenty-nine seeking lessons in mathematics from the master's mate of the *Royal Charles*. He began, he says proudly, with a lesson on multiplication tables.[14] The reason for this desire to become proficient in figures was clear: Pepys feared, justifiably, becoming the victim of unscrupulous suppliers if he could not understand accounts, the measurement of timber and the quantities of goods in the naval dockyards.

Pepys's educational progress relied on aspiration and financial support. As is always the case, aspiration came from inside, but it was fuelled by access to lively company at one of the aristocratic houses of England (the home of the Montagus at Hinchingbrooke – albeit often in the servants' quarters), and realized by a quick brain and a resourceful nature. Financial support came from a host of others who, like Mrs Robinson, provided for the education of worthwhile young people of humble means. Michael McDonnell, the school's historian, assessed the membership of St Paul's between the years 1509 and 1748 as follows:

> Of fathers in more humble walks of life we find about fifty, these including a baker, a barber, eight booksellers or publishers, five brewers, a cabinet-maker, three carpenters, a carrier, a confectioner to the King, two cooks, four druggists, a dyer, a farmer, a fellmonger, a hatter, a jeweller, a linen merchant, a mason, four printers, a porter of the School, two shoemakers, a silk-weaver, a silversmith, a soap-boiler, a stationer, eight tailors, a tobacconist, and two wine-merchants.[15]

This list covers most of the main trades of the City of London, and the wares and services provided by these sorts of men feature prominently in Pepys's diary. It is not surprising that Pepys seems so at ease with such a range of individuals, from members of the professions to the military, from the aristocracy to tradespeople – a characteristic often commented upon by readers of his diary – for he was educated in a microcosm of urban society. Perhaps the point should not be overstated, though: where in this list are the sons of labourers, ostlers, beggars, servants, laundresses? Indeed, as the seventeenth century progressed, many of the scholarships designated for 'poor boys' were taken up not by the very poorest in society but, as in the case of Pepys himself, by the offspring of tradesmen and professionals.

Throughout Pepys's time there, St Paul's School was presided over by one of its greatest High Masters, Dr John Langley. Langley's funeral sermon in 1657, preached by his friend Edward Reynolds, celebrated the 'Use of Humane Learning'. Was Pepys present? His brother John attended. If Samuel was there, he would have heard high praise for Langley's great and diverse learning. Langley was widely influential: Hoole recorded that he was consulted by the philanthropist Abraham Calfe, who 'brought him along with him to Sion College, to see what books he judged most convenient to furnish a library withal for the schoolmaster's use'.[16] On Langley's advice, Calfe bestowed at least £100-worth of 'choice books'.

Another figure at St Paul's whose career overlapped intriguingly with Pepys's was William Cox, who became Surmaster in 1651. It is very likely that this was the same Cox who had been admitted as a Sizar at Magdalene College Cambridge in Easter 1636, and who went on to be ordained at Lincoln in 1644.[17] And it was to Magdalene that Pepys went as a student in 1650, after a mysterious false start at Trinity Hall. He attended Magdalene on the Robinson bequest, but under recently imposed regulations there was a limit to the number of awards made annually, and a certificate was required confirming that the recipient had indeed been resident in Cambridge for the period of term (students in Cambridge are still required to 'keep nights' in order to qualify for their degrees).

What had Cambridge been through by the time Pepys arrived to commence his studies? We can take by way of example an incident from the year Pepys was born, 1633, when tempers had been frayed in the University. Student Justin Pagitt (later a lawyer of the Middle Temple and a friend of Pepys) reported to his uncle, Dr Charles Twysden, that 'a certain Mr [Nathanial] Barnard', a London preacher, had been informed against by the university for words spoken during a sermon the previous summer at the University Church: Barnard had apparently prayed that the queen's eyes might be opened so she could see 'her Saviour whom she hath pierced with her superstition and idolatry'; he claimed there was a 'broad difference between the substance of religion and purity thereof'.[18] He accused the university of 'idolatry' for bowing before the high altar and he stated, according to the indictment, that 'You thinke treason to be only against the king; but I can tell of a farre worse treason than that, to witt, the treason against the commonwealth, which is so much the worse by how much the body is better than a member, and the whole is better than a parte'. Barnard was condemned for his republican sentiments; but the seeds were apparent of the growing religious conflicts that were to lead to the execution of the king, the establishment of a commonwealth and, in Cambridge and Oxford, the expulsion of numerous heads of houses and Fellows in a series of aggressive inspections or 'purges'.

Still, Pepys's undergraduate years coincided with a resurgence of the university, at least in terms of numbers. There had been a sharp decline in the 1640s, owing to the upheavals of the Civil War, but in 1651 Pepys was one of 2,848 students studying in Cambridge, almost a thousand more than a decade earlier. The university was making a concerted effort to offer a period of stability.[19] Pepys was a beneficiary of this. Stability was certainly needed in Magdalene, recently deprived of its Master, Edward Rainbow, in the purge of 1650. Rainbow tried to avoid his expulsion by offering to live peaceably; but unable in the end to subscribe to the demands of the Commonwealth, he was

The record for Pepys's entry in Magdalene's admission register, 1 October 1650

Magdalene College, Cambridge, Archives, B.422, f. 12b.

deprived of the Mastership. He kept a low profile for the next ten years at the helm of small parishes until he was spectacularly reinstated in 1660.

The new head of Magdalene, installed a few months before Pepys arrived, was John Sadler. Sadler was a very different figure from the peaceable Dr Rainbow: with strong links to the City of London (he maintained the office of Town Clerk throughout his time in Magdalene) and a lively attitude to contemporary theological and legal disputes, Sadler presided over a varied fellowship where general conformity to the requirements of the Commonwealth did not completely stifle debate. He wrote what the college history describes as a 'dull but solid book', attempting to give a legal justification for the execution of Charles I (perhaps not surprisingly, at the Restoration of 1660 he was removed from the Mastership in favour of the rehabilitated Dr Rainbow). Pepys's arrival with ten other students also coincided with a change to the social composition of the college: there was no longer a predominance of Lincolnshire-born students; 'different accents, different names, different heraldry, and a different society were now in possession of Magdalene'.[20]

The Cambridge in which Pepys arrived was a place of change in many ways, but especially in its growing academic aspirations. For many, the provision of books for study was a marker of this. The modest medieval holdings of the university library had been seriously damaged in the sixteenth century, when arcane rules of access and use hampered scholarship; but now the library possessed both a scholarly and resourceful librarian in Abraham Whelock and a powerful supporter in the historian John Seldon. In Magdalene College, with a relatively young fellowship, academic life was also undergoing steady improvement.[21] Benefactors considered the provision of books to be as important as that of fellowships. In 1624, Frances, Countess of Warwick, gave a gift of books to the value of £30 or £40, and two years later Barnaby Gooche (a former Master) donated a large civil law library.

Encouragement of private study presupposes private thinking. In 1654, the mathematician and theologian Isaac Barrow recorded the syllabus created by James Duport (later Master of Magdalene): the students read Plato and Aristotle, to be sure, but also the Greek poets, historians and scholiasts (commentators on classical literature).[22] The students would not merely listen to their tutors: they were to think for themselves – within bounds. The young Barrow's interpretation of Greek theatre, for example, did not go down well. As he lamented, 'I and my Sophocles acted in an empty theatre'.[23]

It is worth noting that outside the university there was a parallel movement: private writing by an individual, recording his or her inner thoughts, became valued. The 'Digger' Gerrard Winstanley, who believed passionately in a more equal society, described in 1649 how he would leave all other duties and responsibilities to write his ideas: the value placed on private thoughts was as important to Pepys's literary development as were the social freedoms afforded by the Restoration.[24] 'The mind makes the person' became Samuel's motto. Like so many students, Pepys even wrote a novel, *Love a Cheate*, which he subsequently destroyed.

Pepys's tutor, Samuel Morland, was one of the longer-serving Fellows, at a time when Fellows were relatively young and tended to move on quickly. Oddly, given Pepys's deficiency in basic arithmetic,

S^r. Samuel Moreland
Engraving, by Pierre Lombart (1613–82) after a painting by Sir Peter Lely, 1658.

Pepys Library, Magdalene College, Cambridge, PL2979/118f.

Morland was a mathematician. Pepys was later to purchase his treatise, *Arithmetical instruments ... and perpetual almanac* (1673), which advertised itself as 'a most useful instrument for the addition and subtraction of pounds, shillings, pence and farthings'.[25] After the Restoration, Pepys decided that Morland was 'not so much a fool as I took him for' – something of a double-edged compliment.[26]

There are limited records of Pepys's Cambridge days, though a picture of close friendships, learning and the pursuit of female company emerges retrospectively in his diary. However, the Magdalene Registrar, John Wood, noted one incident which was recorded formally: 'Pepys and Hind were solemnly admonished by myself and Mr Hill for having been scandalously overseen in drink the night before; this was done in the presence of all the fellows then resident in Mr Hills chamber'. It must have been a serious matter in a college at the height of Puritanism in Cambridge; but this is an isolated entry. Despite his troubles with the tutors, Pepys acquitted himself well at Magdalene, winning the prestigious Spendluffe scholarship in 1653. He stayed in touch with the college throughout his life, bestowing numerous gifts, and he often broke the journey from London to Huntingdon to spend an evening with the Fellows. When he died, he left a magnificent benefaction to his old college: his library, which is still housed in the building to which he subscribed.

Claire Tomalin, in her biography of Pepys, points out that it is surprising that he did not enter the legal profession when he left Cambridge. Opportunities were not straightforward, however, and Pepys must have seen other young men flounder in those difficult times as they waited for fellowships, legal positions or preferment. It is perhaps understandable that when an opportunity arose to work as a clerk and 'general dogsbody'[27] in the London house of his relative Edward Montagu, Pepys accepted it.

Pepys still had much to learn. This period saw a rise in the professionalism of clerking, and an aspect of this was the production of handbooks and guides.[28] Pepys added several exemplars to his albums, his interest in penmanship coinciding perfectly with the requirements of his chosen career. In his calligraphy collection referred to above we find a rare survival: Mr Billingsly's copybook, *The pen's excellencie; or the secretaries delightes, wherein as well the abuses wch are offered unto ye worthines of ye pen by unworthie penmen are trulie discovered: as ye dignity of ye art itself by ye antiquitie, excellencie & diversitie therof is breifly demonstrated.*

Pepys's career was moving along well, if slowly, when he set off with his cousin Montagu in 1660 to accompany Charles II back to England. It was surely an audacious move, for there was no guarantee that either the king or the liberties he brought with him would survive, but it brought Pepys dramatically to the attention of the fledgling court. Promotion followed: as Clerk of the Acts to the Navy Board in the new regime, he now commanded an annual salary of £350. In the same year, he took the degree of Master of Arts at Magdalene College, which cost him '9 pounds and 16 shillings'.[29]

The stage was set for the tailor's son to be recognized as, to use A. L. Rowse's term, the 'complete gentleman'– and something, too, of a scholar.[30]

Note of Pepys being 'deaned' for drunkenness, 21 October 1653

Magdalene College, Cambridge, Archives, B.422, f. 3a.

Pepys and the Worlds of Medicine

Mark Jenner

Sir Charles Scarburgh
Oil on canvas, attributed to Jean
Demetrius, c.1660.

Royal College of Physicians, X80.

Illustration from *A Treatise of
Lithotomy, or, of the Extraction of the
Stone out of the Bladder*
By François Tolet (London, 1683).

British Library, 1189.d.10.

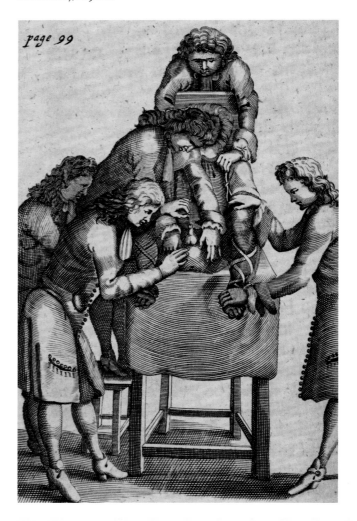

Pepys went under the knife twice. The second time, at his post-mortem, doctors found that his bladder was inflamed, that there were black spots on his lungs, and that one kidney was grossly deformed and discharged 'most foetid matter'.[1] The first time was arguably worse. He was alive, sentient and in agony when in March 1658 the London surgeon Thomas Hollier tied him down, slid a probe up his penis, made a 3-inch (7.5 cm) incision between his scrotum and his anus, cut into his bladder, reached in and pulled out a stone the size of a snooker ball.

Pepys not only recovered, but was glad that he had decided to undergo this operation. He recalled that the stone had caused him 'insufferable' pain, but also knew that he had been fortunate. The experience doubtless intensified his keen interest in the workings of the body. He acquired medical books, including a copy of the Danish physician Thomas Bartholin's *Anatomia*. In February 1663, he went to Barber Surgeons' Hall and heard the lecture on 'the Kidnys, Ureters, and yard [penis]' read over the dissected body of a recently hanged criminal. He was then taken into a private room where he could quiz the physician Charles Scarburgh (1615–95) about the disease of the stone and the mechanics of ejaculation.

It is tempting to assume that when learned men like Scarburgh, Fellow of the College of Physicians and friend of William Harvey, who discovered the circulation of the blood, spoke on health matters they commanded general assent. They did not. The medical world of later seventeenth-century England was bitterly divided over basic questions concerning the functioning of the body, the nature of disease and the best cures for afflictions. Some considered anatomy, which had made great advances since the sixteenth century, to be a secure foundation for more reliable knowledge. Others, like the influential physician Thomas Sydenham, thought that cutting up cadavers told you little about how the body worked while it was alive. The 1665 plague generated public disputes about the nature of the epidemic. An abortive new Society of Chemical Physicians, for whom chemical processes were key to the understanding of the workings of the human frame, directly challenged the more conservative college.

This lack of intellectual consensus fostered a culture of medical pluralism. A myriad practitioners and lay people claimed an ability to diagnose and to heal

The Royal Gift of Healing

bodily maladies. Such assertions of competence could be found at every level of society. Charles II, for instance, promoted the idea that as an anointed monarch he had therapeutic powers; thousands of people queued up to be touched by him in order to be cured of scrofula, also known as the King's Evil. Such rituals were potent displays of royal legitimacy. Not all were convinced: Thomas Hollier was, Pepys noted, a sceptic.

Pepys knew the surgeon's opinion because he had continued to consult him. Hollier's care went far beyond conventional surgical concerns: he bled Pepys, advised him about diet, and prescribed and prepared pills for him. But Pepys's medical relationships were far from exclusive. While still seeing Hollier, he starting taking other pills recommended by Alexander Burnet, a physician he first met at a dinner party. Like every seventeenth-century Londoner, he also sought and received medical advice in all sorts of informal social settings. Wanting to know how to improve his chances of getting his wife pregnant, he asked a group of women at a christening party. Their recommendations ranged from drinking sage juice to wearing 'cool Holland drawers'. When he was troubled by constipation and by painful urination, his colleague in the Navy Office Sir William Batten sent for his wife's juniper

water. Drinking it, Pepys managed 'a couple of stools' and 'a fart or two'. After he complained of a fever, the musician Cesare Morelli, who knew him well, told him of a man who could cure it 'with simpathetical power' if Pepys sent him clippings of hair, toe and finger nails.

In England, patterns of medicinal care changed significantly over the seventeenth century. These transformations were driven by cash, commerce and the international drug trade. In Pepys's lifetime, a broad-based medical market emerged. The proportion of the population who, in sickness, relied on familial and neighbourly assistance or simply sought spiritual consolation declined. With increasing frequency they also purchased medical services, as Pepys did from Hollier, Burnet and others. Surviving probate accounts, which detail the cost of a deceased's care and funeral, suggest that, in the last quarter of the sixteenth century, fewer than 10 per cent of Kentish people with some moveable property paid for medical assistance in their final illness. In the first decade of the eighteenth century, over half of them did so.

The practitioners who attended ever more sickbeds and deathbeds were not just offering advice. They were supplying more kinds and greater quantities of medicaments. They prepared some of these themselves; apothecaries made up others according to their prescriptions. Over the century, diverse new remedies, many of them proprietary brands like Daffy's Elixir and Anderson's Pills, came on to the market. These were intensively promoted with printed handbills and, by the 1690s, in the press. (John Evelyn wrote to Pepys about a powder he had seen advertised in a newspaper.) The ingredients of this new pharmacopoeia came from all over the globe. In around 1700, seventeen times more medicinal drugs were imported into London than in about 1600. Pepys swallowed syrups containing Asian cinnamon and nutmeg, and pills of Mediterranean turpentine; when he first saw a house marked with a red cross, he purchased tobacco (from the Americas) to sniff and chew in order to preserve himself from the possible airborne dangers of plague. With every such purchase, he made a small contribution to the growth of English drug culture and the commercialization of healthcare. We know Pepys as a lithotomy survivor. We should also think of him as a pioneering medical consumer.

Pepys the Witness

In January 1649, the teenage Pepys watched the execution of Charles I, which was nothing if not bloody, as the king's arterial blood jetted forward on decapitation. After the restoration of Charles II, Pepys saw those who had signed the king's death warrant, now found guilty of regicide, hanged, drawn and quartered (see p. 22). He wrote a description of the execution at Charing Cross in October 1660 of one regicide, Major-General Thomas Harrison, who was, according to proper form, hanged, lowered and cut open while still conscious. Moments earlier, Harrison had generously forgiven his executioner, even giving him the money from his pocket. Now Harrison hit out at him, which resulted in the swift removal of his head. His entrails were thrown on a fire nearby. Pepys recorded in his diary that, during this process, Harrison was 'looking as cheerful as any man could do in that condition'. Pepys's bravado may be a kind of defence against the horror of the spectacle.

In his lifetime, Pepys saw many bloody reversals, sudden deaths, the destruction of the London he knew, and human desolation and dislocation. He was no naive innocent. His zest for life was in part a reaction to the transience he noted in the pleasures around him and in part a response to his own good fortune in surviving a dangerous operation to remove a bladder stone. He observed men carefully, and was acutely aware of how they responded to him and the impression he made on them. If Pepys could be wonderfully ebullient and animated, he was also watchful and wary.

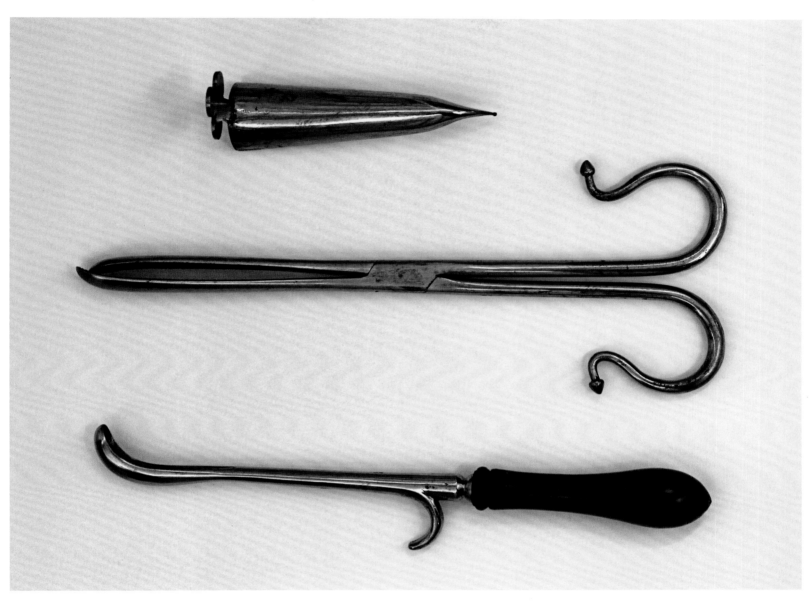

1

Gorget, forceps and scoop for performing a lithotomy

*c.*1650
Richard Kettlebuter or Kettlebetter
(forceps)
Steel and wood
Royal College of Physicians,
X311/36, 30, 52

Pepys suffered such debilitating pain from a bladder stone that he took the extreme step of having an operation (a lithotomy) to remove it. This was performed on 26 March 1658 by Thomas Hollier, an experienced surgeon at the height of his powers. He made an incision into the bladder between the scrotum and the anus through which the stone was extracted. With no anaesthetic or sterilization, the risk of death from shock or infection was considerable. Despite the extreme delicacy of the task, speed was essential to lessen the patient's trauma. The procedure was a

success: Hollier removed a stone the size of a modern snooker ball and, after an uncomfortable convalescence, Pepys felt recovered five weeks later.

Pepys occasionally marked the anniversary of the operation with a celebratory feast. That of 1662, for example, involved stewed carp, roast chicken, salmon, tongue and cheese, among other things. Pepys retained the stone: it was mounted in gold and kept in a special case as a reminder of the ordeal and as an object of curiosity. RB

LITERATURE: Tomalin, pp. 62–65; *Diary*, III, 53.

2

A Tutor to Tachygraphy, or Short-Writing ...

By Thomas Shelton (London, 1642)
British Library, C.31.a.49.2.

Pepys wrote his famous diary, and some draft letters and copies, in shorthand. He used a system devised by Thomas Shelton, who called it 'tachygraphy' from the Greek for 'quick writing' and made his living by teaching it. Shelton's system had limitations, which encouraged Pepys to favour words easily written in the shorthand, and the simpler and more easily remembered signs. This explains why so much of the diary is characterized by stock phrases. It also explains why echoes of Pepys's voice occur in the diary, because speech tends to use the simpler terms that were easier to record in shorthand. ML

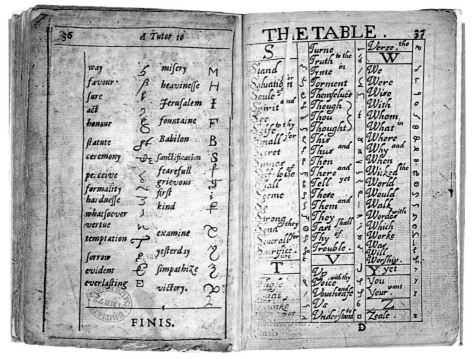

3

Letter-book of the official correspondence of Samuel Pepys

1662–79
Ink on paper
National Maritime Museum, LBK/8

Pepys was meticulous by nature: he and his clerk would make duplicate copies of official correspondence for retention. This letter-book holds items both in Pepys's longhand and in the same shorthand he used for his diary (which concealed information even from close associates). It includes a letter written at the time of the plague in 1665, when the Navy Board retreated to Greenwich. Pepys's careful record-keeping paid off. Faced with an investigation into the humiliating Dutch raid on the Medway in 1667, he had the files and letter-books to defend his position with detailed evidence. MB

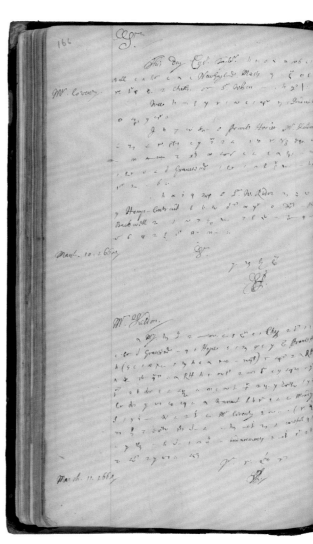

4

....

The Execution of Charles I

....

*c.*1649
Possibly Dutch
Oil on canvas, 1632 × 2968
Scottish National Portrait Gallery, on loan
from Lord Dalmeny since 1951, PGL 208

This view of Charles I's execution on 30 January 1649 is a potent piece of Royalist propaganda designed to shock. The central scene shows the king's head being held aloft in front of the crowd. The fifteen-year-old republican Samuel Pepys skipped school to watch the grisly event. In his diary, he later recalled 'the words that I said the day that the king was beheaded (that were I to preach upon him, my text should be: "The memory of the wicked shall rot")'. Four cartouches show the king at his trial and walking to the scaffold, the unknown executioner, and spectators dipping handkerchiefs in the royal blood. Some believed that it would cure illness. KM

LITERATURE: van Beneden and de Pooter, cat. 1, pp. 112–13; *Diary*, I, 280.

5

Charles I's gloves

c.1649
Leather, gold and silver thread
Lambeth Palace Library

Charles I is said to have handed these gloves to his chaplain William Juxon, Bishop of London (later Archbishop of Canterbury under Charles II), just before his execution. They are one of several pairs that supposedly belonged to Charles. Made of fine leather embroidered with gold and silver thread, they are heavily worn and stained. Juxon, whom Pepys referred to as 'a man well spoken of by all for a good man', spent most of the day of the execution with Charles, accompanying him on to the scaffold where they prayed together. His last words to the king were reported as 'you are exchanged from a temporal to an eternal crown, a good exchange'. KM

LITERATURE: *Diary*, IV, 173; *King Charls His Speech Made upon the Scaffold at Whitehall-Gate …* (London, 1649), p. 13.

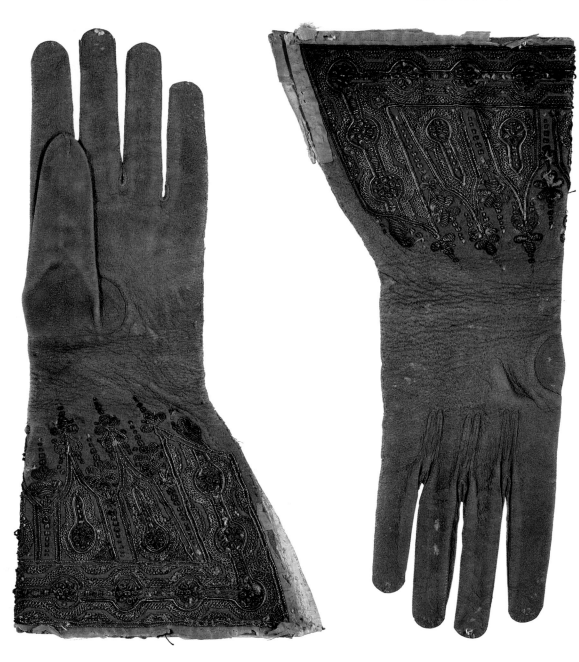

6

Waistcoat worn by Charles I at his execution

c.1649
Knitted silk
Museum of London, A.27050

On the bitterly cold morning of his execution, Charles I is said to have requested two shirts as he worried that any shivering would be misconstrued as fear. This fine, originally blue-green sleeved waistcoat or vest, an exceptional survival, has traditionally been identified as one of the garments he wore that day, probably over a linen undershirt. After the beheading it was passed to the king's physician, Dr Hobbs, who attended to the body. The staining on the front of the waistcoat could be the faded remains of the king's blood, the majority of which may have been absorbed by the shirt underneath. Forensic tests have confirmed that the stains are bodily fluids. KM

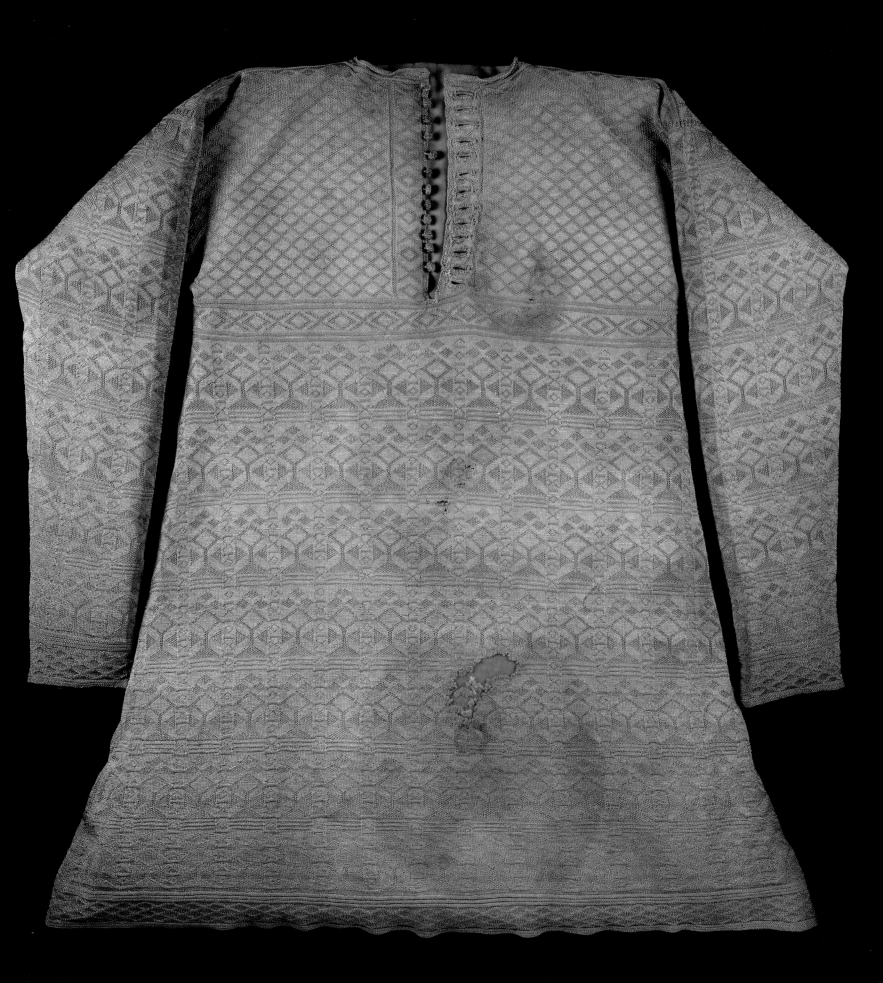

7

**Official Parliamentary report of the trial
of Charles I**

January 1649
Ink on paper
The National Archives, SP 16/517

Charles I's trial at Westminster Hall in January 1649 lasted just seven days. About seventy commissioners, appointed by the Rump Parliament, sat in judgment. The Act of Parliament passed so that Charles could be put on trial accused him of high treason and 'a wicked design totally to subvert the ancient and fundamental laws and liberties of this nation'. He refused to cooperate, enter a plea or recognize the legitimacy of the court. On 27 January, he was found guilty, sentenced to death and was beheaded three days later. This report records the trial, overseen by Judge John Bradshaw, President of the High Court of Justice. It minutes attendees at each session and the exchanges between Bradshaw and the king. KM

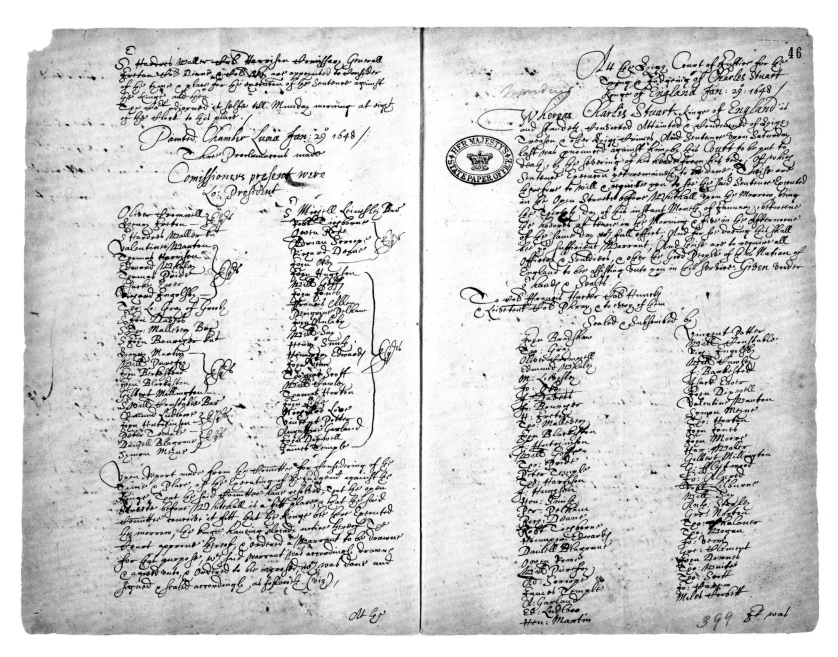

8

Eikon Basilike, The Pourtracture of His Sacred Majestie in His Solitudes and Sufferings

By Charles I [?] and John Gauden (London, 1649)
Royal Collection, RCIN 1080417

Eikon Basilike ('The Image of the King') was supposedly written by Charles I in prison before his execution. It was a powerful piece of Royalist propaganda, published just days afterwards. In it, Charles justified his reign, advised his heir and shared his thoughts on imminent death. The frontispiece, engraved by William Marshall, shows him kneeling in sacrifice, exchanging his earthly crown for a heavenly one. The book helped to promulgate the notion of Charles as a religious martyr. Pepys had his own copy, and referred to it as 'a noble book'. This edition, printed in March 1649, has a total of four lengths of blue ribbon attached to the binding. An inscription inside identifies them as the ribbon from the Order of the Garter worn by Charles I. KM

LITERATURE: *Diary*, VI, 204.

9

Eikonoklastes, In Answer to a Book Intitl'd Eikon Basilike ...

By I. [John] Milton (London, 1649)
British Library, G.11717

Eikonoklastes ('Image-Breaker') appeared nine months after Charles I's execution. It is traditionally seen as a piece of Parliamentary propaganda in response to the best-selling *Eikon Basilike*. The poet John Milton, a staunch advocate of the Commonwealth, was commissioned to write the tract, which justifies Charles I's death by emphasizing the inherent tyranny of monarchy. He criticizes every aspect of Charles's *Eikon* and tries to destroy the idea, promulgated by the Royalists, that the king was a Christian martyr. His tract was not as widely read as the *Eikon Basilike* and, after the Restoration, Charles II decreed that all copies should be burned. KM

10

Miniature of Charles I, with overlays

1650–70
Netherlandish
Oil on copper and on mica, 80 × 63
Royal Collection, RCIN 422099

Charles I (1600–49), second son of King James I, became heir apparent after the death of his brother, Henry, in 1612 and was crowned in 1625. Political, economic and religious tensions between king and Parliament began soon after his accession and culminated in civil war and his imprisonment, trial and execution. This miniature has twelve transparent mica overlays which commemorate that sequence of events. The base miniature is set in a shagreen (ray-skin) case and shows the king wearing his Garter ribbon. It is likely that the set originally had more overlays – perhaps up to twenty-four – which have not survived due to their fragility. KM

LITERATURE: Reynolds, cat. 446, pp. 294–96.

11

Finger ring concealing a miniature portrait of Charles I

c.1650
Gold, enamel and diamond
British Museum, AF.1439

This ring was probably worn by a loyal supporter of Charles I following his execution. It is set with a large table-cut diamond and opens to reveal a locket containing an exquisite miniature portrait of the king. The miniature was wisely hidden from view to keep the wearer's allegiance a secret at a time when it was dangerous to show support for the Royalist cause. The black enamel on the shoulders of the ring is in keeping with contemporary mourning jewellery, suggesting that it was made just after the King's death. KM

12

Pendant or slide, set with a miniature double portrait of Charles I and Charles II

1650–60
Gold and enamel, with a painted and varnished miniature under rock crystal
Victoria and Albert Museum, M.253-1975

Political jewellery was sometimes sold to raise money for the Royalist cause or was given as gifts to faithful supporters of the Stuarts. It was worn during the Civil Wars, Charles I's trial and the Interregnum, although often concealed from the Parliamentarian gaze. This enamel double portrait of Charles I and Charles II commemorates the execution of the king while supporting his heir in exile. It could be worn as a pendant or as a slide on a ribbon and may have originally had a pearl suspended from the loop at the bottom. KM

LITERATURE: Scarisbrick, pp. 189–90.

13

Reliquary of the blood of Charles I

c.1649, ornament added c.1660
Silver-gilt, enamel, crystal, fabric and human hair
Private collection

This reliquary, in the form of a miniature book, is connected to the cult of Charles I as king and martyr. Inside, it has a chased and engraved profile portrait of him, surmounted by two tiny cherubs carrying a skull. The facing compartment contains a piece of fabric said to be stained with his blood. The ornament on the outside, a tree of life decorated with forget-me-nots, crystals and the crowned 'CR' (Carolus Rex or King Charles), may have been added later. KM

LITERATURE: Dicks, cat. 2/3, p. 9.

Commonwealth, 1649–60

On 19 May 1649, the so-called Rump Parliament, swayed by Oliver Cromwell's New Model Army, declared that Britain would be a commonwealth, governed by the people's representatives in Parliament, without any king or House of Lords (the New Model Army was independent of Parliament and therefore willing to help overthrow its authority and that of the Crown). The regime endured for the next eleven years, during which time Charles II was an exile in Europe.

People's everyday lives were transformed by Puritan views. Bull-baiting and bear-baiting pits were outlawed. Cock fighting was forbidden. Theatres were closed. Traditional maypoles were pulled down and religious festivals, including Christmas, were banned. Fast days and Sunday worship were strictly enforced.

From 1653, Cromwell, as Lord Protector, dismissed Parliament and in effect ruled by military dictatorship. He also kept up an aggressive foreign policy: he strengthened the navy, as Charles I had done before him, and encouraged trade. This policy meant war with Holland and Spain, both powerful nations, but Cromwell enjoyed some success. He won control of the seas around England, forced the Dutch to accept an English monopoly on trade between England and the English colonies, and seized Jamaica from the Spanish in 1655.

When Cromwell died in September 1658, few people mourned. According to the diarist John Evelyn, who saw the funeral procession through the streets of London on 22 October, it was 'the joyfullest … that ever I saw, for there were none that cried but dogs, which soldiers hooted away with a barbarous noise, drinking and taking tobacco in the streetes as they went'. Yet, after the restoration of Charles II, people were soon disillusioned with his rule and remembered Cromwell with sneaking admiration. Pepys confided to his diary on 12 July 1667, 'every body do now-a-days reflect upon Oliver, and commend him, what brave things he did, and made all the neighbour princes fear him'.

Civil War pikeman's armour

*c.*1635
Iron
Royal Armouries, II.352

From the late sixteenth century, pikemen began discarding the cumbersome protection for their arms. By the time of the Civil Wars they were simply equipped with breastplates and backplates, thigh and neck defences, and helmets known as pots, though many pikemen wore even less. As well as pikemen, foot regiments now also contained musketeers, who were predominantly armed with matchlock muskets. Regiments usually contained two musketeers for every pikeman; the fearsome pikes provided a bristling defensive shield against charging cavalry, while the musketeers fired around two shots a minute. RB

A PROCLAMATION

OF THE

Parliament of the Commonwealth of England,

Declaring *CHARLS STVART* and his Abettors, Agents and Complices, to be Traytors, Rebels and Publique Enemies.

Hereas divers of the Scotish Nation, and some English Fugitives, being lately come out of Scotland into England with their Leader CHARLS STUART, Son to the late Tyrant, do here Levy War against the Commonwealth, and commit many Outrages, Spoils and Murthers upon the people of this Nation; And the said Charls Stuart hath caused himself by the said Men of Scotland and English Fugitives to be Proclaimed King of England, and by Declarations proscribing some who have performed great and excellent Service to the Publique, and offering his Indulgences to others, would draw Adherents to him in his wicked and trayterous Practises, particularly by Letters in his Name directed to the City of London, and spread abroad by some of his Clandestine Agents, he labors to court them to his Party, by boasting his own Condition, and by endeavoring to annihilate the Honor and Esteem of the Parliament and their Forces, who through Gods Mercy have been so often Instrumental to Chastise him and his Confederates, and will, through Gods Blessing we trust, still prove a burthensom Stone unto them; Hoping it seems in the mean time, That that famous City (whose Faithfulness and eminent Services in behalf of Religion, Laws and Liberties are ever to be acknowledged) and that others of this Land and Nation, into whom by his Cunning and Flatteries he would thus insinuate, can forget the horrid and Bloody War raised by the late Tyrant his Father, and the Devastations attending it, and by his Delusions and Impostures be perswaded to betray Themselves and their Liberties again into Vassalage and Bondage, which through the Goodness of God, and at so great an Expence of Blood and Treasure have been vindicated from the Pride and Tyranny of that Man and his Fathers House : Which laborious Fraud and Falshood of him the said Charls Stuart hath hitherto notwithstanding, through the Favor of God to his People, proved of small or no effect but to aggravate his own Guilt, he being a Traytor of a former Date, and to render Himself and his Complices more and more obnoxious to the Penalties of the Laws of England, Declaring and Adjudging High Treason, wherein they are so deeply and desperately involved : And whereas by a late Act and Declaration of Parliament, All persons have been warned and Commanded not to give any Countenance or Assistance to the said Charls Stuart or his Party, but to Oppose them, and to Assist the Forces of this Commonwealth for the apprehending of them, to which a most chearful and general Obedience hath been given by the People according to their Duty, wherein the Parliament doth humbly acknowledge the Goodness of God to this Nation, and shall not fail to manifest their good Acceptance of the Peoples Affections herein; All which the Parliament of England having taken into their serious Consideration, although they cannot conceive that any true English-man can be debauched from the Duty and Fidelity which they owe to their Native Countrey, upon such Deluding and false Pretences as the Enemy hath used, and that therefore it is not necessary to make any further Declaration herein; Yet for the more Notoriety of the Fact to all persons concerned to take knowledge of the same, and to avoid all pretence of Ignorance in any touching the Condition of this Man and his Followers, have thought fit to Publish and Declare, And do hereby Publish and Declare the said Charls Stuart to be a Rebel, Traytor and Publique Enemy to the Commonwealth of England, and all his Abettors, Agents and Complices to be Rebels, Traytors and publique Enemies to the Commonwealth of England; And do hereby Command all Officers Civil and Military, in all Market-Towns and convenient places, to cause this Declaration to be proclaimed and published.

Monday, 25th August, 1651.

ORdered by the Parliament, That this Proclamation be forthwith Printed and published.

Hen: Scobel, Cleric. Parliamenti.

London, Printed by John Field, Printer to the Parliament of England. 1651.

A Proclamation Of The Parliament of the Commonwealth of England, Declaring Charls Stuart and his Abettors, Agents and Complices, to be Traytors, Rebels and Publique Enemies

....

25 August 1651
English Parliament
British Library, 669.f.16.21.

This declaration was published by Parliament just before the Battle of Worcester (3 September 1651), the last major engagement of the Civil Wars. In June 1651, Charles II landed in Scotland from exile in France in an audacious attempt to regain the English crown. This proclamation was intended to deter potential English supporters from joining Charles's army of mainly Scottish loyalists. It states that 'All Persons have been Warned and Commanded not to give any Countenance or Alliance to the said *Charls Stuart* or his Party, but to Oppose them'. By this time, Charles and his army of around 15,000 men were already at Worcester fortifying the town against Parliamentarian attack. KM

16

Commemorative dish

....

1670–80
Thomas Toft (d. 1698)
Lead-glazed earthenware
British Museum, 1935,0716.1.CR

This slipware display dish
commemorates Charles's escape
following his defeat at the Battle of
Worcester by Cromwell's much larger
army. It shows him hiding in an oak
tree in the grounds of Boscobel House,
in Shropshire, flanked by the lion and
unicorn from the royal coat of arms. The
story, and the oak tree, became symbolic
of his restoration. Pepys first heard
Charles recount how he escaped into
exile abroad after Worcester while they
were on board the *Royal Charles*, returning
to England in May 1660. Pepys wrote,
'it made me ready to weep to hear the
stories that he told of his difficulties that
he had passed through'. KM

LITERATURE: *Diary*, I, 155.

A
DIRECTORY
FOR
The Publique VVorship of *GOD*,
Throughout the Three
KINGDOMS
OF
England, Scotland, and *Ireland.*

Together with an Ordinance of Parlia-
ment for the taking away of the Book of
COMMON-PRAYER:
AND
For eſtabliſhing and obſerving of this preſent DIRECTORY
throughout the Kingdom of *England*, and Dominion of *Wales*.

Die Jovis, 13. *Martii,* 1644.

ORdered by the Lords and Commons aſſembled in
Parliament, That this *Ordinance* and *Directory* bee
forthwith Printed and Publiſhed:

Joh: Brown, Cleric.   *H: Elſynge, Cler.*
Parliamentorum.   *Parl.D.Com.*

LONDON:
Printed for *Evan Tyler, Alexander Fifield, Ralph Smith,* and
John Field ; And are to be ſold at the Sign of the Bible
in Cornhill, neer the ROYALL-EXCHANGE. 1644.

17

....

*A Directory for The Publique Worship of
God, Throughout the Three Kingdoms of
England, Scotland, and Ireland ...*

....

English Parliament (London, 1645)
British Library, 695.e.4.1.

As part of its religious reforms, early
in 1645, the Long Parliament approved
replacing the Book of Common Prayer
with the *Directory for The Publique
Worship of God*. The *Directory* was a
manual of instructions for ministers in
all places of public worship. It avoided
a prescribed form of worship, or liturgy,
and rejected certain ceremonies, such
as bowing to the east. It was denounced
by Charles I and was unpopular with the
Church of England. The Book of Common
Prayer, which Parliament considered
too 'Romish', continued to be used in
secret until its reinstatement after the
Restoration. Pepys's friend John Evelyn
was imprisoned for using a copy at
Christmas 1657. KM

LITERATURE: *Diary*, I, 282.

18

Oliver Cromwell

c.1650
Robert Walker (1599–1658)
Oil on canvas, 1257 × 1016
National Portrait Gallery, NPG 536

Oliver Cromwell (1599–1658) was the
fifth of ten children born to Robert
Cromwell and Elizabeth Steward of
Huntingdon. At the outbreak of civil
war in 1642, Cromwell, Member of
Parliament for Cambridge with a
reforming agenda, joined Parliamentarian
troops. This portrait shows him when he
was foremost general in the New Model
Army, a professional and religiously
committed force, about three years
before he became Lord Protector. Despite
Cromwell's unpopularity with some,
Pepys remained a supporter until well
after the Restoration: in his diary in
February 1667 he wrote that, 'we talked
much of Cromwell, all saying he was a
brave fellow and did owe his Crowne he
got to himself as much as any man that
ever got one'. KM

LITERATURE: *ODNB*; *Diary*, VIII, 50.

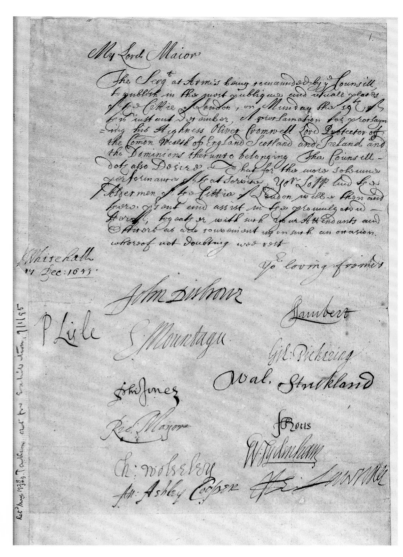

19

Dunbar medals

1650
Thomas Simon (c.1623–65), London
Bronze
British Museum, M.7330 and M.7334

Victory medals were issued to the
officers and men of Cromwell's army
who fought at the Battle of Dunbar
in September 1650. Officers received
gold versions; ordinary soldiers bronze.
Dunbar was part of the conflict between
England and Scotland, after the latter
acclaimed Charles II king. Charles's
attempt to take the throne ended in
failure with the rout of Royalist forces
at Worcester in 1651. The medal shows
Cromwell in profile with a scene on the
reverse of Parliament sitting in a single
chamber, the House of Lords having been
abolished in 1649. RB

20

**Order of the Council of State
proclaiming Oliver Cromwell as Lord
Protector of the Commonwealth**

17 December 1653
English Parliament
Ink on paper
British Library, Add. MS 18739, f.1

In 1653, Cromwell formally accepted
the title of Lord Protector of the
Commonwealth in a new constitution
called the 'Instrument of Government'.
It was an elective post but gave him
executive power for life. This is the
official proclamation of him as Lord
Protector, prepared the day after
he was invested. It is signed by the
thirteen members of the Council of
State, appointed by Parliament to act
as the executive of the government in
place of the king. It included Pepys's
cousin and patron, Edward Montagu,
who served as MP for Huntingdonshire
in the first Protectorate Parliament. In
1657, Cromwell was offered the crown
but turned it down saying, 'I would not
seek to set up that which Providence
hath destroyed and laid in the dust'. KM

21

Naval reward medal

1653
Thomas Simon (*c*.1623–65), London
Gold
National Maritime Museum, on loan
from a private collection, MEC1115

This naval reward medal, presented
to Admiral Sir William Penn, is one
of a small number struck in gold for
senior naval officers during the First
Anglo-Dutch War (1652–54). On the
obverse, an anchor, with the emblems
of England, Scotland and Ireland, is set
within a decorated border consisting of
rigging, flags, cannon and other naval
attributes. The reverse depicts a battle,
with a sinking Dutch ship to the fore.
Penn was appointed general-at-sea in
1653 and played a prominent role in
advancing Cromwell's colonial ambitions
in the Caribbean. He was one of several
senior officers who, despite earlier
Parliamentary sympathies, continued
to serve in the Restoration navy; Pepys
knew him well through his work at the
Navy Board. RB

22

Naval reward medal

1653
Thomas Simon (*c*.1623–65), London
Gold
National Maritime Museum, MEC1118

A gold medal, smaller than object 21, was
presented to junior flag officers (officers
above the rank of captain) serving in the
First Anglo-Dutch War. Of similar design
to the larger version, it features a simpler,
laurel-leaf design around the border. This
medal is believed to have been awarded
to Captain William Haddock, a member
of a distinguished naval family. RB

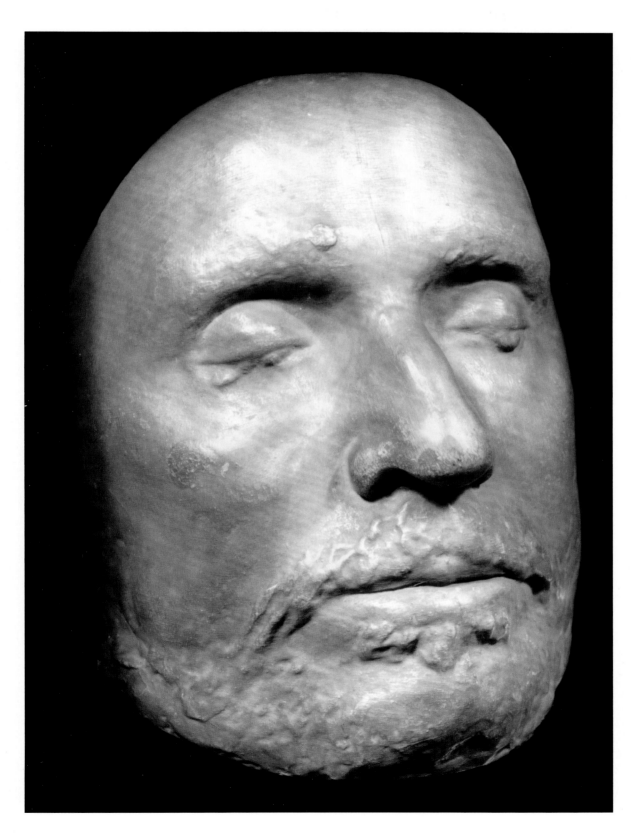

23

....

Cast of the death mask of Oliver Cromwell

....

Late seventeenth century
Plaster
National Portrait Gallery, NPG 4025

After a steep decline in health, Cromwell died on 3 September 1658, probably from pneumonia associated with malarial fever. He was fifty-nine. A wooden effigy, wearing a wax mask and dressed in robes with a crown, orb and sceptre, lay in state at Somerset House. Cromwell was buried at Westminster Abbey, but his body was not left in peace. In 1661, the vengeful Convention Parliament ordered that the regicides should suffer a traitor's death: Cromwell's corpse was disinterred, hanged and beheaded. His head was displayed on a spike at Westminster Hall, where Pepys saw it in 1669. RB

LITERATURE: *ODNB*; *Diary*, II, 31.

24

Miniature of Richard Cromwell

1650–55
Unknown artist
Watercolour on vellum, 54 × 44
National Portrait Gallery, NPG 4350

It is likely that Cromwell intended Richard
(1626–1712), his eldest son, to follow
him as Lord Protector. The succession
was publicly declared on 4 September
1658, but Richard lacked the military and
Parliamentary experience of his father.
Difficulties soon arose with the army
and the Protectorate finances. Unable to
control the situation, Richard abdicated
under pressure from the army on 8 June
1659. The Protectorate was over and the
serious political plotting that would lead
to the Restoration now began. RB

LITERATURE: *ODNB*; Tomalin, pp. 73–75.

25

Miniatures of Edward Montagu,
1st Earl of Sandwich
and Jemima Montagu (née Crew),
1st Countess of Sandwich

....

*c.*1661
Richard Gibson (1615–90)
Watercolour on vellum: 80 × 70; 75 × 65
Private collection

Edward Montagu (1625–72) and Jemima
Crew (1625–74) were married at St
Margaret's, Westminster, on 7 November
1642 and moved to Hinchingbrooke
House, near Huntingdon, where they
raised their family. Pepys respected his
cousin and patron, referring in his diary to
Montagu as 'my Lord'. Their relationship
was not simply one of employer and
employee – they shared a close social
bond and had mutual interests in music,
art and science. Pepys also admired
Jemima Montagu, the 'most excellent,
good, discreet lady that ever was'. The
miniaturist Richard Gibson was also
known as 'Dwarf' Gibson, being only
3 feet 10 inches tall (1.17 metres). RB

LITERATURE: *ODNB*; *Diary*, V, 257.

THE
RESTORATION

At about three o'clock on the morning of Sunday, 2 September 1666, Pepys was awoken by his maid Jane with news that there was a great fire in the City of London. The fire had started a couple of hours earlier at the house of Thomas Farriner, the king's baker, in Pudding Lane: Pepys being over a quarter of a mile (0.4 km) to the east in Seething Lane thought the fire too far away to worry about, 'and so went back to bed again to sleep'.[1] Londoners were used to small fires breaking out all the time, and at first the fire at Farriner's place seemed little to worry about. When the Lord Mayor, Sir Thomas Bludworth, arrived in Pudding Lane just before 3 a.m., he dismissed the danger, saying 'that a woman might piss it out'.[2] However, it had been an unusually dry summer, and the City's densely packed wooden buildings proved the perfect fuel. As a strong east wind fanned the flames, the fire quickly got out of control, raging for several days until the wind finally dropped late on Tuesday and the firebreaks created by tearing down properties at last began to prove effective. By the evening of Wednesday 5 September the main threat was finally over, although small fires continued to burn in various places.

In the course of almost four days, the Great Fire had destroyed some 85 per cent of the area of the City of London proper (the famous 'square mile'), including eighty-seven churches, fifty-two company halls, and over 13,200 houses, the homes of perhaps 75,000 of the City's 90,000 inhabitants.[3] Surveying the damage, Pepys observed 'the saddest sight of desolation' he had ever seen.[4] Nothing remained, lamented George Hall, Bishop of Chester, 'but a strange maze and labyrinth of naked Steeples, useless Chimneys and pitiful fragments of ragged Walls, amidst perpetual heaps of Ashes, Stones and Rubbish'.[5] It is not clear how many died: perhaps very few (the figure normally given is eight), though it is likely that many deaths were unrecorded and that many more died from indirect causes, such as hunger or exposure in the aftermath of being made homeless.[6]

At the time, London was still reeling from a renewed outbreak of plague. The Black Death had first come to England in 1348 and been

Tim Harris

The Dissolute Court and Retribution

endemic ever since, although the last serious outbreaks had occurred in the 1630s. However, by November 1663 the plague was back in Yarmouth, in Norfolk, introduced by a ship from Holland, and the following spring cases were being reported in London. It was in the summer of 1665 that the contagion really took hold in the capital. The nonconformist preacher Thomas Vincent wrote of death riding 'triumphantly on his pale Horse through our streets' and of people falling 'as thick as leaves from the Trees in Autumn'.[7] For the week of 22–29 August, the Bills of Mortality listed 6,102 deaths from the plague in the City of London alone, although Pepys believed the true figure was nearer 10,000, since not all poor people or Quakers had been recorded. The official number the next week was even higher – just shy of 7,000. By the end of the year, perhaps as many as 100,000 Londoners had died, some 15 per cent of the greater-metropolitan population. Nationwide, the figure was twice that many.[8]

The Great Fire the following year was a double blow. Moreover, the fire happened when England was at war with the Dutch and the French. Naturally, Londoners looked to blame their enemies. Several Dutch and French visitors, as well as English Catholics, were assaulted by angry crowds and dragged before magistrates on suspicion of firing the City; one woman was killed for having something in her apron which the crowd feared were fire-balls.[9] A mentally unbalanced watchmaker from Rouen by the name of Robert Hubert subsequently confessed to having started the fire, as part of an international Catholic conspiracy, and was duly executed. The presiding judge at the trial did not believe Hubert's story – it was discovered a year later that Hubert was not even in the country when the fire broke out – but the country needed a scapegoat and Hubert himself seemed bent on suicide. Despite this, the government concluded there was no evidence of 'any other cause of that woful fire than the displeasure of God Almighty',[10] and duly appointed Wednesday 10 October to be a day of 'Fasting and Humiliation' to implore God to 'pardon the crying sins of this Nation' – this to fall a week after the monthly fast that was still being held for deliverance from the plague.[11]

The restoration of the monarchy in 1660 – achieved, as it had been, without the least bloodshed – had seemed a miracle wrought by God. By 1665–66, God appeared to be deserting England, punishing the nation for its sins. But for what sort of sins, and who were the greatest sinners? After the repressive moralism of the mid-century Puritan revolution, the return of the monarchy was greeted with a sense of release – a feeling that people were free at last to have a good time. Back came the maypoles, church ales and village feasts. Back came the theatre. Yet to some it seemed that the pursuit of pleasure was being carried to excess. Most worrying in this regard was the hedonism of the royal court itself. As early as the summer of 1661, Pepys noted the prevalence of 'swearing, drinking and whoring' at court, and the fact that 'the pox' was 'as common there … as eating and swearing'.[12] Charles II and his brother James, Duke of York, seemed to be leading the way: both were notorious womanizers, and it was said that success at court depended upon an ability 'to pimp, cheat, forswear thyself, and lie'.[13]

It was not just that the debauchery of the court risked provoking God's wrath. The temptations on offer seemed to be distracting those at the top from the business of running the country. Government incompetence was highlighted in June 1667, when the Dutch fleet sailed up the Medway to Chatham, destroyed four of the English navy's largest vessels and captured the flagship, the *Royal Charles*. Yet Pepys had had his doubts for some time: in his diary he recorded how, at a meeting at Greenwich in September 1665 to discuss the war, they talked of 'the ill-government of our Kingdom, nobody setting to heart the business of the Kingdom, but everybody minding their perticular profit or pleasures, the King himself minding nothing but his ease … so we let things go to wrack'.[14]

The triple disasters of the plague, Great Fire and the Medway provoked the first major crisis of the Restoration monarchy. This crisis led to the downfall of the Earl of Clarendon, one of the key architects of the Restoration settlement and someone who, ironically, had opposed the Second Anglo-Dutch War; impeached by the Commons, Clarendon fled to France and lived out the remainder of his life in exile. Yet there were some who felt the blame lay higher up. Anonymous satires began to circulate, suggesting that the king was responsible for England's woes. One compared Charles II to the Roman tyrant Nero, who had fiddled while Rome burned, and noted (in reference to the Medway disaster) how 'our great Prince, when the Dutch fleet arriv'd, / Saw his ships burn'd and, as they burn'd, he swiv'd.' 'So kind was he in our extremest need,' the poet concluded, 'He would those flames extinguish with his seed.'[15] In August 1667, Pepys claimed that people were beginning to look back favourably on the Interregnum and even predicted that England would 'fall back again to a commonwealth', since the Stuarts were 'doing all that silly men can do to make themselfes unable to support their Kingdom – minding their lust and their pleasure, and making their government so chargeable,

that people do well remember better things were done, and better managed and with much less charge, under a commonwealth than they have been by this King'.[16]

The mood of the nation had changed dramatically since 1660. Then, the collapse of the republic and the return of the monarchy had been greeted with widespread rejoicing across the three kingdoms. Crowds in London celebrated the downfall of the Rump Parliament in February 1660 by roasting the hind quarters of animals in derision of the republican regime. When the Rump's successor, the Convention Parliament, voted on 1 May 1660 to restore the king, there was 'great joy' across London, 'and at night more bonefires then ever and ringing of bells', with people 'drinking of the King's health upon their knees in the streets'.[17] There were jubilant celebrations when Charles was proclaimed king in the capital on the 8th and in the provinces a week later, when he reached Dover on the 25th and when he made his triumphal entry into London on the 29th, his thirtieth birthday.[18]

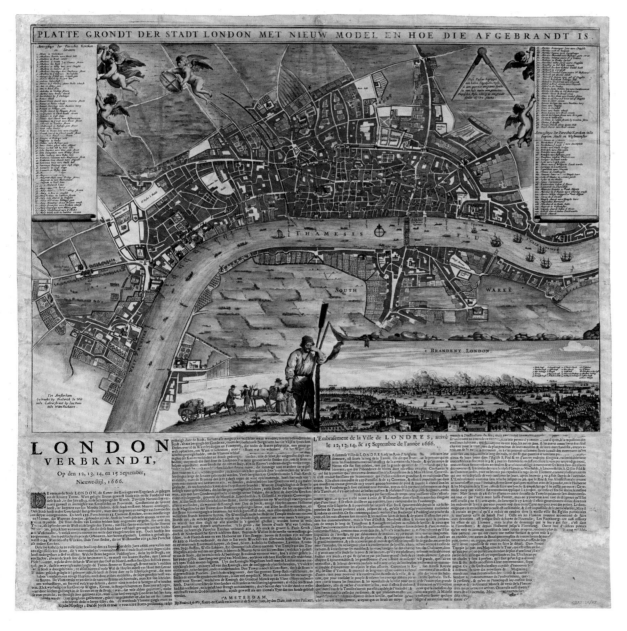

London Verbrandt ... 1666
('London Burns ... 1666')
Hand-coloured engraving, by Frederick de Wit (1629/30–1706).
This engraving shows the extent of the Great Fire and people fleeing.

National Maritime Museum, G297:20/27.

Not that everyone rejoiced. A few Cromwellian veterans made idle boasts that they would run Charles through with their rusty old swords given half the chance. In Newcastle upon Tyne, up near the border with Scotland, an area that had suffered much from the depredations of Scottish forces during the 1640s, a woman named Margaret Dixon was outraged that they could 'finde noe other man to bring in then [than] a Scotsman', believing there were none who loved Charles Stuart 'but drunk whores and whoremongers' and that he would 'sett on fire the three kingdoms as his father before him has done'.[19] But diehard republicans were a tiny minority. Even most Protestant separatists, those who had been the keenest supporters of the republic, were prepared to accept the inevitable and make their peace with the Restoration, putting their faith in the promise Charles had made in his declaration issued from Breda in April 1660 that he would allow people to worship as they wished.

Yet although the vast majority did welcome the return of monarchy, different people had different expectations of the Restoration. Some wanted limited monarchy, others a return to the more absolute style of kingship practised by Charles I in the 1630s. Separatists desired religious toleration. Presbyterians favoured a settlement in the church sufficiently comprehensive to allow moderate Puritans like themselves to conform, but with no toleration for the sects. Anglicans wanted the return of the old church of bishops and prayer book, with neither toleration nor comprehension. All, of course, hoped that the return of Charles II would lead to political stability and economic recovery. In the end, Charles was restored without conditions, albeit the reforming legislation enacted by the Long Parliament in 1641 was left on the statute books – leaving plenty of room for debate as to whether or not the king's power needed to be limited further, and ambiguity over exactly how much power the restored monarchy had. In the church, the Anglican vision won out, leaving Presbyterians and separatists alike liable to persecution. Some 2,000 ministers in England were ejected from their livings for failing to conform to the Restoration Church, while the Five Mile Act of 1665 aimed at driving nonconformist ministers from urban centres and the Quaker Act (1662) and two Conventicle Acts (1664, 1670) subjected those who preached at or attended nonconformist meetings to a series of gradated fines (with those unable to pay facing the possibility of imprisonment and seizure of goods). Moreover, not only did the economy fail to pick up, but taxes remained high, with a new tax imposed on fireplaces in 1662 – the Hearth Tax – proving particularly unpopular.

Disillusionment with the restored monarchy began to manifest itself quite soon after 1660. 'If the King did side with the Bishopps, the Divell take King and Bishops too,' one Londoner warned in August 1662. 'Wee were made to believe when the King came in That we should never pay any more taxes. If wee had thought that he would have taxed us thus, hee should never have come in,' complained another in July 1663.[20] The biggest grievance was the settlement in the church and the ensuing persecution of nonconformists. Many who had welcomed the Restoration felt betrayed. A few of the more radical types engaged in conspiracies against the state, although this merely served to confirm the government's belief that severe measures against Protestant dissenters were justified.

Religious persecution divided the nation. Some thought the dissenters deserved all they got for having begun the troubles that led to the outbreak of civil war, the downfall of the Church of England and the execution of Charles I. Others felt only the more radical sectarians, those who posed a genuine threat to national security, should be targeted. Yet many believed it was wrong that 'the godly', the overwhelming majority of whom were peaceful, should be persecuted merely for worshipping God – especially when the royal court appeared to be giving free licence to rakes and libertines who had turned their back on God.

What was going on at court became a cause for concern for a number of reasons. There was moral outrage. Yet people were also worried about the threat of 'popery'. There were some powerful figures at court who were either Catholics or sympathetic to Catholicism, including

Medal commemorating the landing of King Charles II at Dover
Silver, by John Roettier (1631–1703), 1660.

National Maritime Museum, MEC0867.

Text beneath the engraving:

That beastly Rabble that came down	To cry the Cause — up heretofore	And all ye Grandees of our Members		That serve for Characters & Badges,	And 'tis a Miracle we are not	Some on the Sign Post of an Ale house
From all the Garretts in the Town	And bawl the Bishops out of Door	Are Carbonading on the Embers;	Burning ye **Rumps**	To Represent their Personages	Already Sacrific'd Incarnate	Hang in Effigie, on the Gallows,
And stalls & shop boards in vast num	Are now drawn up in greater Shoals	Knights Citizens and Burgesses	at TEMPLE-BARR.	Such Bonfire is a Funeral Pile,	For while we wrangle here & jar,	Made up of Rags to personate
With new chalk'd Bills & rusty Arms	To Roast and Broil is on the Coals	Ride forth by Rumps, & Pigs & Geese.		In which they Roast & Scorch & Broil	Ware Grylld all at Temple-Bar	Respective Officers of State

Burning ye Rumps at Temple Barr
Etching and engraving, by
William Hogarth (1697–1764), 1725–26.

Fitzwilliam Museum, PDP, 22.K.3-68.

Madam Elinora Gwynne.

P: Lely pinx: N: Visscher exc: A De Blois fecit

George Digby, Earl of Bristol, and Henry Bennet, Earl of Arlington, and of course the king's brother and heir to the throne, the Duke of York (who converted to Catholicism sometime in the late 1660s). Charles's mother, Henrietta Maria, who as the French and Catholic wife of Charles I had never been a popular figure in England, was back at court in the early 1660s, until the damp British weather forced her to retire to France in 1665. In 1662, Charles married a Catholic, the Portuguese princess Catherine of Braganza, a match which many feared would bring England into the French orbit, since both France and Portugal had a common enemy in Spain. Charles, of course, was never faithful to Catherine, and continued to have numerous affairs. His favourite mistress from 1660 to 1668 was Barbara Villiers, Countess of Castlemaine and later Duchess of Cleveland, whose husband, Roger Palmer, Earl of Castlemaine, was a Catholic and who herself converted to Catholicism in 1663. From about 1663, Charles developed a passion for Frances Stuart (or Stewart), later Duchess of Richmond, who had been raised in France as a Catholic, although it is not clear that they ever became lovers. (Frances is best known for having been the model for Britannia on coinage.) From the early 1670s, the king's most influential mistress was the French Catholic Louise de Kéroualle, Duchess of Portsmouth. Given English people's views of Catholicism and of France, Charles was quite literally sleeping with the enemy. Nell Gwyn, the orange-seller and actress who became Charles's mistress from the late 1660s, was 'the Protestant whore'.[21]

Furthermore, all this was not cheap. Charles had fourteen illegitimate children by his various mistresses over the course of his lifetime, and these had to be supported: during the 1670s, Cleveland and Portsmouth and their children were in receipt of permanent grants worth more than £45,000 a year (several million pounds today).[22] As one satirist later rhymed: 'Why art thou poor, O King?' Embezzling Cunt, / That wide-mouthed, greedy monster, that has done't.'[23] Then there was the issue of pillow talk. Did those who had closest access to the king's body perhaps have an undue influence in shaping royal policy? As the notorious court libertine John Wilmot, Earl of Rochester, observed in the early 1670s, Charles's 'sceptre and his prick are of a length, / And she may sway the one who plays with t'other'.[24]

As early as 1662, at the time of the Braganza match, Clarendon warned Charles that his behaviour was costing him politically, and if he continued like this it 'would break the hearts of all his friends' and please only 'those who wished the destruction of monarchy'.[25] Radical separatists began to warn that God would visit his judgment upon 'all the workers of Iniquity', as the Quaker Charles Bayley put it in 1663. He included Charles himself, who had provoked God's anger by the excesses and wantonness he allowed at court and 'the great and grievous Oppressions' suffered by the 'Lord's People'.[26] It was the double visitation of plague and the Great Fire that seemed to offer confirmation that God was punishing England for its sins – a view shared by people of all religious and political persuasions. They differed, however, on where they apportioned blame. There were distinct separatist, moderate Puritan and Anglican perspectives on what was responsible for provoking God's wrath. Rather than creating a united front, the plague and Great Fire instead revealed how little unity the Restoration had brought to England.

Of the sects, the Quakers were the most outspoken. In late 1666, a Quaker whom we know only as J.C. claimed to have had a vision in which 'a bright Cloud came about him' and a shrill, childlike voice said: 'They [the inhabitants of London] have had the pestilence and fier, and other Callamitys and yett are not Amended, but a worse plauge is it to Come on them (and the Nattion)'.[27] The following year, the Quaker James Parke sounded *Another Trumpet ... in the Ears of the Inhabitants of England, Rulers, Priests and People*, warning the 'Nation of England' that 'a great Destruction and Calamity' had 'begun in thee', because of 'thy Oaths, Drunkenness, Covetousness and ... Whoredoms' and persecution of 'them that fear the Lord' (i.e. the Quakers), and calling on the wicked to repent.[28]

Madam Elinora Gwynne [Nell Gwyn]
Mezzotint, by Abraham de Blois (active 1679–1720) after Sir Peter Lely, 1670s.

National Maritime Museum, PBE9953/3.

Presbyterians and moderate Puritans, however, tended to blame not just the court rakes but also the radical sects. The work that best illustrates the moderate Puritan position is *God's Terrible Voice in the City*, published in 1667 by the ejected minister Thomas Vincent (see 73). Vincent was one among many nonconformist clerics who had returned to London following the outbreak of the plague, preaching in various churches vacated by Anglican ministers who had fled the capital, and attending to the sick and dying. Huge crowds attended his sermons, and *God's Terrible Voice* proved so popular that it ran to sixteen editions in just eight years. Vincent lambasted the 'Gallants' and 'Atheists' of 'our times', the 'notoriously ungodly of this generation' who wallowed in drunkenness and 'filthy fornication and adultery'. Yet he also condemned Quakers, Ranters, Seekers, Antinomians, Brownists and Anabaptists – those 'false teachers' whom he believed were Jesuits and Catholic priests in disguise sent by Rome to 'tear our Protestant Church to pieces' and 'make way for the introduction of Popery' – as well as Catholics more generally: indeed, he thought the Great Fire of London smelled 'of a Popish design', akin to the Gunpowder Plot of 1605. Nevertheless, Vincent proclaimed, whoever might have been the instruments, ultimately God was the author of the fire, as well as the plague. Terrible though these were, they could have been worse: more people could have died, more of London could have been destroyed.

England therefore needed to hearken to God's terrible voice and mend its ways. Vincent concluded by condemning those responsible for persecuting the godly (though to judge from his earlier remarks he presumably thought the sects were fair game), imploring 'persecutors' to 'turn from your evil ways'.[29]

Anglican clergy were also deeply critical of the debauchery of the court. Indeed, they had been since the early years of the Restoration. On Christmas Day 1662, the Bishop of Winchester and Dean of the Chapel Royal, George Morley, a man who had served the Royalist court in exile in the 1650s, preached a lengthy sermon at Whitehall condemning the excesses of the court, albeit only to be laughed at by his congregation.[30] The royal chaplain Richard Allestree, Regius Professor of Divinity at Oxford from 1663, preached a number of sermons at court over the course of the 1660s attacking the sensualists and atheists of the age, who showed no 'restraint of Appetites or Passions' and who scoffed at religion.[31] In 1667, the Archbishop of Canterbury, Gilbert Sheldon, was brazen enough to tell Charles to his face to 'put away this woman that you keep' (Barbara Villiers).[32]

The Anglican establishment thus also saw the plague and Great Fire as divine retribution upon a reprobate nation. Preaching before the king on 10 October 1666, the solemn fast day for the fire, William

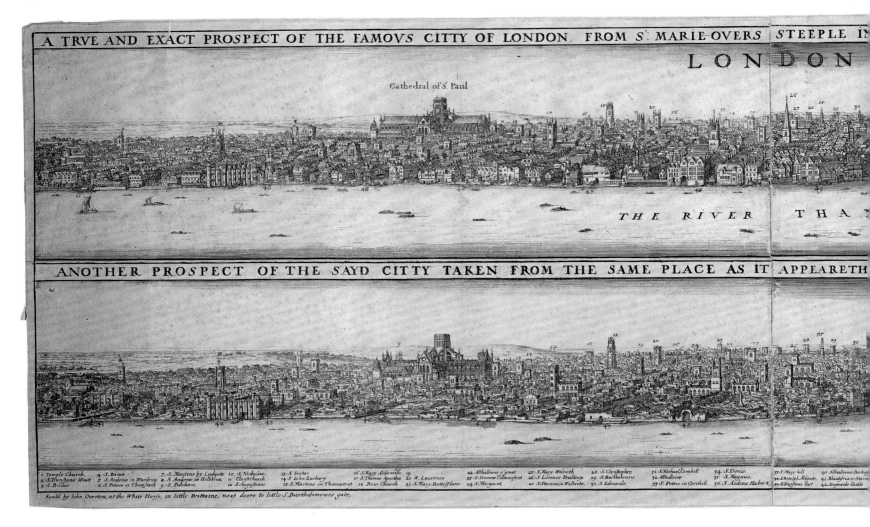

Sancroft, Dean of St Paul's, urged his listeners to 'dream no longer of ... Incendiaries, Dutch or French', since the fire was evidence of God's 'Displeasure for our Sins'. Sancroft, in fact, refused to identify the particular sins that had 'occasioned this heavy Judgment': ''Tis a slippery place', he said; the judgment fell 'upon us All', so 'every Man' should 'suspect himself'.[33] Others, however, seized the opportunity to attack the nonconformists. At Greenwich on 4 October 1665, one of the monthly fast days for the plague, the vicar Dr Thomas Plume chose to preach 'of the sinn of rebellion against Magistrates and Ministers'.[34] At St Martin-in-the-Fields, Westminster, on the Sunday after the Great Fire, the royal chaplain Nathaniel Hardy accepted that it was 'the effect of Gods wrath' for the sins of 'the whole Kingdom'. Yet those who had provoked God's anger were not just those 'guilty of Sodoms sins', but also those who had raised 'a Rebellious War against their Sovereign' that had ended in regicide and who had 'made wide breaches in Church and State, between the King and His People' and 'set the whole Kingdom on flames'.[35] The Master of the Savoy hospital, Dr Henry Killigrew, preaching before the king on the first Sunday in Advent 1666, lamented the fact that recent judgments of God, such as the plague, had seemingly had little effect 'upon the hearts of the People', who 'in their holding fast of their Iniquities' were trying 'what will be the Issue of [God's] Threats and Denunciations against sin'. He lambasted those 'immers'd in Lust and Sensuality', condemned the pride of 'Great Ones', urging them to 'to practice Self-denyal', and was even prepared to offer the reminder that 'Outward Pomp and Magnificence was annext to Kings' simply 'to preserve Reverance and Awe in the Vulgar, not to puff up their own Spirits'. Yet Killigrew reserved his venom for those 'false teachers' who advanced nothing but 'schisme and Sedition', urging his listeners and readers 'not so much as to admit such persons into their Houses, or bid them God-speed'; such types, he insisted, deserved 'only the Entertainment of the Whipping-Post, and the welcome of a Hot Iron to bore their Tounges' (tongue-boring was the punishment in England for blasphemy).[36] Allestree was another Anglican cleric who linked his attacks on the sensualists of the age with a condemnation of all those he took to be enemies of true religion, whether atheists, Roman Catholics or Protestant dissenters.

The events of 1665–66 were deeply traumatizing. Yes, London would be rebuilt and the Restoration regime would soldier on. Yet the honeymoon period was over. Disillusionment had crept in, and people had started to look nostalgically back to the days of the republic. Most worrying of all, it seemed that the old battle lines were being redrawn. It was as if the Restoration had solved little.

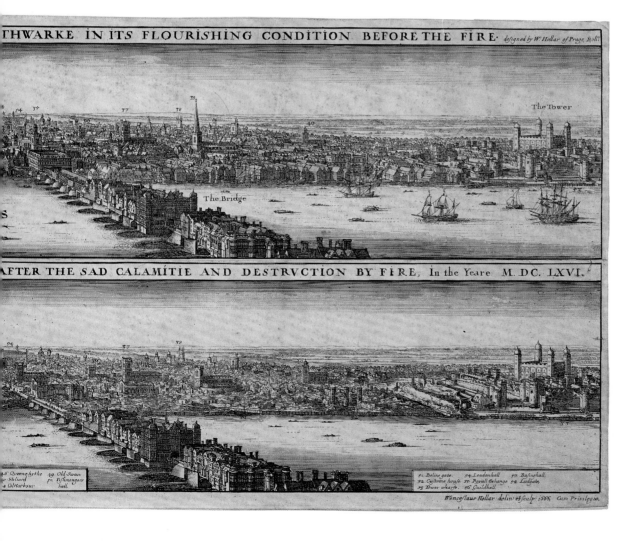

A True and Exact Prospect of the Famous Citty of London ... Before the Fire and Another Prospect of the Sayd Citty ... After the ... Fire Etching, by Wenceslaus Hollar (1607–77), 1666.

National Maritime Museum, PAH9901.

Laura Gowing

Women

in the World

of Pepys

Elizabeth de St Michel and her husband, Samuel Pepys, were children of an extraordinary generation. As they grew up – Samuel in London, Elizabeth in Devon and Paris – they witnessed the world turned upside down. Elizabeth was eight years old when Charles I was executed, Sam fifteen; over the next decade they lived through the creation of a militarized state and saw the old familial politics in which the king stood for the head of household replaced by a republican ideal of male citizens. Their short, intense marriage, which lasted only from 1655 to Elizabeth's death in 1669, took place against a backdrop of national crises with corresponding shifts in sexual politics.

During the Puritan revolution, women's activism was symptomatic of a world overturned. Ordinary women joined sects and spoke as prophets. Groups of women petitioned Parliament for peace. City women helped build defences, and gentlewomen defended their country houses against besieging armies. With print censorship removed, the mass of cheap pamphlets included, for the first time, significant numbers of texts written by women, many of them Quakers and members of other radical sects in which women played prominent speaking and writing roles. All this public activity was paralleled by a print culture peopled by stories of witches and monstrous births, in which the vicissitudes of warfare and religious change were projected onto views of the female body.

Yet in the midst of political cataclysm, much remained unaltered for women. The democratic dreams of the Levellers did not anticipate levelling the distinctions of gender. Marriage defined a woman's identity. English common law, stricter than elsewhere in Europe, imposed considerable restrictions on a wife: once married, she was, as one contemporary legal treatise memorably put it, like a stream that flowed into her husband's river and became part of it. Her business actions were legally assumed to be on behalf of her husband; her ability to hold property was limited; her husband was entitled to beat her (within limits) and she had no right to refuse sex with him. Marriage was truly 'until death us do part', for it was still against church law

Elizabeth, Wife of Samuel Pepys, Esqr.
Engraving, by James Thomson
(1788–1850) after John Hayls, 1825.

National Maritime Museum, PBE9953/4.

for a couple to live apart. Separation might be granted on the grounds of women's adultery, or men's violence, but it still did not allow remarriage, and was unlikely to be financially practicable for women without family support.

But of course neither law nor rhetoric determined the whole shape of women's lives. Many married women worked independently, kept their own property and used the variety of law courts and informal routes to justice to protect themselves and their goods. A late average age of marriage and a high mortality rate also meant that at any one time at least half the female adult population were single: spinsters and widows were always visible and active in urban and rural communities. Women did not, usually, train for work as men might, nor in an age of growing wage labour did they often work for a living wage, but

they occupied a well-established part of the labour market. On farms they were likely to be doing dairy work, looking after smaller animals, working close to the house or taking goods to market. In towns and cities, many worked in the service sector: selling food and drink, laundering clothes, nursing.

Especially visible in Pepys's diary are the women who made and sold clothes, because he liked to buy from them and pursue them. Ribbons, haberdashery, stockings, bands, buttons – all these were the province of the women who traded, either independently or with their husbands, in the Royal Exchange and the shops of the City and Westminster, conveniently provided with counters and chairs. It was at the end of the seventeenth century that shoplifting became a recognizable crime, one particularly associated with women; and the stories of those arrested

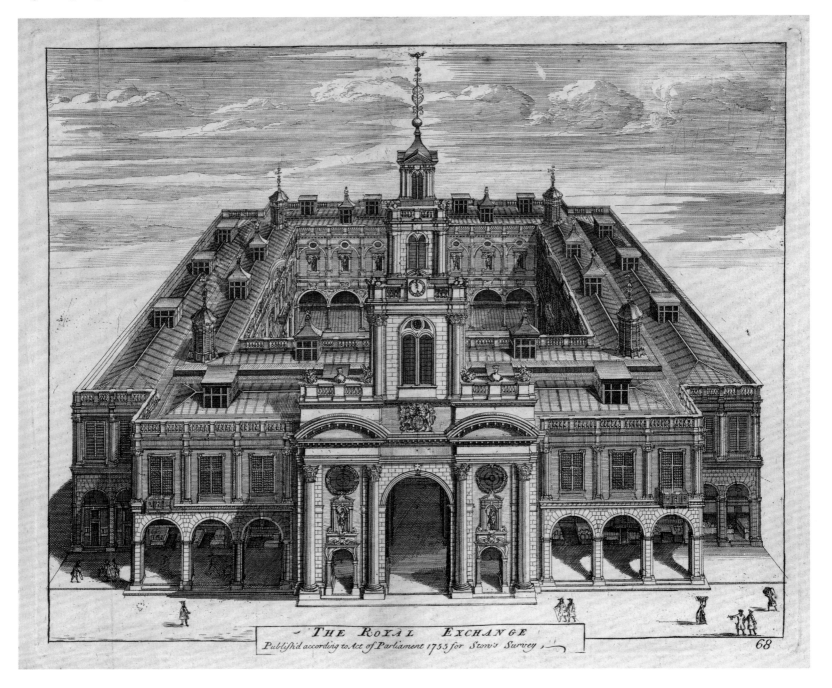

THE ROYAL EXCHANGE
Publish'd according to Act of Parliament 1755 for Stow's Survey

68

convey something of the engrossing new world of cheap patterned cottons, ribbons, lace and gloves. Those who traded in this world were the new middle class, the daughters of clergy, tradesmen and even gentry, and they were not so far away from the Pepyses.

Within the families of this world, as in the political universe, hierarchy was rarely questioned. Male dominance over women was institutionalized by natural law as well as by virtue of a symbolic analogy between family and state, father and monarch. But this was also a world of complementary roles, in which marriage was still all but essential to economic success for men as well as women, and the working partnership of husband and wife was crucial at all social levels. The majority of the population married in their late twenties, when they were able to support themselves. Most had already lost at least one parent by then, and they married to suit themselves as much as their families, balancing attraction with economic viability. As many as 20 per cent of people never married. Those who did mostly lived in small, nuclear households, with an average of between two and three surviving children. Among the elites, early marriages were more common, but neither Samuel nor Elizabeth had the finances to support the household they had created so young.

Pepys's first diary entry in January 1660 recorded the inhabitants of the house he was renting in Axe Yard, in Westminster, as 'my wife and servant Jane, and no more in family than us three'. His turn of speech reflected the domestic arrangements of typical households, where servants were part of the family. Service was not a career or a status, but a stage in the life cycle, occupying and housing the young until they had amassed the skills and savings to marry, and servants were often not far removed in status from their employers, though this was to change as service roles became more specialized and domestic hierarchies developed. By the late seventeenth century, female domestic service was at a high point, and so many young women came to London to work that the city's ratio of men to women was something like 40:60. Service often enabled rural and urban women to advance themselves, and to

live in the city, but the low pay and the risk of domestic disagreement, harassment and potential pregnancy made it also a risky move.

Late-seventeenth-century houses were crowded, with rooms used for multiple purposes. Privacy was limited and servants often ended up moving from room to room, sleeping in truckle beds alongside their employers, or being housed in kitchens or attics. When marriages went wrong, the servants' testimony, garnered from hours of close work and company, always took pride of place and, for many, marital conflict left them in positions of great awkwardness. The closeness of family life raised suspicions and dangers for single-women servants, and sometimes for men too. Samuel's apparent assumption of a right to touch and kiss female servants was not uncommon.

As the Pepys household increased in substance, the intimacies of domesticity often led to rage and jealousy. Elizabeth rarely, it seems, had enough knowledge of Samuel's sexual life outside the home with which to tax him, nor did contemporary sexual culture often expect a man to be held sexually accountable in the way a woman was. On domestic turf, though, he was more culpable, and the row when Elizabeth caught him with the maid, Deb Willet, in 1668 cast a long shadow. Nor did Samuel entirely trust Elizabeth. On 15 May 1663, jealousy of Elizabeth's dancing master reached a peak when he found himself trying to discover whether or not she was wearing drawers during his visits. (The drawers were another of Elizabeth's exceptionalities, perhaps a French habit: most English women at this point were still wearing no lower undergarments. A Somerset servant in the same period described wearing drawers especially to protect her from her master's groping as she went upstairs.)

Pepys was fascinated by lurid stories of court life – the woman who 'dropped' a baby while dancing at a ball, the king's guards being allowed a weekly absence to visit their whores. Only a few years earlier, at the time of the Pepyses' marriage, adulterous sex had been classed with incest and bestiality as a capital offence: by the 1660s, men from the king downwards were declaring in public that lusts of the body were a minor affair. This sexual atmosphere undoubtedly shaped their relationship, and the lives of all women in London and its environs. Rarely, in seventeenth-century records, do we read women's words on sex. But Pepys's encounters with his female partners, as he recorded them, fascinated by his own sexual sins and adventures, convey in exceptional detail the sexual culture in which he lived. For centuries, women's pleasure had been deemed essential to conception, and women had been held to be the more lustful sex. Pepys, like other men, seems to have sometimes actually tried to avoid giving pleasure to his partners: not, surely, because of a Puritan horror at women's lust, but in order to protect against illegitimate pregnancy. Noting his 'great pleasure' with his long-time sexual partner Betty Martin on 16 January 1664, he added: 'j'ai grand peur que je l'ay fait faire aussi elle meme' ('I fear that I have given the same to her'). Careful calculations about sexual activity, its timing and its consequences were part of the regular conversations between them.

Alongside a belief in the powerful effects of women's desire ran another, increasingly prevalent aspect of male libertinism. The plays the Pepyses saw commonly featured rape as a plot device, depicting women as helpless victims of male lust. It is apparent from many diary entries that Samuel's idea of a woman's consent was minimal. His sexuality, and his own sense of it, reflected an era in which force was to a man's credit, and women's ability to consent or dissent was severely restricted by both law and custom. A revealing moment comes on 6 July 1667,

as Samuel celebrated with Betty Martin, at the draper's stall she ran in Westminster Hall, the happy news that she was not pregnant by him. Their pleasure was ruined by the arrival of Betty's sister (also one of his lovers):

> But here happened the best instance of a woman's falseness in the world, that her sister Doll, who went for a bottle of wine, did come home all blubbering and swearing against one Captain Vandener, a Dutchman of the Rhenish Wine House, that pulled her into a stable by the Dog tavern, and there did tumble her and toss her, calling him all the rogues and toads in the world, when she knows that elle hath suffered me to do any thing with her a hundred times.

Not only did Samuel apparently believe that Doll's having had sex with him meant she had no right to complain when a random Dutchman 'tumbled' her; but his very phrasing, 'elle hath suffered me to do any thing with her', depicts her as the passive object of his desire. Pepys's stories echoed the new sexual narrative of the times, in which men were insatiable, and women were their victims. Eventually this helped enable charity towards single mothers and reformed prostitutes, but not soon enough to inhibit Pepys's forceful repudiation of his brother's illegitimate daughter by his servant.

The name of 'whore' continued to carry criminal significance. Elizabeth, it seems, insisted not only that Deb Willet would leave their service, but that Samuel would formally repudiate her and call her a whore in writing. She threatened, according to Sam, 'to slit the girl's

nose'. Her words harked back to an old customary punishment for whoredom, meant to mark out dishonest women. It featured in Roman and Byzantine law against sexual sin, and had been invoked in street talk throughout the sixteenth century. Elizabeth's threats echoed an older world than that of Restoration sexual freedom.

Pepys's life after Elizabeth's death in 1669 brought him a sustained quasi-conjugal relationship with another woman, Mary Skinner. They never married, but they shared a household: she was both known as his housekeeper and called by some 'Mrs Pepys' or 'the second Mrs Pepys'. It was an era when clandestine and illicit marriages were rife. In the 1680s, two women married in a church and lived together, one dressed as a man, and when the deception was discovered, the older of the two passed it off as a 'frolic'. In Mary Skinner's case, her own income eventually assured her an independence that marriage would have imperilled.

Pepys's sex life was intimately entwined with the economic and marital lives of the women he pursued. Patronage oiled the wheels of the economies of city, court and navy. Mrs Bagwell, in Flagon Row, Deptford, pressed Pepys for a job for her husband as a ship's carpenter. Betty Michell, daughter of an old family friend, grew up knowing Pepys, who called her 'wife' because she reminded him of Elizabeth. Once she married a sailor, Pepys was able to help her husband by getting one of his pay tickets cashed. Alongside this, he constantly harassed her, groping and grabbing at every meeting. Finally she managed to tell him to stop. Another of Pepys's victims suggests the means women might have had to protect themselves. Standing next to a young woman during a sermon at St Dunstan's Church, in the City, he tried again and again to touch her. She wriggled away, and eventually reached in the pocket that hung from her dress and took out some pins to prick him. He gave up, glad to have noticed in time.

Despite the lack of any reliable protection against pregnancy, infertility was a familiar concern for both women and men. Elizabeth and Samuel's childlessness was not extraordinary for the time. Both of them had serious medical issues that may well have got in the way: Elizabeth a painful Bartholin's cyst, Samuel bladder stones and a lithotomy in the earliest days of their married life. Far from being a private matter, though, their childlessness was apparently the subject of discussion and attempts to help. Samuel's uncle used it as an excuse to proposition Elizabeth on 11 May 1664, suggesting that they should have a child together and saying 'that for all he knew the thing was lawful'.

Mary Skinner
Oil on canvas, English school,
seventeenth century.

Pepys Library, Magdalene College,
Cambridge, College portrait, no. 92.

Advice to Young Gentlemen; or,
An Answer to the Ladies of London
c.1685–88.
This is one of the ballads in
Pepys's collection.

Pepys Library, Magdalene College,
Cambridge, Ballads, IV.87.

She gave him a sharp 'warm answer'. Samuel, in turn, asked for and received advice from their female neighbours on how to improve his chances of fathering a child: sage juice, sleeping with the feet higher than the head, and wearing cool drawers. He noted the advice with care, as he did Elizabeth's regular and often painful periods. These matters were not yet too private to record, though he only asked the women when they were 'very merry' at a dinner after a christening.

Like almost all women of the era, Elizabeth Pepys left no personal records; her story, like so many others, must be reconstructed from the words of others. Yet we know that Elizabeth, like her husband, had written about her daily life. By the 1660s, a literate woman who wrote as well as read was no longer so unusual. English women of the middle class and elites were increasingly likely to use private writings as well as letters to record and reflect upon their intellectual, social and family lives. Few of these writings survive; in Elizabeth's case we at least know why. Twice in the years of the diary she had written of her frustrations at her withdrawn life, and her lack of companionship. That she wrote in English, rather than the more private French she knew well, horrified him as much as what she said. The first time she presented her account to Samuel, he refused to read it and burned it; but she had kept a copy, and when she read it to her husband on 9 January 1663, he was enraged, he wrote, by how its contents disgraced him. It was 'so picquant, and wrote in English and most of it true, of the retirednesse of her life and how unpleasant it was, that being writ in English and so in danger of being met with and read by others'. He tore it to pieces, along with a bundle of his old love letters to her and the will in which, when he went to sea in 1660, he had left her everything. However, by bedtime, he said, they were in accord again.

If all this records a tempestuous relationship in which both of them veered from jealous rage to comfortable happiness, it also suggests that, like many women, Elizabeth had a strong sense of the rights and wrongs of marriage, and that a life of 'retirednesse' was to her both impossible and unreasonable. Instead, Elizabeth tried to change the terms of her domestic life. Again and again in 1662–63 her desire for a companion arose, and despite Sam's many reservations, a series of women joined the family both to serve Elizabeth and to keep her company. Winifred Gosnell was the first: the Pepyses called her their 'marmot' and dressed a bed with red hangings for her. She was followed by Mary Ashwell, who had worked in a Chelsea school and was daughter of one of Pepys's old clerking friends. Both delighted the couple with their dancing and singing, and pleased Samuel by providing respectable companionship for Elizabeth's trips to church and elsewhere, though he also fretted about Winifred's predilection for more liberty than suited his family. Predictably enough, almost all Elizabeth's companionships ran into trouble with her husband, but they provide a good sample of the kind of young women who might join a prosperous middle-class household. This kind of paid companionship, which was to flourish in the eighteenth century, was a recent development. It drew on the old-fashioned intimacy between servants and employers, but it also represented a new order in which elite and middle-class women needed a sociable safeguard into the outside world.

Like Samuel, and both with and without him, Elizabeth joined in the social life of her London neighbourhood, going to christenings, operas, plays, dinners, and music-making. Samuel's diary records a world of Restoration sociability. Elizabeth and he witnessed the birth of urban leisure: music, theatre, gardens, coffeehouses. Yet Sam did not, it seems, expect women of his wife's status to move freely round the city. After Winifred Gosnell had left them, he saw her at an entertainment at the house of the Duke of York on 26 December 1662 – Elizabeth being at home baking Christmas pies – and noted that Winifred, her sister and another woman had come 'alone, without any man, and did go over the fields a foot'. Urban life was imagined as a threat to female respectability, and some of Pepys's worst stories, of himself and of others, demonstrated the risks of nocturnal streets and open spaces for women on their own.

Flagon Row, Deptford, from the north side, 1896

London Metropolitan Archives, SC_PHL_01_079_76_12311.

One gets the idea that Sam wanted his wife to be private and modest, in a way that distinguished her from both the court ladies and the working women whom he met so regularly. In this he was participating in the creation of a powerful rhetorical division: the public vs. private binary that was to dominate gender politics in the next two centuries. Pepys's ideal of a woman who kept at home had increasing traction for the middle class, as the ideology of public and private was fleshed out in politics and social life. The growth of party and the politicized public sphere were predicated in part on the exclusion of women. Femininity was defined, instead, in terms of religion and domesticity. Citizenship was becoming by definition masculine, and in the party politics of the 1680s women took sides and demonstrated their support, but rarely had a formal public role. At the same time, the growth of the market, especially in London and other large cities, was partly facilitated by the business enterprise of women and their work in the city's shops and stalls.

Pepys's diary often offers glimpses of Elizabeth's domestic work. We see her burning her hands on a turkey, or doing the washing alone at home on a rainy day. In January 1663, that turbulent month for the couple, Elizabeth had a new gown she was pleased with, but Sam was angry she had not prepared their feast for the following day. She compensated by getting up before five, going to market and buying the meat, with which he was 'highly pleased'. Housewifery, like fashion, was a performance for both of them. Less obvious is the richness of the interior life that Elizabeth Pepys, with her husband's help, made for herself. Like many women of her class, she had a room of her own, a 'closet', furnished with costly cabinets and some scientific instruments. Despite their exclusion from the male networks of late-seventeenth-century science, exemplified by the Royal Society, many women participated in the excitement of discovery and experiment.

In reality, far from being excluded from street life, women in Pepys's London were integral to neighbourhood politics. The high levels of mobility that had long characterized the city made reputation paramount. A keen concern for sexual morals typified the era of Reformation, Civil War and Commonwealth, and women retained an authority over neighbourhood life and social interactions that focused particularly on illegitimacy and the conduct of servants and apprentices. Sam noted on 21 November 1667, as his wife lay ill with period pain in her chamber, that she had told him 'great stories of the gossiping women of the parish – what this, and what that woman was'. So strong was the power of rumour that London's church court saw a regular procession of men and women suing each other, and most of all women suing women, for insults against their reputations. Business, marriage chances, and social life depended on the credit that was often brokered on the street between women.

Women's collective voice also carried political and economic weight. At the Navy Office on 10 July 1666, Elizabeth and Samuel found themselves besieged by a crowd of 300 or so women, 'clamouring and swearing, and cursing us'. They were the wives of sailors imprisoned in Holland in the course of the ongoing Second Anglo-Dutch War, pleading for their husbands' pay. The Pepyses feared for the safety of the venison pie they were hoping to send out to be baked for supper. The pie survived, but the women carried on pressing their case through Samuel's closet windows, petitioning him with accounts of their ill-usage. Eventually he gave some money to one, and the same day the Navy Office ordered that relief should be given. The women of seafaring communities were frequently driven to plead and protest by the hard-pressed navy's system of giving 'tickets' as partial, delayed, pay, which could be exchanged for goods. Sailors' wives kept their households afloat by working in taverns and shops, taking in laundry or cooking; many had powers of attorney for their husbands, and some women made a business of buying multiple pay tickets, or pawning or swapping them. All these arrangements brought dockside women into a close engagement with the apparatus of the naval state – a reminder that Pepys's navy was also a world of women.

Warren Chernaik

Pepys and the Restoration Theatre

The diary of Samuel Pepys is the main source of information we have about the Restoration theatre in the 1660s – its repertory, staging, actors and audience. During this decade, Pepys attended and commented on 140 different plays, and made at least 338 separate visits to see performances. That includes 118 performances in the theatrical year 1667–68 alone, after the theatres had been closed because of the plague for most of 1666. Pepys saw *Macbeth* nine times, the same number of times he saw John Dryden's *Sir Martin Mar-all*; he also saw William Davenant's spectacular 'opera', *The Siege of Rhodes*, eleven times and Ben Jonson's *Epicoene, or The Silent Woman* eight times.

In several diary entries, Pepys speaks of playgoing as his greatest pleasure in life. On Twelfth Night 1668, after attending a production of *The Tempest* and then returning home 'to a very good supper, and mighty merry and good music playing; and after supper to dancing and singing till about 12 at night', Pepys wrote:

> And so away to bed, weary and mightily pleased; and have the happiness to reflect … going to a play or the like, to be the greatest real comforts that I am to expect in the world, and that it is that that we do really labour in the hopes of; and so I do really enjoy myself, and understand that if I do not do it now, I shall not hereafter, it may be, be able to pay for it or have health to take pleasure in it, and so fool myself with vain expectation of pleasure and go without it.[1]

At various times, as in September 1662, Pepys expressed feelings of guilt about addiction to the pleasure of attending plays, and made an oath to limit his attendance at the theatre, vowing to stay away from the playhouses for the next three months:

> Strange to see how easily my mind doth revert to its former practice of loving plays and wine, having given myself a liberty to them both these two days; but this night I have again bound myself to Christmas next, in which I desire God to bless me and preserve me, for under God I find it to be the best course that ever I could take to bring myself to mind my business.[2]

Thomas Killigrew (detail)
Oil on canvas, by William Sheppard, 1650.

National Portrait Gallery, NPG 3795.

On 26 December, the temptation to ignore his oath proved too great when faced with a chance to see *The Villain*, which was a success at the Duke's Theatre. After wrestling with his conscience, he decided that he could now resume theatre-going: 'sense' won out over 'reason':

> With the greatest reluctancy and dispute (two or three times my reason stopping my Sence and I would go back again) within myself, to the Duke's house and saw *The Villaine* – which I ought not to do without my wife, but that my time is now out that I did undertake it [my vow] for. But Lord, to consider how my natural desire is to pleasure, which God be praised that he has given me the power by my late oaths to curbe so well as I have done, and will do so again, after two or three plays more.[3]

In Restoration London, only two theatrical companies were authorized to give public performances of plays: the King's Company, under Thomas Killigrew, and the Duke's Company, under Sir William Davenant. Both Davenant and Killigrew had served Charles II in exile. The royal grant of 1660 licensing them to provide 'innocent and harmless divertissement for many of our subjects' had the intention of suppressing all other playhouses. Even so, a rival company under George Jolly attempted to compete intermittently for several years.[4] Pepys wrote of a performance of this company in 1661:

> And then out to the Red Bull (where I have not been since plays came up again) ... where I was led ... up to the tiring-room; where strange the confusion and disorder that there is among them in fitting themselfs, especially here, where the clothes are very poore and the actors but common fellows. At last into the pitt, where I think there was not above ten more than myself, and not 100 in the whole house. And the play (which is called *All's lost by Lust*), poorly done.[5]

Davenant and Killigrew were given licence to 'build, and erect or hire at their charge as they shall thinke fitt two Houses or Theaters',[6] and the new playhouses they built in 1660 and 1661 were small, with room for about 400 spectators, in refurbished buildings formerly used for tennis courts – the King's Company in Vere Street, and the

Duke's Company, several months later, in Lincoln's Inn Fields. The King's Company subsequently moved to a new theatre in Bridges Street in 1663. From the outset, Restoration theatres, unlike those of Shakespeare and his contemporaries, featured a proscenium arch, a stage that jutted out into the auditorium, and elaborate scenic effects. The patent awarded to Davenant and Killigrew referred to 'the great expences of scenes, musick, and such new decorations as have not been formerly used'.[7] In 1667, Killigrew bragged to Pepys:

> That the stage is now by his pains a thousand times better and more glorious than ever heretofore. Now, wax-candles, and many of them; then, not above 3lb. of tallow. Now, all things civil, no rudeness anywhere; then, as in a bear-garden. Then, two or three fiddlers; now nine or ten of the best. Then, nothing but rushes upon the ground, and everything else mean; and now, all otherwise. Then, the Queen seldom and the King never would come; now, not the King only for state, but all civil people do think they may come as well as any.[8]

When the Duke's Company moved to larger premises in Dorset Garden in 1671, after Davenant's death, and the King's Company to

Thomas Killigrew
Mezzotint, by William Faithorne
(1616–91) after William Sheppard, 1664.

National Maritime Museum, PBE9953/1.

the Theatre Royal, Drury Lane, in 1674, it was in part to allow for more spectacular scenic effects. Comments on individual productions by Pepys frequently characterized the 'scenes' or 'shows' as somehow separable from the plays to which they were attached:

> Here we saw *The Faithfull Shepheardess*, a most simple thing and yet much thronged after and often shown; but it is only for the Scenes sake, which is very fine endeed and worth seeing. But I am quite out of opinion with any of their actings but Lacy's, compared with the other house.

> Here saw the so much cried-up play of *Henry the 8th* – which, though I went with resolution to like it, is so simple a thing made up of a great many patches, that, besides the shows and processions in it, there is nothing in the world good or well done.[9]

Thomas Shadwell in the preface to *Psyche* (1675) told his readers 'the grand Design was to entertain the Town with variety of Musick, curious Dances, splendid Scenes and Machines'. The 'machines', as well as allowing for spectacular entrances by gods and goddesses ('The Clouds divide, and Juno appears in a Machine drawn by Peacocks; while a Symphony is playing, it moves gently forward and … descends'), included flying machines.[10] In Davenant's adaptation of *Macbeth*, the three witches flew on and off stage.

The principal innovation in staging was moveable scenery, where Davenant and Killigrew built on the example of the lavish masques designed by Inigo Jones for the Jacobean and Caroline court. Painted stage sets, on shutters and wings that could be opened or closed between scenes, gave the illusion of perspective. This painted scenery could be elaborate. Davenant's *The Siege of Rhodes*, with its 'new Scenes and Decorations, being the first that e're were Introduc'd in England', opened the new theatre in Lincoln's Inn Fields in 1661, and enjoyed a successful run of twelve consecutive nights. The plot was based on the Ottoman siege of the island by the fleet of Suleyman the Magnificent in 1522. The set designs featured three different scenes painted on shutters, and two further scenes revealed on an inner stage once

Sir William Davenant K[t].
Engraving, by William Faithorne
(1616–91) after John Greenhill, 1672.

National Maritime Museum, PBE9953/5.

Mr. Thomas Betterton

Totus Mundus Agit Histrionem

G. Kneller pinx.   E. Cooper Ex.   R. Williams fc.

the shutters had been opened. They included a 'prospect of the city of Rhodes'; a further prospect, where 'the scene is changed and the city of Rhodes appears beleaguered at sea and land'; and a 'relieve', in which 'the further part of the Scene is opened and a Royal Pavilion appears displayed, representing Solyman's imperial throne'.[11] Detailed stage-setting illustrations survive for Elkanah Settle's *The Empress of Morocco* at Dorset Garden Theatre in 1673 (see 63). In Act 1, Scene 1, set in a dungeon, 'the scene opens' and 'Muly Labas appears bound in chains', joined by a second prisoner, Morena. Receding wings provide perspective, with a back wall at the rear of the stage, revealed when the shutters are opened. In Act 2, after Muly Labas has been released from prison and crowned king, 'the scene open'd is represented the Prospect of a large River with a glorious Fleet of Ships', again in perspective. The action takes place on the forestage, in front of the painted scenery.[12]

In the 1660s, the repertory of the two licensed theatrical companies consisted mostly of older plays from before the Restoration. In the theatrical season of 1661–62, four new plays and fifty-four pre-Restoration plays were put on; whereas in 1667–68, there were roughly equal numbers of older plays (thirty-seven) and new (thirty-three).[13] The plays of the pre-Restoration dramatists were not divided equally between the companies. Killigrew, arguing that the King's Company was an extension of the old King's Company for which Shakespeare, Jonson and John Fletcher had written, laid claim to nearly all the plays by Beaumont and Fletcher, and by Jonson. During the period of his diary, Pepys saw and commented on five Jonson plays: *The Silent Woman, Bartholomew Fair, Volpone, The Alchemist* and *Catiline*. He enjoyed *Bartholomew Fair*, 'as it is acted, the best comedy in the world I believe', but found 'no pleasure at all' in seeing *Catiline*, 'A play of much good sense and words to read, but that doth appear the worst upon the stage, I mean the least divertising … the play is only to be read'.[14]

The King's Company owned the rights to most plays in the Shakespeare canon. Pepys remarked on the company's productions of *Othello, 1 Henry IV, The Merry Wives of Windsor, A Midsummer Night's Dream,*

and *The Taming of the Shrew* (rewritten by the comic actor and playwright John Lacy in 1667 as *Sauny the Scot*). Yet the Duke's Company put on productions of *Hamlet, Macbeth, The Tempest, Romeo and Juliet, Twelfth Night, Henry VIII,* and an amalgam of *Measure for Measure* and *Much Ado about Nothing,* under the title *The Law against Lovers.*

Pepys's comments on productions by the Duke's Company of *Macbeth* and *Hamlet* were uniformly enthusiastic. Both featured performances by Thomas Betterton, Pepys's favourite actor:

> To the Opera, and there saw *Hamlet Prince of Denmarke*, done with Scenes very well. But above all, Batterton did the Prince's part beyond imagination.

> To the Dukes house and there saw *Hamlett* done, giving us fresh reason never to think enough of Baterton.[15]

Although the Duke's Company version of *Hamlet*, revived in 1661, included cuts of over 800 lines, it was not substantially rewritten. Davenant, who was Shakespeare's godson and at times said he was Shakespeare's illegitimate son – claiming a form of theatrical lineage as well – was reported to have coached Betterton in the part.[16]

Several other Shakespeare plays, including *Macbeth*, were performed in revised versions, differing considerably from the received text. Davenant's licence was based on his proposal to modernize older plays for the contemporary stage and listed Shakespeare plays that his company was authorized to perform.[17] Davenant's *Macbeth*, first performed in November 1664, 'With all the Alterations, Amendments, Additions, and New Songs, As it's now Acted at the Dukes Theatre', was published in 1674 and frequently reprinted. The major changes, along with radically reducing the cast and adding several songs for the witches, included larger roles for Macduff and Lady Macduff, who debated such topics of contemporary interest as ambition and usurpation. Pepys, who saw this production many times, felt that the additions, including the 'dancing and music', did not detract from the overall tragic effect: 'though I have seen it often, yet it is one of the best plays for a stage, and variety of dancing and music, that ever I saw'.[18] Pepys also commented explicitly on the odd mixture of elements that nevertheless seemed to work dramatically:

> And thence to the Duke's house and saw *Macbeth*; which though I saw it lately, yet appears a most excellent play in all respects, but especially in divertissement, though it be a deep tragedy; which is a strange perfection in a tragedy, it being most proper here and suitable.[19]

The adaptation of *The Tempest* by Davenant and Dryden, first performed in 1667, had even more extensive changes. Miranda was doubled by a young man, Hippolito, 'one that never saw Woman', and given a sister, Dorinda, who like her 'never saw Man'. 'By this means,' Dryden said in his preface, 'those two Characters of Innocence and Love might the more illustrate and commend each other'. The production had elaborate scenic effects, 'many dreadful Objects in it, as several Spirits in horrid shapes flying down amongst the Sailers, then rising and crossing in the Air', and music for a 'Band of 24 Violins, with the Harpsichals and Theorbo's which accompany the Voices'.[20] Pepys saw the production nine times, commenting at its first performance that the house was 'full, the King and Court there', and later: 'The Tempest which we have often seen; but yet I was pleased again, and shall be again to see it, it is so full of variety'.[21] He was much less complimentary about *Twelfth Night*, as put on by the Duke's Company, and *A Midsummer Night's Dream*, by the King's Company. Both were unaltered.

> After dinner to the Dukes house and there saw *Twelfth night* acted well, though it be but a silly play and not relating at all to the name or day.

> Then to the King's Theatre, where we saw *Midsummer nights dream*, which I have never seen before, nor shall ever again, for it is the most insipid ridiculous play that ever I saw in my life. I saw, I confess, some good dancing and some handsome women, which was all my pleasure.[22]

Romeo and Juliet was rewritten 'as a Tragi-comedy' by James Howard, 'preserving *Romeo* and *Juliet* alive': the two versions were 'Play'd

Alternatively, Tragical one Day, and Tragicomical another; for several Days together'.[23] Pepys saw the first performance on 1 March 1662 and thought it 'the worst acted that ever I heard in my life'.[24]

Of new plays, Pepys commented in detail only on George Etherege's *She Would If She Could*, Dryden's *Sir Martin Mar-all*, and a third comedy, Sir Samuel Tuke's *The Adventures of Five Hours*, all performed before full houses. He seems to have particularly appreciated skill in constructing a plot, and the ability to make one laugh. He praised the 'variety and the most excellence continuance of the plot to the very end' in Tuke's play, which premiered in 1663, and remarked of *Sir Martin Mar-all*, 'I never laughed so in my life; I laughed till my head [ached] all the evening and night with my laughing'.[25] Etherege's comedy, however, was disappointing: 'But Lord … how silly the play, there being nothing in the world good in it'. The actors had not perfectly learned their lines and the play's composition and finale were both 'mighty insipid'.[26] However, as Pepys's diary ends in 1669, we have no comment from him on Etherege's now-classic comedy, *The Man of Mode*, or any of the plays by Aphra Behn, William Wycherley and Thomas Otway from the 1670s and 1680s.

Despite this fact, Pepys is an invaluable source of information about performers, and particularly popular actresses such as Nell Gwyn, Rebecca Marshall, Mary Betterton and Elizabeth Knipp. The Restoration theatre was the earliest in England to cast women in female roles. The Elizabethan, Jacobean and earlier Caroline stages had all used boy actors: Edward Kynaston, a principal actor with the King's Company noted for his looks, had started out as a boy actor, as had James Nokes, a comedian with the Duke's Company. Pepys thought Kynaston made 'the loveliest lady that ever I saw in my life' when he saw him perform in 1660.[27] On several occasions, Pepys spoke of his pleasure in seeing attractive women, especially semi-undressed, both on- and backstage. Without doubt, there was an element of voyeurism in the way women's bodies were displayed in Restoration drama. Breeches roles, with female curves provocatively revealed by male dress, were

Kynaston, Comedian [Edward Kynaston]
Engraving, by Richard Cooper (1740?–1814?), possibly after Sir Peter Lely, 1818.

National Portrait Gallery, NPG D18327.

1619 1687

Sr P. Lely   Cooper

KYNASTON, COMEDIAN.

a staple of Restoration plays, as were scenes of threatened rape, with innocent heroines 'much disordered' in their dress, breasts exposed. Contemporary lampoons often associated the profession of actress with prostitution, and prologues and epilogues to the plays tended to blur distinctions between the lives of the actresses offstage and the roles they played, hinting at sexual availability. Dryden's prologue to *The Tempest* ends with the lines, spoken by a cross-dressed actress:

> Whate'er she was before the Play began
> All you shall see of her is perfect man.
> Or, if your fancy will be further led
> To find her woman, it must be abed.[28]

Pepys mentioned several visits backstage, where 'Nell was dressing herself and was all unready'.[29] On one such occasion:

> I did see Becke Marshall come dressed off of the stage, and looks mighty fine and pretty, and noble – and also Nell, in her boy's clothes, mighty pretty; but Lord, their confidence, and how many men do hover about them as soon as they come off the stage.[30]

Nell Gwyn, whose career as a leading actress with the King's Company lasted only six years, became the mistress of Charles II in 1669, bearing him two sons. Pepys, when he heard that the king lavished expensive gifts on Nell and other actresses, could 'hope for no good to the State from having a prince so devoted to his pleasure'.[31] Aphra Behn, on the other hand, dedicated *The Feign'd Curtizans* to 'Mrs Ellen Gwin' in 1679,

praising 'the Power of that Illustrious Beauty ... who has subdu'd the most powerfull and Glorious Monarch of the world'.[32]

As an actress, Nell Gwyn specialized in comic parts. A series of roles for what were termed 'gay couples' (rather like Shakespeare's Beatrice and Benedick) were written for her and Charles Hart, the King's Company's principal male actor. Pepys was particularly smitten by her cross-dressing performance in Dryden's tragicomedy *Secret Love*:

> There is a comical part done by Nell, which is Florimell, that I never can hope ever to see the like done again by man or woman ... Nell does this, both as a mad girle and then, most and best of all, when she comes in like a young gallant; and hath both the motions and carriage of a spark the most that ever I saw any man have. It makes me, I confess, admire her.[33]

According to Pepys, she was less impressive in serious parts: it 'makes a miracle to me to think how ill she doth any serious part, as the other day, just like a fool or changeling; and in a mad part, doth beyond all imitation almost'.[34]

After the death of Davenant in 1668, Betterton took over the management of the Duke's Company, which on the whole was run more efficiently than Killigrew's company. In 1692, the two companies were united under Betterton's direction (Charles Hart, the leading actor of the King's Company, retired at that time). In his

Portrait of a Young Woman and Child as Venus and Cupid
Oil on canvas, by Sir Peter Lely (1618–80), after 1670.
The identity of the sitter has been questioned, but it is likely that this painting depicts Nell Gwyn (1650–87) with her eldest son, Charles Beauclerk, later Duke of St Albans.

Private collection.

THE

Feign'd Curtizans,

OR,

A Nights Intrigue.

A

COMEDY.

As it is Acted at the

Dukes Theatre.

Written by Mrs. *A. BEHN*.

Licenſed *Mar.* 27. 1679. *ROGER L'ESTRANGE*.

LONDON,

Printed for *Jacob Tonſon* at the *Judges Head*
in *Chancery-Lane* near *Fleet-ſtreet*. 1679.

Title page of *The Feign'd Curtizans, or,*
A Nights Intrigue ... by Aphra Behn
(London, 1679).

British Library, 11774.e.9.

long career, lasting from 1661 to 1706, Betterton played at least 180 roles, many of them, in tragedy and comedy, opposite Elizabeth Barry.

During the period covered by Pepys's diary, between 500 and 600 people attended performances at the two London theatres each day. Ticket prices, more expensive than for the Shakespearean stage, were 2 shillings and 6 pence for the pit (favoured by the aristocracy and gentry of both sexes), 1 shilling and 6 pence in the middle gallery, 1 shilling in the upper gallery and 4 shillings in boxes. Royalty attended regularly: between 1666 and 1669, the king, the queen, and the Duke and Duchess of York, together with their attendants in the royal household, attended an average of thirty-five plays in each theatrical season. To some extent, the new plays and adaptations of older plays reflected the ideology of the Restoration court. Prologues and epilogues suggest that members of the audience might expect to find idealized or satirized versions of themselves onstage. Dryden, in his epilogue to Etherege's *The Man of Mode*, described the play as a composite portrait of its audience: 'From each he meets', the dramatist 'culls what e're he can'. The play's title character, a slave to fashion, 'represents ye all'.[35] But it is clear from some of Pepys's comments that the audiences were more socially inclusive, whatever the ideological assumptions behind the plays. In December 1662, Pepys complained that he was 'not so well pleased with the company of the house ... full of citizens, there hardly being a gentleman or woman in the house', and those that were there were 'jostled and crowded by prentices'.[36] And again, on 1 January 1668:

> Here a mighty company of citizens, prentices and others; and it makes me observe that when I begin first to be able to bestow a play on myself, I do not remember that I saw so many by half of the ordinary prentices and mean people in the pit, at 2s-6d apiece, as now; I going for several years no higher than the 12d, and then the 18d places, and though I strained hard to go in then when I did – so much the vanity and prodigality of the age is to be observed in this particular.[37]

However much Pepys saw 'vanity and prodigality' in playgoing, he never ceased to derive enjoyment from it.

Stuart Portraiture

Catherine MacLeod

Peter Lely
Oil on canvas, by Sir Peter Lely (1618–80),
c.1660.

National Portrait Gallery, NPG 3897.

Barbara Villiers, Countess of Castlemaine,
later Duchess of Cleveland, with her son,
Charles Fitzroy
Oil on canvas, by Sir Peter Lely (1618–80),
c.1664.

National Portrait Gallery, NPG 6725.

Samuel Pepys's commission of John Hayls to paint his own portrait and that of
his wife in 1666 was a characteristic act of an ambitious and upwardly mobile
man in the Restoration period, a reflection of his achievements and aspirations
(see 41). Portraiture had been the dominant genre of painting in England since
the Reformation in the sixteenth century led to the widespread destruction
of religious images; this dominance was reinforced by a second wave of such
iconoclasm in the period of the Civil Wars and Interregnum. The commissioning of
portraits had spread from elite groups in early Tudor times to become increasingly
widespread in the gentry and professional middle classes during the late sixteenth
and seventeenth centuries. While sometimes used to mark an important event
like a marriage, it seems to have often been undertaken simply because it was
fashionable, reflecting the patron's financial means, artistic discrimination or
appreciation of the sitter. English portraiture had been dominated by continental
artists since its inception, as skilled immigrant painters, particularly from the Low
Countries, arrived in significant numbers during Tudor and Stuart times. Initially
mainly escaping religious persecution or excess competition at home, artists at
the Restoration court were also attracted by patrons whose years in exile during
the Interregnum had given them a taste for continental art. Pepys greatly admired
various foreign artists working at Charles II's court, but his choice of Hayls at this
stage in his career was probably influenced by the lower prices charged by the
English artist compared with his continentally trained contemporaries.

Pepys hired an 'Indian gown' to wear in his portrait by Hayls, a garment that
provided a degree of informality and simplicity suitable for a fashionable portrait in
the 1660s. In the sixteenth and early seventeenth centuries, most British portrait
artists had prioritized the representation of elaborate surface detail, including
intricate embroidery, lace and precious jewels, over the depiction of individual
character, movement or space. However, this approach had changed dramatically
in the second quarter of the seventeenth century. Dutch and Flemish painters in
Britain had begun to introduce a more sophisticated use of perspective and broader
handling of paint, and the Flemish artist Sir Anthony Van Dyck (1599–1641),

The Right Honble: Lady Barbara,
Countesse of Castlemaine
Engraving, by William Faithorne
(1616–91) after Sir Peter Lely, 1666.

British Museum, P,8.30.

Catherine of Braganza as
St Catherine
Oil on canvas, by Jacob Huysmans
(c.1633–96), c.1664–70.

Royal Collection, RCIN 405880.

Principal Painter to Charles I, finally turned British painting decisively away from its previous path. His elegant compositions created a sense of movement and space, and his sitters were often shown dressed in simplified versions of the elaborate fashions of the day, with swathes of shimmering fabric across their shoulders suggesting the garments of classical antiquity. Hayls was renowned as a copyist of Van Dyck and, in his own compositions, like most of his contemporaries, he reflected Van Dyck's approach to portraiture. Pepys's simple gown and cravat give Hayls's painting a relatively timeless air, and they also allowed the artist to focus on depicting the play of light and shade across the folds of fabric rather than meticulously reproducing the rich trimmings of contemporary court dress.

Hayls's most successful and influential contemporary was Peter Lely (1618–80), a Dutch émigré artist who came to England in the early 1640s and worked for sitters with a range of political affiliations during the Interregnum. Appointed Principal Painter to the King at the Restoration in 1660, Lely responded to the permissive tone of Charles II's court by developing a luxuriant and sensuous style that took the unstructured costumes of Van Dyck's images a stage further, especially in female portraiture. Both well-known courtesans and respectable married women were shown in varying degrees of 'undress', often in their shifts, their gowns slipping from their shoulders. Lely also popularized a continental type of portraiture, the *portrait historié*, in which women in particular were shown in the guise of saints, classical deities or eminent historical figures. Being painted in this way helped to justify a looser, more revealing but more timeless form of dress, and also associated the sitters with the virtues of their 'historical' counterparts. The most prominent woman to be portrayed thus was Charles II's chief mistress of the 1660s, Barbara Villiers, Countess of Castlemaine, who was in effect Lely's muse: the artist painted her as St Catherine, St Barbara, Mary Magdalen, Minerva and, exceptionally, as the Virgin Mary, with her son by the king as the Christ Child. When Hayls painted Elizabeth Pepys as St Catherine, he was using the most popular such guise, a homage to the queen, Catherine of Braganza, whose favoured portraitist, the Dutch Jacob Huysmans, had painted her as her patron saint in about 1664.[1]

Pepys's admiration of the beautiful Barbara Villiers led to protracted attempts to acquire her portrait, which reveal much about the way in which artists' studios operated in the seventeenth century and about the spread of images. Many studios were run rather like commercial galleries today, places where new commissions could be arranged, but also where existing works could be bought from stock, or simply admired. Painters were often collectors in their own right and also dealers in paintings and drawings by others. In Restoration London, many painters in oils, miniaturists and others in related trades lived in and around Covent Garden: Lely's house, including his studio, was in the Piazza, and several of those who worked for him or produced copies of his work lived nearby. Pepys saw Barbara's portrait at Lely's studio, and he also saw a copy of it in coloured chalks when he visited the printmaker William Faithorne on the edge of the City of London.[2] Faithorne had made the drawing as a basis for an engraving, of which Pepys was eventually to buy three impressions.

Printmaking was then at the start of an enormous and rapid expansion in England, providing a means by which both artists' compositions and the appearance of famous individuals could be transmitted to a wide public. Pepys pasted one of his prints of Barbara Villiers into a frame, had it varnished and the frame gilded, illustrating the use of prints as inexpensive alternatives to paintings. However, the huge collection of portrait prints that Pepys had assembled by his death was mostly arranged in large albums. Like his other prints, they were ordered by subject rather than artist. For in spite of his admiration of artists, Pepys's fascination with portraits – like that of most of his contemporaries – stemmed primarily from his interest in the people they depicted.

Charles II's Restoration and Marriage

The Restoration in 1660 was celebrated with pomp and symbolism intended to secure public support for the new king. Charles II was, in any case, fully aware of the political importance of ceremonial majesty. For instance, he soon reinstated the practice of touching for the King's Evil (scrofula), an ancient ritual which advertised the saintly character of the monarchy. In the next twenty-five years, he touched some 100,000 people desperate for a cure. However, advisers early in his reign were anxious to rectify one awkward detail that counted against the king: rather than being chastely married, as his father had been, he openly kept mistresses.

Negotiations for Charles II's marriage to the daughter of the King of Portugal had begun before the Civil Wars. Now they were purposefully renewed and concluded. Charles married Catherine of Braganza by proxy in Lisbon on 23 April 1662. Their pictures were carried in procession through the Lisbon streets in public celebration. On 14 May, Catherine landed at Portsmouth, where Charles met her for the first time a few days later. It was a political match. Portugal set great store by the alliance and commissioned a print series, which was promulgated across Europe, of the marriage and Catherine's arrival in England. England was pleased with Catherine's large dowry, but her devotion to Catholicism ensured that she remained unpopular. She also suffered at least three miscarriages and did not produce any heirs. Charles was routinely unfaithful and negligent, but always formally honoured Catherine as his wife.

26

Letter from Charles II and the Declaration of Breda

4–14 April 1660
Signed by Charles II
Ink on paper, with wafer seal
Parliamentary Archives, HL/PO/
JO/10/1/283A

On 29 April 1660, Pepys noted in his diary, 'a letter is come from the King to the House [of Commons]'. That letter included the Declaration of Breda, which set out the terms for the restoration of the monarchy. Drawn up by the exiled Charles II and his closest advisers in Breda in Holland, it offered a general pardon for all offences committed during the Civil Wars, Commonwealth and Protectorate. Only the regicides were to be excepted. KM

LITERATURE: *Diary*, I, 118, 124.

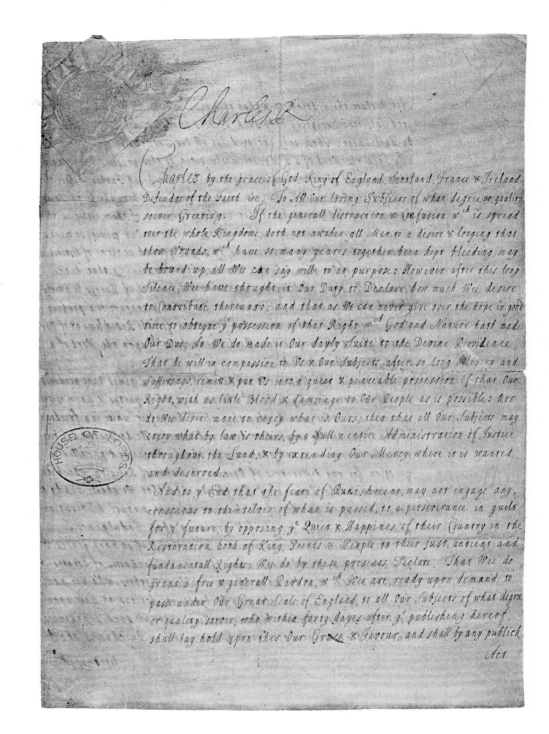

27

**The Embarkation of Charles II
at Scheveningen**

c.1660–70
Johannes Lingelbach (1622–34)
Oil on canvas, 965 × 1478
Royal Collection, RCIN 404975

Charles II lived in exile from 1646. On May Day 1660, he was proclaimed king in London. Two weeks later, he arrived at Scheveningen to sail for England. This painting shows the crowd gathered on the beach to see his departure on 23 May. Charles was seemingly apprehensive about his return. Pepys recorded: 'we weighed Ancre [anchor], and with a fresh gale and most happy weather we set sail for England – all the afternoon the King walking here and there, up and down (quite contrary to what I thought him to have been), very active and stirring.' KM
LITERATURE: *Diary*, I, 155.

28

Miniature of George Monck,
1st Duke of Albemarle

c.1658
Samuel Cooper (1609–72)
Watercolour sketch on vellum laid on
card, with a gessoed back, 123 × 98
Royal Collection, RCIN 420086

Despite supporting the Royalist cause
in the early Civil War, George Monck
(1608–71) served the Commonwealth
on the battlefield in Scotland and later
as a general-at-sea during the First
Anglo-Dutch War. After the collapse of
the Protectorate following Cromwell's
death, a disillusioned Monck entered into
secret negotiations with representatives
of Charles II for the restoration of the
monarchy. Pepys mentioned seeing this
unfinished miniature, 'my Lord Generall's
picture', during a visit to Cooper's studio
in March 1668. KM

LITERATURE: Reynolds, cat. 116, pp. 138–39;
ODNB; *Diary*, I, 158; IX, 139.

29

Model of the *Naseby* (1655)

1943
Robert Spence
Fruit wood, brass, paint and gilt
National Maritime Museum, SLR0001

Named after a major Parliamentary victory in the Civil War, and with a figurehead of Cromwell, the *Naseby* was perhaps a surprising choice to bring Charles II home from exile: he immediately ordered it to be renamed the *Charles* (though it became known as the *Royal Charles*). When the figurehead was also later removed and symbolically hanged, Pepys complained that its Neptune replacement would cost the king £100. The *Naseby/Royal Charles* was a three-deck warship of 80–86 guns, built at Woolwich by the Master Shipwright there, Peter Pett. RB

LITERATURE: *Diary*, I, 154–55; IV, 418.

30

....

Journal of Edward Barlow

....

1659–1703
Ink on paper
National Maritime Museum, JOD/4 f.24

In 1660, Edward Barlow was an ordinary seaman who had recently joined the Royal Navy. He served in the *Naseby* and recorded the events of Charles II's return to Britain from Holland in his illustrated journal. Later he rose to become a captain in the East India Company. The men drank toasts to the king's health, each being given a pint of wine. Pepys, also on board, discussed business with the Duke of York, who promised him 'his future favour'. When going ashore, he saw the king's favourite dog 'shit in the boat, which made us laugh and me to think that a King and all that belong to him are but just as others are'. RB

LITERATURE: *Diary*, I, 157–58.

31

Charles II's cavalcade through the City of London, 22 April 1661

1662
Dirck Stoop (c.1615–86)
Oil on canvas, 668 × 2015
Museum of London, 79.18

The day before Charles II's coronation on St George's Day (23 April) 1661, the king made a state entry into London. The extraordinary procession wound its way from the Tower of London to Westminster, passing through huge triumphal arches which had been specially erected at Leadenhall, Cornhill, Cheapside and Whitefriars. Along the route, the king was lauded with pageants and festivities that symbolized the renewed Stuart monarchy and restored royal government. Pepys was overwhelmed, writing 'it is impossible to relate the glory of that this day'. KM

LITERATURE: Sharpe, pp. 103–04; *Diary*, II, 82–83.

32

....
Cope

....
*c.*1661
Velvet embroidered with gold and
silver thread
Westminster Abbey, WAM 2497

The delay of almost a year after his return
from exile before Charles II was crowned
at Westminster Abbey in April 1661
was due to the extensive preparations
needed. Pepys watched the ceremony
from a scaffold at the Abbey's north
end, noting the arrival of 'the Deane
and prebends of Westminster with the
Bishops (many of them in cloth-of-gold
Copes) ... which was a most magnificent
sight'. This cope, a cape or mantle worn
by a bishop over his cassock and surplice,
was probably commissioned for Charles's
coronation. KM

LITERATURE: *Diary*, II, 84.

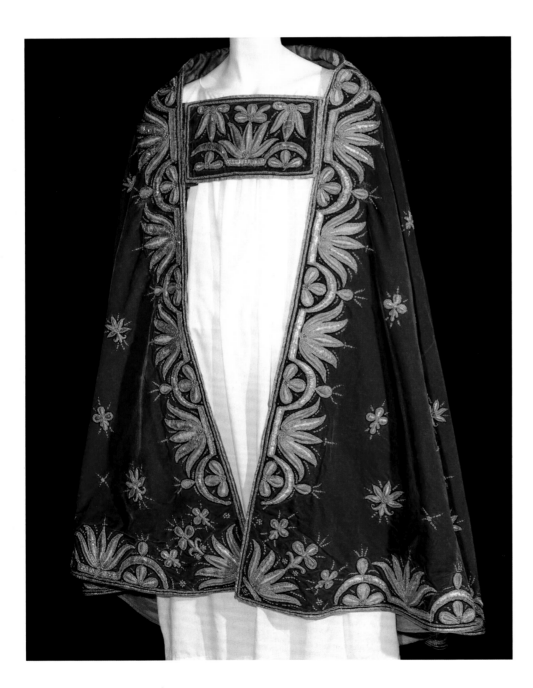

33

....
Charles II

....
1661–62
John Michael Wright (1617–94)
Oil on canvas, 2819 × 2392
Royal Collection, RCIN 404951

This painting is a powerful image of the
restored monarchy. Enthroned under
a canopy of state, Charles II (1630–85)
is shown surrounded by the trappings
of kingship. He is dressed in coronation
robes and the distinctive suit, collar
and Great George of the Order of the
Garter (see 34). He also holds the new
orb and sceptre and wears St Edward's
Crown. These were remade by the royal
goldsmith, Robert Vyner, to replace the
medieval regalia broken up during the
Interregnum. KM

LITERATURE: Sharpe, pp. 104–05; *Diary*, III, 113.

34

....

Great George and Garter collar

....

1661 (George) and c.1685 (collar)
Robert Vyner (1631–88)
Gold, enamel and diamonds
Royal Collection, RCIN 441924

At the Restoration, Charles II resurrected
the symbols and traditions of monarchy
abolished under the Commonwealth.
These included the Most Noble Order
of the Garter, the oldest and most senior
order of chivalry in Britain, reserved for
the monarch and twenty-five knights.
The insignia of the order principally
consist of a garter bearing the royal
motto *Honi soit qui mal y pense* ('shame
on him who thinks evil of it'), a badge
depicting St George and the Dragon (the
'Great George') and a collar of knots
and roses. This George was supplied to
Charles II; the collar was probably made
for James II. KM

LITERATURE: Piacenti and Boardman, cat. 297,
p. 218; *Diary*, I, 160–61.

35

....

Alms dish

....

1660–61
Attributed to Henry Greenway (*fl.* 1648–
70) and Wolfgang Houser (*fl.* 1652–88)
Silver-gilt
Royal Collection, RCIN 92012

....

Pair of 'feathered' flagons

....

1660–61
Possibly by James Beacham (*fl.* 1660)
Silver-gilt
Royal Collection, RCIN 31756.1–2

These pieces of altar plate were
commissioned to replace ones melted
down during the Interregnum. The alms
dish was made for Charles II's coronation
in 1661; the flagons were supplied to the
Chapel Royal at Whitehall around the
same time. The embossed decoration at
the centre of the dish depicts the Last
Supper. The unusual flagons, decorated
with engraved ostrich feathers, may
have been made by James Beacham or
Beauchamp, who was known to Pepys.
On 14 November 1660, Pepys 'went
into Cheapside to Mr. Beachamp's the
goldsmith to look out a piece of plate to
give Mr. Fox from my Lord [Sandwich] …
and did choose a guilt Tankard'. KM

LITERATURE: Roberts, cat. 170 and 171,
pp. 250–52; *Diary*, I, 292.

36

The Holy Bible: containing the bookes of the Old & New Testament

Cambridge, 1659–60
Royal Collection, RCIN 1142247

This lavish Bible, bound in blue velvet, embroidered with coloured silks, silver and silver-gilt wire, was probably made for the Chapel Royal in Whitehall Palace around the time of Charles II's Restoration. With its companion prayer book, it is a potent symbol of the king's reassertion of his position as supreme governor of the Church of England. The velvet binding is finely embroidered in metallic thread with the Stuart coat of arms on a ground of roses and thistles, a decorative theme that continues on the Bible's fore-edge. On the binding, above the arms, is the king's cipher, 'C2R', which flanks a crowned lion standing beneath two angels. The Bible, by the printer to the University of Cambridge, is illustrated with seven plates by Wenceslaus Hollar. KM

LITERATURE: Roberts, cat. 328, pp. 378–79.

37

Commemorative mug

1662
Southwark, London
Tin-glazed earthenware
Inscribed: 'C R 2'
British Museum, 1938,0314.108.CR

This mug is a high-end souvenir celebrating the restoration of the monarchy and showing the owner's loyalty to the king. It is painted with a portrait of Charles II holding an orb and sceptre, and wearing his crown and coronation robes. This type of pottery is called English delftware, after the Dutch town of Delft, where it was produced from the early 1500s. Numerous delftware commemorative pieces from the 1660s survive, suggesting that many were produced to mark the king's restoration, coronation and marriage. KM

LITERATURE: Archer, cat. 29, p. 21; Dawson, cat. 1, pp. 30–31.

38

Commemorative charger

1661
Pewter
Inscribed: 'Vivat Rex Carolus Secundus
Beati Pacifici' ('Long Live King Charles II
of Blessed Peace')
British Museum, 1869,0501.1

This pewter charger or dish commemorates
Charles II's coronation. It was a display
piece, probably not used for food. It is
incised with a repeated zig-zag pattern
made using a flat-bladed tool, a technique
called 'wriggle work'. The central well is
decorated with the Stuart coat of arms
while the broad rim has a running band of
oak leaves and acorns. In the seventeenth
century, pewter ware was found in even

the most modest homes. Pepys bought
pewter, including tableware, and wall
sconces for the candles on his stairway,
from a 'French pewterers' in the city. KM

LITERATURE: Homer, p. 124; *Diary*, IX, 115.

39

....

Catherine of Braganza

....

*c.*1660–61
By or after Dirck Stoop (*c.*1615–86)
Oil on canvas, 1232 × 1003
National Portrait Gallery, NPG 2563

Catherine of Braganza (1638–1705), third daughter of King John IV of Portugal and Luisa de Guzman, is depicted in the austere and conservative dress of the Portuguese royal household. She married Charles II in Portsmouth on 21 May 1662. Pepys wrote of his first sighting of Catherine in September 1662, 'she be not very charming, yet she hath a good, modest, and innocent look, which is pleasing'. The Dutch artist Dirck Stoop worked for Portugal's royal court and accompanied Catherine to England in 1662. KM

LITERATURE: MacLeod and Alexander, pp. 82–83; *ODNB*.

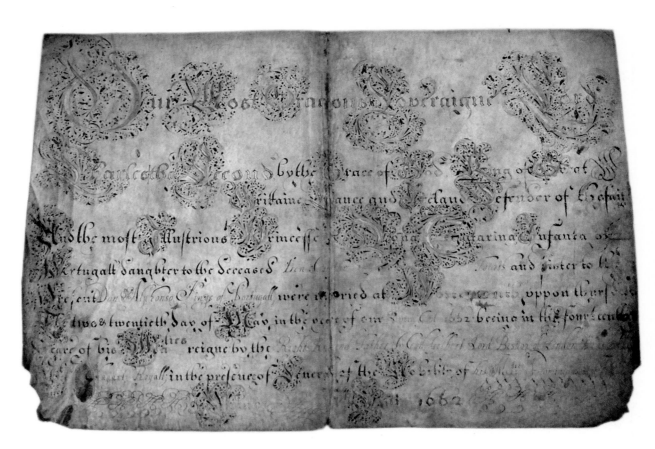

40

....

Marriage certificate of Charles II and Catherine of Braganza

....

22 May 1662
Ink on paper mounted on parchment
Portsmouth Cathedral, chu 12/8/1

This illuminated certificate records the marriage of 'Our Most Gracious Sovereign Lord Charles the Second' to 'the most Illustrious Princess Dona Catarina Infanta of Portugal'. Although it is dated 22 May 1662, the couple actually married the day before. A brief and secret Catholic ceremony, a concession to Catherine's faith, was followed by a public Protestant service. On the back of the certificate, added in 1687, is an inscription that records James II's gift of silver to the parish church, later cathedral, in Portsmouth (see 100). The plate was removed from Tangier, which had formed part of Catherine's dowry, when the English colony there was abandoned in 1683. KM

Pepys, King and Court

Royalists had long signalled their defiance of the Puritan movement by swearing, hard drinking and shameless merriment. This addictively enjoyable lifestyle was hard to give up: the court of Charles II was, to put it simply, debauched. Pepys, in his diary, often accused the king of neglecting business for leisure.

The court was also a dangerous place of intrigue. If Pepys relished looking at Lady Castlemaine's lace petticoats, drying on the washing line in the Privy Garden at Whitehall, 'the finest ... that ever I saw; and did me good to look upon them', he also took care to glean as much court gossip as possible that might help him stay out of trouble. During the fallout from the supposed Popish Plot, when anti-Catholic hysteria extended to supporters of the Catholic Duke of York, Pepys and Will Hewer, now his chief clerk, became targets of malicious, personal satire. Two pamphlets, *Plain Truth, or, A Private discourse betwixt P. & H.* and *A Hue and Cry after P. and H.* (1679), deftly misrepresented some of Pepys's administrative reforms at the Admiralty. The authors accused him, in *A Hue and Cry*, of taking bribes: 'Jarrs of Oyle, the Boxes of Chocolate ... Chests of Syracuse wines & Potts of Anchovies'. They mocked his presumption, as son of a mere tailor, in daring to maintain a richly furnished barge and coach and hobnob with powerful merchants. It was difficult for Pepys to be closely associated with the royal brothers and still maintain a reputation for integrity.

Yet, while Pepys accumulated worldly goods, he also placed a high value on furnishing his mind. His motto, which appears with his portrait on his bookplate, was *Mens cujusque is est Quisque*: 'the mind is the man'. His diary gives the impression of a man driven to pack his days with activity, exhibiting the zeal of someone who has narrowly escaped death and is determined to make the most of life.

41

Samuel Pepys, aged thirty-three

1666
John Hayls (1600–79)
Oil on canvas, 756 × 629
Inscribed: '1666'
National Portrait Gallery, NPG 211

This is the most famous of Pepys's portraits. In his diary, he recorded his sittings for Hayls, complaining, 'I sit to have it full of shadows, and do almost break my neck looking over my shoulder to make the posture for him to work by'. Pepys is presented as a fashionable, cultured, musical man. He hired the Eastern-style tunic and made Hayls repaint the piece of music in his hand with greater accuracy: it is his own setting of 'Beauty, retire', a lyric from Sir William Davenant's *The Siege of Rhodes*. KB

LITERATURE: Barber, pp. 2, 6; Ingamells, pp. 210–11; *Diary* VII, 74–75.

42

Guitar

Seventeenth century
Wood, ivory and mother-of-pearl, Italian
Horniman Museum, M15.10.48/88

Lute

Seventeenth century
Rosewood and bone, possibly by Bassano
Pardini
Horniman Museum, M15.10.48/60

Flageolet and case

Seventeenth century
Ivory, wood
Horniman Museum, M15.10.48/118 and
M15.10.48/118a

Music was one of the great passions of
Pepys's life. His interest was not simply
that of an appreciative listener: he played
several musical instruments, was keen to
learn composition and immersed himself,
as well as he could, in the theory of
music. A lute, flageolet, recorder, spinet,
viol, violin and theorbo were all, at some
point, in his possession. From 1673,
he employed an Italian musician,
Cesare Morelli, not only to
perform for him but also to
create arrangements that
he could play. This allowed
him to play favourite but
more technically demanding
songs. He also acquired an
extensive, and now important,
collection of popular ballads.
Overall, his musical expenditure
was considerable.
RB

LITERATURE: *Diary*, X
(Companion), 258–82.

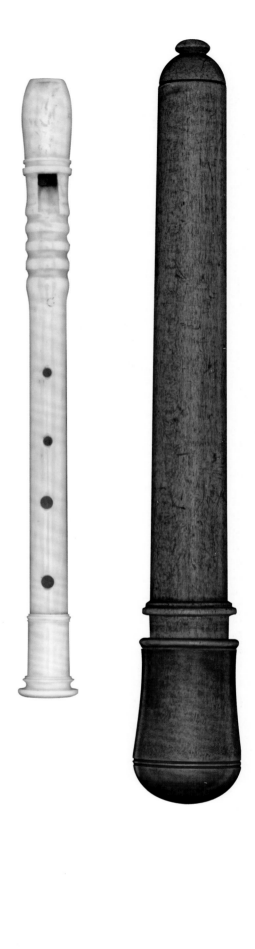

43

Ayres and Dialogues, for One, Two, and Three Voyces. The Third Book

By Henry Lawes (London, 1658)
British Library, K.3.m.18

Pepys collected books written by the popular songwriters of the day, of whom Henry Lawes was perhaps the most famous. Pepys owned all three volumes of his *Ayres and Dialogues*, published between 1653 and 1658. The third volume appears to have been one of two songbooks Pepys took with him on the *Royal Charles* when he brought the restored king back to England in 1660. Pepys, a bass-baritone, enjoyed singing with friends. In February 1665, he wrote, 'After supper, a song, or three or four (I having to that purpose carried Lawes's book); and staying here till 12 a-clock got the watch to light me home'. KM

LITERATURE: *ODNB*; *Diary*, VI, 27; X (Companion), 267.

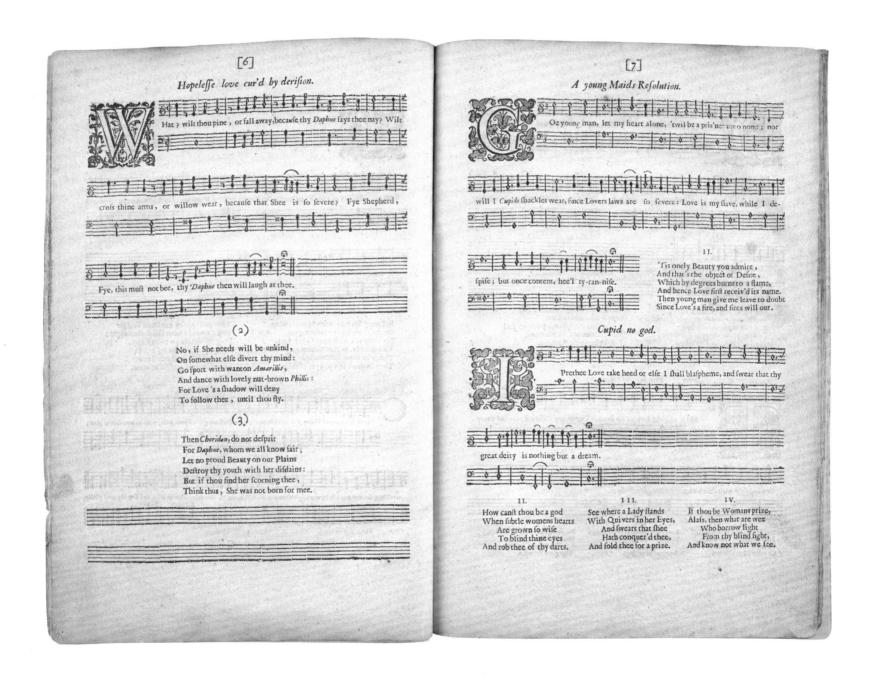

44

Whitehall from St James's Park

c.1674-75
Hendrick Danckerts (c.1625-80)
Oil on canvas, 1055 × 2270
Government Art Collection, 12211

Pepys's work at the Navy Board brought him into close association with James, Duke of York, when James was Lord High Admiral. Pepys also spent much time in the courtly and governmental centre at Whitehall Palace. Danckerts's view shows Charles II and James walking with courtiers in the foreground: the Banqueting House, where Charles I had been beheaded over twenty years before, is visible behind. A popular court painter, Danckerts was commissioned by Charles II to paint views of his palaces and harbours. In 1669, Pepys followed suit, commissioning from Danckerts 'the four houses of the King – White-hall, Hampton-court, Greenwich and Windsor' to hang in his dining room. KB

LITERATURE: *Diary*, IX, 423.

45

Silver furniture supplied to Charles II

*c.*1670
English table and mirror; possibly
Dutch stands
Silver, wood, iron and mirror glass
Royal Collection, RCIN 35299, 35298.1–2,
35300

Silver firedogs

*c.*1670
Inscribed: 'C. C. or G. C.'
Silver
National Maritime Museum,
AAA3471.1–2

This spectacular furniture was probably
inspired by similar sets that Charles II
saw at the court of King Louis XIV of
France in the mid-1640s and 1650s.
These pieces are likely to have been
part of a larger suite, of a type displayed
in palaces during the late seventeenth
century, when such opulent furniture was
the height of royal fashion. The dense
decoration of tulips, acanthus, foliage
swags and garlands of fruit also suggests
Charles's love of Dutch-style ornament,
possibly acquired in The Hague when in
exile. The table is made of oak encased
in embossed sheets of silver. The mirror
was intended to reflect light into the
room from candelabra placed on the
two candle stands. The firedogs have a
shaped pedestal supported by two paw
feet. Each is surmounted by a draped
female figure. KM

46

Snuffbox given to Nell Gwyn by Charles II

....

*c.*1670–80
Silver
Inscribed: 'The Gift of K. Charles .2. to M^rs: Gwin. Her Son Charles Duke of St. Albans Gave this to Me Lawrance Answorth 1720 Who had then the Honour to be Head Butler to Him'
Victoria and Albert Museum, M.700-1926

Taking snuff, finely ground tobacco, grew in popularity among men and women during the seventeenth century, partly because it was believed to prevent diseases such as plague. This snuffbox is decorated with an imagined Chinese scene. 'Chinoiserie' ceramics, silverware and furniture, decorated with fantastic landscapes, figures and buildings, were fashionable. Although inspired by exotic objects imported from the Far East, much of the decoration was drawn from the imagination. This box was inherited by Charles Beauclerk, Duke of St Albans, the eldest of the two illegitimate sons of Charles II and Nell Gwyn. KM

47

....

Snuffbox given to Nell Gwyn by Charles II

....

*c.*1668
Silver
Inscribed: 'OUID DE ARTE AMAND[A]' ('Ovid The Art of Love')
Royal Cornwall Museum, TRURI: 1928.17

In January 1668, Pepys wrote in his diary, 'the King did send several times for Nelly'. Eleanor ('Nell') Gwyn (*c.*1651–87), was one of Charles II's principal mistresses. Little is known about her early life. In 1663, she was selling oranges at the King's Playhouse and the following year became one of the first women on the English stage. Her unusual portrait by Lely (see p. 88), probably commissioned by Charles II, epitomizes the lasciviousness associated with the Restoration court. This snuffbox shows Charles's love for her, but is also a playful reflection on their relationship. The box is in the form of a book, *The Art of Love* (*Ars Amatoria*), written by the Roman poet Ovid. Condemned for its immorality, the poem is a guide on how to find, seduce and keep a woman. KM

LITERATURE: *Diary*, VI, 73; VII, 401; IX, 19; *ODNB*; Millar, *Peter Lely*, cat. 44, p. 62.

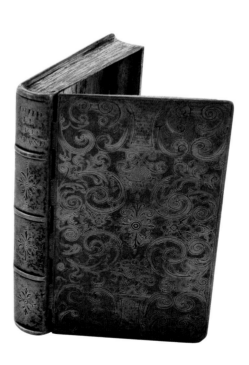

48

Barbara Villiers, Countess of Castlemaine, later Duchess of Cleveland

*c.*1662
Sir Peter Lely (1618–80)
Oil on canvas, 1910 × 1315
Knole, The Sackville Collection
(The National Trust), NT 129855

Barbara Villiers (1640–79) dominated English court life in the first decade following the Restoration. Despite her marriage in 1659 to Roger Palmer, Earl of Castlemaine, she became Charles II's mistress shortly after his arrival in England. Like the king, Pepys was seduced by Barbara's beauty and appeal. On one occasion he confided in his diary a dream 'that I had my Lady Castlemayne in my armes and was admitted to use all the dalliance I desired with her'. This portrait is probably the one Pepys saw in Lely's studio in October 1662, where, 'among other pictures, I saw the so much by me desired picture of my Lady Castlemayne, which is a most blessed picture and that I must have a copy of'. KM

LITERATURE: MacLeod and Alexander, cat. 33, pp. 118–20; *ODNB; Diary*, VI, 191; III, 230.

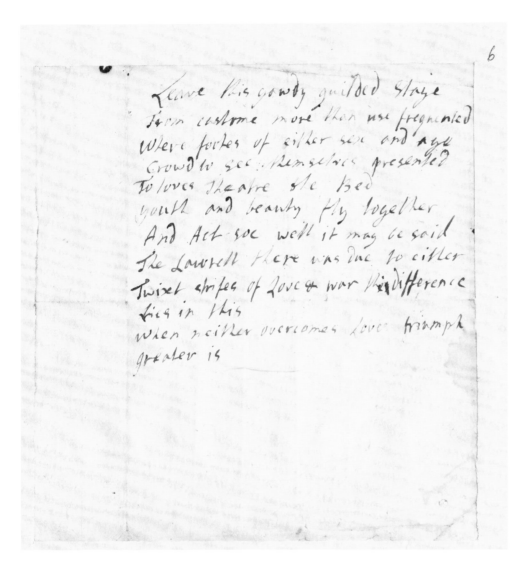

6

Leave this gawdy guilded stage
From custome more than use frequented
Where fopes of either sex and age
Crowd to see themselves presented
To loves Theatre the Bed
youth and beauty fly together
And Act soe well it may be said
The Lawrell there was due to either
Twixt strifes of Love & war the difference
lies in this
when neither overcomes Loves triumph
greater is

49

**Manuscript folio of John Wilmot,
2nd Earl of Rochester**

....

*c.*1660s–80
John Wilmot, 2nd Earl of Rochester
(1647–80)
Ink on paper
University of Nottingham, Pw V 31
(Portland MSS)

The Earl of Rochester's verse was characterized by its lewdness, wit and brutal satire. Many poems were circulated anonymously; few survive written in his own hand. Rochester criticized politics, the aristocracy, king and court, a world in which he played an active part. In 1673, he mistakenly delivered to the king a savagely satirical poem, *In the Isle of Britain; or, A Satyr on Charles II*, in which he lampooned the king. It saw Rochester expelled from court. This folio contains some of the only known manuscripts in Rochester's hand, as well as work by his wife, Elizabeth. KM

LITERATURE: *ODNB*

50

John Wilmot, 2nd Earl of Rochester

....

*c.*1665–70
Unknown artist
Oil on canvas, 1270 × 991
National Portrait Gallery, NPG 804

John Wilmot inherited the title of Earl of Rochester in 1658, when he was ten, on the premature death of his father, an exiled Royalist army officer. Presented to court at Christmas 1664, he lived the life of the archetypal rake, given to gambling, drinking and women. He was a satirical poet, dramatist, critic and patron, whose outrageous behaviour saw him imprisoned in the Tower of London and banished from court on two occasions. In February 1669, Pepys described one of the episodes that led to his expulsion: 'there was that worthy fellow my Lord of Rochester and T[homas] Killigrew, whose mirth and raillery offended the former so much, that he did give T. Killigrew a box on the ear in the King's presence'. The portrait has a satirical point: Rochester bestows the poet's laurels on a jabbering monkey. KM

LITERATURE: *ODNB*; *Diary*, IX, 451.

51

Love letter from Charles II to Louise de Kéroualle, later Duchess of Portsmouth

....

c.1684
Charles II (1630–85)
Ink on paper with a wax seal
Goodwood Collection, Duchess of
Portsmouth's MSS, Goodwood MS 3,
unfol.

Charles II and Louise de Kéroualle,
from a Breton noble family, began their
affair shortly after she was appointed
maid of honour to Queen Catherine in
1670. Owing to her fashionably plump
face, Charles nicknamed Louise 'Fubbs'
(meaning 'chubby'). This undated love
letter, written from Newmarket, is one of
several sent by Charles to Louise:

> I should do my selfe wrong if I tould you
> that I love you better then [than] all the
> world besides, for that were making a
> comparison where 'tis impossible to
> expresse the true passion and kindnesse
> I have for my dearest dearest fubs.

KM

LITERATURE: *ODNB*.

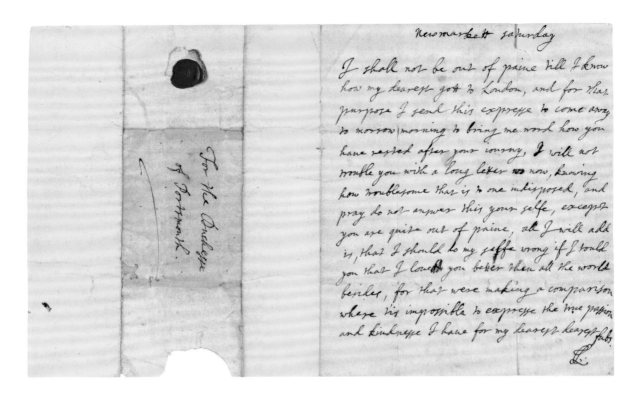

52

Pair of embroidered velvet shoes

....

c.1660
Silk velvet, metal thread and leather
Northampton Museums and Art Gallery,
BS410

Covered with extremely costly
embroidered velvet, shoes like these
were the height of luxury and fashion at
the Restoration court. When venturing
out on filthy streets, shoes would have
been protected with pattens, a type of
platform undershoe that strapped to
the foot and raised the wearer up. Pepys
recorded his wife's difficulties with a new
pair of pattens, which made him 'vexed
to go so slow'. AM

LITERATURE: *Diary*, I, 27.

53

Miniature of a lady, perhaps Louise de Kéroualle, later Duchess of Portsmouth

....

c.1680
British school
Watercolour on vellum with a gessoed back, 73 × 58
Royal Collection, RCIN 420143

The lady shown here in court dress may be Louise de Kéroualle (1649–1734), who was at the centre of Restoration politics. She provided a crucial unofficial channel of communication between the British and French courts, and acted as a political broker for Louis XIV. Her influence over Charles from 1671 was admired and feared by British courtiers, especially as she was, dangerously, both French and a Catholic. Louise brought French fashions and tastes to the British court. She wears her hair in the style that became fashionable in the early 1670s, probably at her instigation. KB

LITERATURE: Reynolds, cat. 166, p. 171.

54

Miniature of Charles II

....

c.1660–65
Samuel Cooper (1609–72)
Watercolour on vellum, 83 × 66
National Maritime Museum, Caird Collection, MNT0188

This miniature shows Charles II in armour, wearing an embroidered lace collar and a blue Garter sash. It was painted early in his reign by Samuel Cooper. The leading miniaturist of his day, Cooper was appointed limner (a painter of miniatures) to the king in 1663. Previously, he had painted Cromwell and leading Parliamentarians, again frequently depicted wearing armour. A profile of Charles by Cooper was employed on the new coinage struck after the Restoration. RB

55

Miniature of Frances Theresa Stuart, later Duchess of Richmond

....

*c.*1663–64
Samuel Cooper (1609–72)
Watercolour on vellum laid on card
with gessoed back, 124 × 99
Royal Collection, RCIN 420085

Frances Stuart (1647–1702) was brought up in Paris in the exiled court of Charles I's widow, Queen Henrietta Maria. She secured a position as maid of honour to Charles II's queen, Catherine of Braganza, after the Restoration. On arrival in England in 1663, she soon caught the attention of the king. Pepys described her as 'the greatest beauty I ever saw I think in my life'. Despite Charles's attentions, Frances never became his mistress, but secretly married the Duke of Richmond in 1667. A year later, she contracted smallpox but escaped serious disfigurement. Pepys probably saw this unfinished miniature when visiting Cooper's house in 1668:

> Here I did see Mrs. Stewards [Stuart's] picture as when a young maid, and now again done just before her having the smallpox; and it would make a man weep to see what she was then, and what she is like to be ... now.

KM

LITERATURE: Reynolds, cat. 114, pp. 136–37; MacLeod and Alexander, cat. 16, p. 94; *ODNB*; *Diary*, IV, 230; IX, 139.

56

Miniature of Catherine of Braganza

....

*c.*1662
Samuel Cooper (1609–72)
Watercolour on vellum laid on card
with gessoed back, 123 × 98
Royal Collection, RCIN 420644

This miniature sketch was probably made shortly after Catherine arrived in England in May 1662. In contrast to Stoop's painting (39), Cooper shows a young woman wearing the daring fashions popular with the English court of the early 1660s. Catherine's arrival threatened the position of Barbara Villiers, Lady Castlemaine, as the principal woman in the king's life. Pepys recognized this, writing in May 1662, 'all people say of her [the queen] to be a very fine and handsome lady, and very discreet, and that the King is pleased enough with her: which I fear will put Madam Castlemaines nose out of Joynt'.
KM

LITERATURE: Reynolds, cat. 113, pp. 135–36; *Diary*, III, 97.

57

Miniature of Barbara Villiers,
Countess of Castlemaine, later
Duchess of Cleveland

1661
Samuel Cooper (1609–72)
Watercolour on vellum laid on card
with gessoed back, 80 × 65
Royal Collection, RCIN 420088

This miniature was probably painted
shortly after Barbara Villiers became
Charles II's mistress. Following the arrival
of Catherine of Braganza in 1662 she was
appointed a Lady of the Bedchamber,
despite the queen's objections. The five
children she bore the king between 1661
and 1665 were a painful reminder to the
childless queen of Barbara's hold over
him. Pepys was fascinated by Barbara's
beauty and changing fortunes. In 1662, he
wrote, 'my Lady Castlemaynes interest at
Court encreases and is more and greater
than the Queenes'. In 1663, 'the King is
grown colder to my Lady Castlemaine
than ordinary, and ... he begins to love
the Queene and doth make much of her,
more than he used to do'. KM

LITERATURE: Reynolds, cat. 117, p. 140; *Diary*,
III, 289; IV, 222.

58

Miniature of Hortense Mancini,
Duchess of Mazarin

c.1670
Unknown artist
Oil on copper, 70 × 56
Royal Collection, RCIN 421603

Hortense Mancini (1646–99), niece
of Cardinal Mazarin, Louis XIV's chief
minister, was suggested in 1659 as
a possible wife for the exiled and
impoverished Charles II. Her uncle did
not approve and she married the wealthy
Marquis de La Porte. She arrived in
England in 1675 to escape her unhappy
marriage. Described by John Evelyn as
'an extraordinary Beauty & Witt', within
a year she had temporarily displaced
Louise de Kéroualle as Charles's favourite
mistress. Scandalous affairs, including
one with Charles II's illegitimate
daughter, Anne, Countess of Sussex,
soured her relationship with the king.
This miniature was probably copied from
a larger painting attributed to the Flemish
artist Jacob Ferdinand Voet. KM

LITERATURE: Reynolds, cat. 439, p. 291; *ODNB*;
Evelyn, *Diary*, V, 330.

59

Doublet and petticoat breeches

1662
Silk damask, metal thread and
silk-and-metal ribbons
Claydon House, The Verney Collection
(The National Trust), NT 1446624.13–5

This suit was made for Edmund ('Mun')
Verney's marriage to Mary Abell at
Westminster Abbey on 1 July 1662. It
shows the extravagance of court fashions
in the 1660s. Flamboyant but short-
lived Dutch and French styles of dress,
popular from the mid-1650s, featured
wide petticoat breeches and a short, full
doublet, trimmed with excessive amounts
of ribbon. Pepys recorded that one
courtier 'put both his legs through one of
his Knees of his breeches, and went so
all day'. Verney's wedding suit has 158
yards (144 metres) of six different types
of ribbon, in colour combinations of lilac,
salmon, silver and ivory. AM

LITERATURE: *Diary*, II, 66.

60

Pair of gauntlet gloves

*c.*1660–90
Leather, silk and metal ribbon
On loan from the Worshipful Company of
Glovers, London, to the Fashion Museum,
Bath, BATMC GLO 233681 + A

These dyed leather men's gloves are
an extremely rare example of the
extravagant continental styles brought to
England by Charles II at his restoration.
The loops of silk-and-metal ribbons are
not restricted to the gauntlet of the glove
but run from wrist to fingers. The fingers
themselves are elongated, a fashion in
use since the reign of Elizabeth I. The
gloves were not meant to be worn but
carried, to display the wealth and fashion
of the owner. AM

61

Court dress

*c.*1660
Silk, silver metallic thread, linen and
cotton lining
On loan from the Vaughan Family Trust
to the Fashion Museum, Bath, BATMC
I.09.1032, LOAN

This court dress, which would have
had an overskirt, is of silver tissue
embellished with silver lace. It marked
a return in the Restoration to the
splendid elegance of court fashions
after the relatively sober period of the
Commonwealth. Much of this fashion
was influenced by continental courts,
and specifically that of Louis XIV, who
devised a richly decorated, rigidly
structured dress, known as the *grand
habite*, which women were obliged to
wear when at court. This dress combines
the elaborate style of the French with the
more relaxed informality of Charles II's
court. AM

62

Aphra Behn

*c.*1670
Sir Peter Lely (1618–80)
Oil on canvas, 768 × 641
Yale Center for British Art, B2002.15

The origin of Aphra Behn (*c.*1640–89) remains shrouded in uncertainty. She was probably a barber's daughter from Kent, and served as a Royalist agent during the final years of the Interregnum. In the 1660s, she travelled (partly as a spy) to the then English colony of Surinam in South America and to the Netherlands. After a brief marriage to a German merchant, and imprisonment for debt, she began in 1670 to support herself as a writer. She became a prolific and celebrated author of poetry, plays, novels and adaptations from French works, her output notable for its political loyalty to Charles II and James II, its exotic romance and libertine bawdiness. Her romantic 'history' of *Oroonoko, or The Royal Slave* (1688) – set in Surinam – preserved her name as an early female novelist and proto-abolitionist. PvdM

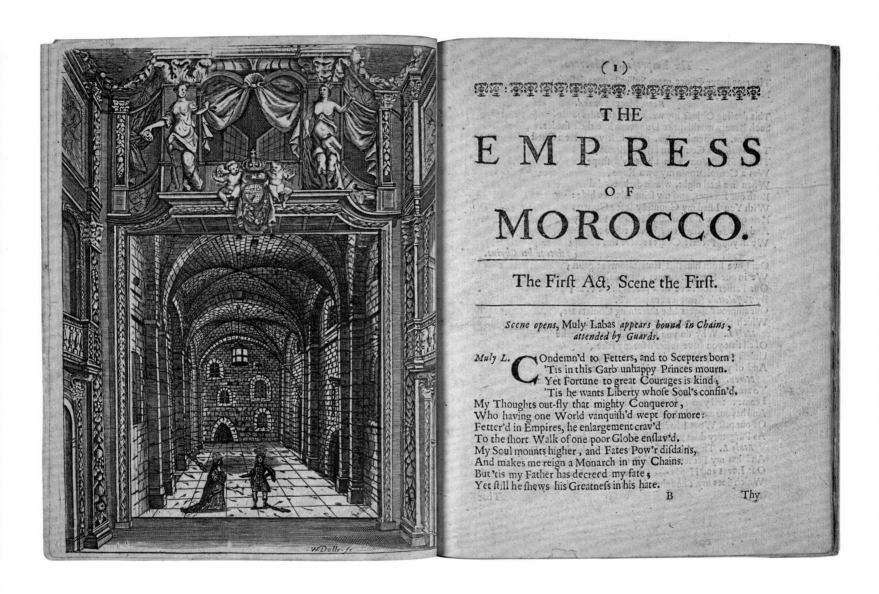

63

The Empress of Morocco, A Tragedy.
With Sculptures ...

By Elkanah Settle (London, 1673)
British Library, 841.c.21

Elkanah Settle was a popular Restoration playwright, although more significant dramatists – especially John Dryden – criticized him as a purveyor of bombast. The exotic settings of his works invited spectacular staging, none more so than this verse tragedy of love and honour. It was first performed by amateurs at court, then publicly in July 1673 at the Duke's Theatre in Dorset Garden, which had recently been refitted with new stage machinery. The six engravings ('sculptures') in the play's printed editions give a good idea of how it appeared there, and are almost the only visual records of how plays were staged in the Restoration theatre. PvdM

64

Mary Davis

*c.*1674
Sir Peter Lely (1618–80)
Oil on canvas, 1245 × 1016
Weston Park

Mary ('Moll') Davis (*c.*1651–1708) was Nell Gwyn's rival on the stage and in the king's bed. An actress with the Duke's Company, she became Charles II's mistress around 1668. Pepys saw her perform on several occasions, commenting in March 1664, 'the little guirle is come to act very prettily and spoke the epilogue most admirably'. Pepys's wife did not share her husband's enthusiasm for Moll, describing her as 'the most impertinent slut … in the world'. KM

LITERATURE: MacLeod and Alexander, cat. 56, p. 155; *ODNB*; *Diary*, III, 2; V, 78–79; IX, 24.

65

....

Thomas Killigrew

....

1650
William Sheppard (1641–60)
Oil on canvas, 1245 × 965
National Portrait Gallery, NPG 3795

The courtier and dramatist Thomas
Killigrew (1612–83) was one of the
leading figures of the Restoration theatre.
In his youth, he served in the household
of Charles I (hence the inclusion of the
martyred king in this portrait); and he
was a Groom of the Bedchamber to
Charles II both in exile and after the
Restoration. In July 1660, Killigrew and
Sir William Davenant were granted
royal warrants to build two theatres
and create companies of players.
Killigrew's 'King's Company' was to be
instrumental in re-establishing the stage
in London after its suppression during the
Commonwealth and Protectorate. As a
theatre-lover, Pepys – who met Killigrew
on the *Royal Charles* in May 1660 – was
very familiar with their work. RB

LITERATURE: *ODNB*.

Plague and Fire

Ring-a-ring of roses,
A pocketful of posies,
A-tishoo! A-tishoo!
We all fall down.

It is commonly thought that the first line of the famous nursery rhyme refers to the sores that often appeared in plague victims' groins and armpits: large circular blotches that could develop into painful, pus-filled sacs. The second line alludes to the flowers people were advised to carry, either to mask a victim's rank breath or to counteract the poisonous gas (or 'miasma') thought to spread the plague. Then the sick, it seems, were seized with a violent fit of sneezing before they died, though many poor people without strength to fight the disease succumbed before that stage. Folklore specialists disagree with this explanation of the rhyme, which was not recorded before the 1950s. But its widespread acceptance is an indication of how powerful the plague of 1665 remains in the popular imagination.

The epidemic's first victims came from the poorer districts of London, where people lived in cramped squalor, and where it was more difficult to isolate sufferers and avoid contact with the disease. The sick were ordered to be locked in their homes for forty days and nights; only 'nurses' were allowed to visit them. Pepys was scathing about local nurses, believing that they abused their position to rob the sick. By the time the worst of the plague had passed with the onset of winter, as many as 100,000 had died. In September 1666 a second awful tragedy befell London when the Great Fire destroyed the medieval city.

66

Pomander and vinaigrette

....

First half seventeenth century
Silver, parcel-gilt
Victoria and Albert Museum,
M.84:1–4-1933

This portable pomander and vinaigrette is engraved with flowers and arabesques, and is surmounted by a dragon. It allowed the owner to insert a variety of perfumed substances. In normal times, pomanders were mostly used to mask the unpleasant smells of everyday seventeenth-century life. In plague years, they took on a medicinal role. With no one certain how plague was contracted, there was a widespread belief that noxious airs were to blame and that particular herbs and spices could protect against infection. The long beaks of bird-like masks, worn by some plague doctors, were stuffed with such a prophylactic potpourri. RB

67

Fumigating torch

Twentieth-century replica
Brass, bamboo, solder and copper
Science Museum (Wellcome Collection),
A115561

With no understanding of what the plague was, various methods were tried to prevent its spread. While most focused on the human body, others looked to the environment. Fumigating torches were used in the belief that their scented smoke would drive off the plague and create a 'cleansed' space for the carrier to occupy. RB

68

Plague bell

Seventeenth century
Iron and wood
Museum of London, C2275

These bells were rung at the funerals of plague victims. They served to remind people of the rules surrounding such burials: they were to take place at night, with no more than six people in attendance, in order to impede the spread of the disease. Church bells were also tolled, as Pepys noted: 'It was a sad noise to hear our Bell to toll and ring so often today, either for deaths or burials; I think five or six times'. By the middle of summer 1665, however, the scale of death in London was so great that burials took place around the clock. RB

LITERATURE: *Diary*, VI, 175.

69

Tobacco box

Seventeenth century
Wood
The Clothworkers' Company, MNT003

This decorated tobacco box is believed to have belonged to Pepys. It bears the initials 'AP', indicating it was probably owned by his great-uncle Apollo Pepys, a noted lawyer. Tobacco was another product thought to ward off the plague. Concerned by the sight of red crosses, which marked the doors of infected houses, Pepys recorded, 'I was forced to buy some roll-tobacco to smell ... and chaw [chew] – which took away the apprehension'. RB

LITERATURE: *Diary*, VI, 120; Bryant, *Pepys: Man in the Making*, p. 14.

70

*Londons Loud Cryes to the Lord by
Prayer: Made by a Reverend Divine ...*

....

(London, 1665)
British Library, 816.m.9.26

Weekly Bills of Mortality were issued in
London, listing the number of burials in
each parish and the causes of death. As
the epidemic took hold, mortality rates
soared, with thousands of plague deaths
each week. Gradually, the numbers began
to decline. Pepys noted on 5 October
1665: 'The Bill, blessed be the Lord, is
less this week by 740 of what it was the
last week.' The accuracy of these bills
was a matter of speculation at the time.
Pepys feared they played down the scale
of mortality, 'which is a very ill practice',
making 'the plague much greater then
[than] people take it to be'. RB

LITERATURE: *Diary*, VI, 253, 207.

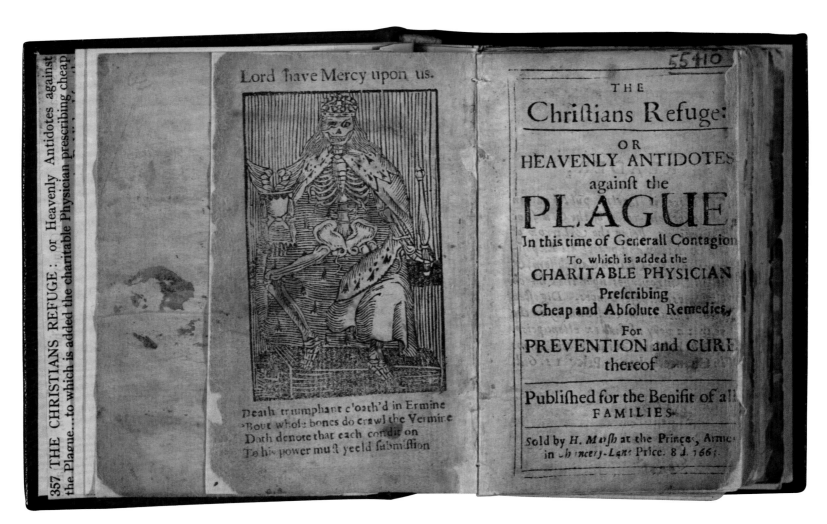

71

*The Christians Refuge: or Heavenly
Antidotes against the Plague In this time
of Generall Contagion ...*

....

By W.W. (London, 1665)
Wellcome Library, EPB/A:53190/A

The author of this small book was
probably the poet and biographer
William Winstanley, better known
as the writer of the comic *Poor Robin*
almanacs. It was just one of a large
number of works hastily compiled
and printed in response to the plague
epidemic. It offers medical and spiritual
advice, while providing contextual
information that compares rates of
mortality with earlier outbreaks. RB

LITERATURE: Miller.

Londons Loud Cryes to the Lord by Prayer:

Made by a Reverend Divine, and Approved of by many others: Most fit to be used by every Master of a Family, both in City and Country. With an Account of several modern Plagues, or Visitations in *London*, With the Number of those that then Dyed, as well of all Diseases, as of the *Plague*, Continued down to this present Day *August*, 8th. 1665.

O London, Repent, Repent.

An exact and true relation of the number of those that were buried in *London*, and the Liberties of all Diseases, from the 17 of *March* 1591; to the 22. of *December* 1592.

1603.			1625. Buried in *London* and the Liberties of all diseases, Anno 1625. the number here following.			1630.			1636.			1637.			1638. Buried 1665 Of the Plague 508

Printed by T. Mabb, for R. Burton, and R. Gilbertson.

**A View of Greenwich and the
Queen's House from the South-East**

1670–75
Hendrick Danckerts, *c.*1625–80
Oil on canvas, 865 × 1210
National Maritime Museum, BHC1818

Pepys obtained the king's permission to move the Navy Office from London to the safety of Greenwich in August 1665, having stayed in the city until the weekly death toll approached 7,000. He visited Greenwich on 16 March 1669 'to see the prospect [from] the hill to judge of Dancre's picture which he hath made thereof for me; I do like it very well and it is a very pretty place'. Pepys ordered from Danckerts paintings of the four palaces of Whitehall, Hampton Court, Windsor and Greenwich. PvdM

LITERATURE: *Diary*, IX, 485.

By T.V. [Thomas Vincent] (London, 1667)
British Library, 4412.bb.47

Ejected from the Church of England by
the Act of Uniformity in 1662, the Puritan
Thomas Vincent was one of a number of
ministers who remained in London during
the plague epidemic of 1665, preaching
and tending to the sick. This lack of
regard for his own personal safety won
him many admirers. *God's Terrible Voice
in the City* is based on a lengthy sermon
cataloguing the sins of Londoners and
ascribing the plague and Great Fire to the
vengeance of a wrathful God. It ran to
sixteen editions within just eight years.
RB

LITERATURE: *ODNB*.

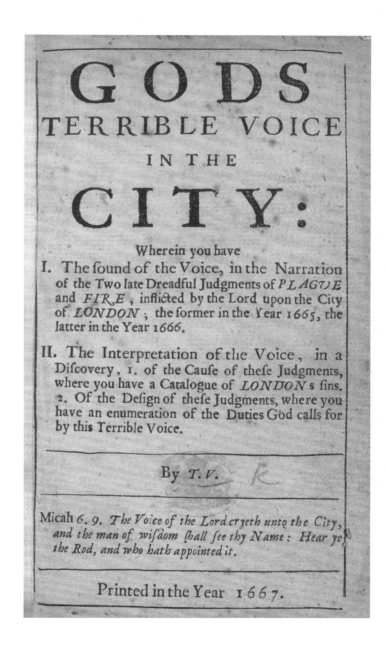

74

The Fire of London, September 1666

....

Possibly eighteenth century
Unknown artist
Oil on panel, 485 × 750
National Maritime Museum, BHC0291

This visualization of the Great Fire of
London captures the extraordinary drama
of the events on 2–6 September 1660.
The view looks up river towards London
Bridge, its arches silhouetted against the
inferno beyond. The Tower of London
is on the right, with a mass of evacuees
escaping the burning City. To the left,
away from the menace of a huge cloud
of flame-lit smoke, the south bank of the
Thames is calmly illuminated
by moonlight.

The entries for the fire in Pepys's
diary are some of its most memorable.
On 2 September, he recorded the chaos
on the river with people 'running into
boats or clambering from one pair of stair
by the water-side to another'. That day,
he travelled to Whitehall, relaying his
account of the situation to the king and
the Duke of York. The king, upon Pepys's
suggestion, commanded that houses be
pulled down to impede the progress of
the blaze. Having taken to the river, Pepys
then observed the scene from the safety
of the opposite bank:

When we could endure no more upon
the water, we to a little alehouse on the
Bankside ... and stayed there till it was
dark almost and saw the fire grow; and as
it grow darker, appeared more and more,
and in Corners and upon steeples and
between churches and houses, as far as
we could see up the hill of the City, in a
most horrid malicious flame.

On 5 September, with the flames
drawing ever nearer, Pepys took Elizabeth
down river to Woolwich. Later, he
climbed the steeple of the church of All
Hallows, Barking, and gazed out at 'the
saddest sight of desolation that I ever
saw'. Then he 'Walked into Moore-fields
(our feet ready to burn, walking through
the town among the hot coles) and find
that full of people, and poor wretches
carry their goods there, and everybody
keeping his goods by themselfs'.

The fire had by now reached its
greatest extent and began to recede.
In the charred confusion of London,
Pepys was unable to buy a clean shirt on
6 September and resorted to borrowing
one the next day. In company that
evening, the conversation turned to
property prices: 'Strange to hear', he
wrote, 'what is bid for houses all up and
down here – a friend of Sir W. Riders [a
colleague] having £150 for what he used
to let for £40 per annum.' Pepys's home
and office were saved, but the house of
his birth was one of more than 13,200
destroyed. After the fire, only a fifth of
the City of London remained standing
and about 100,000 people were left
homeless, many having lost everything.
RB

LITERATURE: *Diary*, VII, 267–80.

PEPYS
AND
THE NAVY

Samuel Pepys's perceptive observations on the Stuart age, so carefully recorded in his diary, represent the epitome of seventeenth-century social commentary. Pepys, though, was more than an insightful eyewitness. The year that he began his diary was also the year that he joined the ranks of the Royal Navy's administration, establishing a career path that ultimately saw him take a leading role in English national affairs. Alongside his diary's more colourful entries are regular and detailed descriptions of his working life, which offer a very different view of the man. In these passages, we find Pepys poring over documents at the Navy Board, visiting naval dockyards, consulting with royalty and even standing up in Parliament to defend the service against its most strident political critics. Pepys emerges as a man of remarkable talent and diligence, who left a discernible impact upon the times in which he lived. In due course, he came to define the navy of his era: to this day, the late seventeenth-century Royal Navy continues to be termed 'Pepys's navy'. How this particular institution came to be identified with a humble administrator is a remarkable story. It is made all the more so when we consider that, in the course of a few years, an individual who initially had little knowledge of ships or navigation rose to the heights of the naval bureaucracy, and made a lasting contribution to both the service and the nation it served.

Pepys entered the administration of the Royal Navy in 1660, the year that Charles II was restored to the throne. The new king took a deep interest in the navy – Charles himself was an experienced yachtsman with a keen knowledge of navigation and ship design – and he was determined to wrest back control of the force after years of Parliamentary regulation. He appointed his brother, James, Duke of York, as Lord High Admiral of England, making him the effective head of the navy, responsible for naval policy, discipline and the command of the fleet. He was assisted by the Navy Board, a group of permanent officials who were charged with the day-to-day running of the navy: building and maintaining the navy's ships, managing the Royal Dockyards and contracting for supplies of naval stores.

James Davey

'... and so to the office': Pepys at Work

James immediately restored the four principal officers of the navy – the Treasurer, Comptroller, Surveyor and the Clerk of the Acts – which had been absent under the Commonwealth. Pepys was appointed Clerk of the Acts, the most junior of the four positions, with a salary that befitted his status: while £350 was hardly a small sum at the time, it was dwarfed by the £2,000 earned by the Treasurer.

Pepys's employment owed nothing to knowledge or proficiency, and everything to his contacts. 'Chance without merit brought me in', he confessed to his diary, years later. Appointed thanks to the intervention of his cousin and employer, the Earl of Sandwich, he had little experience of the maritime world, and no real qualifications for the job. Preferment of this sort was not unusual in a society built around patronage and favour, but it immediately set him apart from his more expert colleagues on the Navy Board. Pepys quickly began to absorb everything he could about his new trade. The Clerk of the Acts was tasked with attending meetings, recording decisions, keeping minutes and preparing agendas and correspondence. Intelligent, and with a prodigious appetite for learning, he rapidly mastered the practices and routines of his office. Pepys's ability to store and retrieve information was unparalleled – indeed, it was almost obsessive – and formed a knowledge base he maintained through a series of interrelated registers. In addition, his work ethic set him apart from all of his peers: 'Living as I do among so many lazy people,' he wrote, 'the diligent man becomes necessary, that they cannot do anything without him.'[1] He soon began to assume greater responsibilities, and even encroach on his colleagues' roles, visiting dockyards, and delving into the complex world of contracts, stores and markets.[2] Within a few years he made himself an indispensable part of the navy's administration: in 1662, he was told by a colleague, with little exaggeration, that he was 'the life of this office'.[3]

Pepys's increasing authority gave him a central role in the reform of the naval departments. The navy of the 1660s was in turmoil, following years of financial neglect. Wracked with debt, it owed £1.25 million, and some ships in commission had been unpaid for over four years.[4] Pepys

Miniature of James, Duke of York
Watercolour on vellum, by
Samuel Cooper (1609–72), 1670–72.

National Maritime Museum,
Caird Collection, MNT0191.

made frequent allusions to the state of the navy in his diary, criticizing both the systems employed and his fellow colleagues on the Board. Much of naval spending was directed to contractors, and involved deals that were susceptible to bribery and fraudulent behaviour. Pepys, like many others, took advantage of such opportunities, and benefited financially from the ambiguous practices. To give one example, he learned much about the timber trade from the merchant Sir William Warren, and repaid this by ensuring that Warren was given several navy mast contracts. He unashamedly highlighted the corrupt practices of Warren's competitors, and failed to mention that he himself had received a £40 present from Warren. National duty and private gain were not mutually exclusive: Pepys could claim with some justification that the king had got a good deal, and in due course he insisted on examining Warren's accounts carefully, calling him out on certain irregularities. Nevertheless, Pepys made considerable sums from these murky dealings: between 1660 and 1669 he received £2,566 'other gain', a substantial supplement to his basic salary.[5]

Throughout the 1660s, the navy continued to struggle with its funding. In 1664, Parliament voted £2.5 million for the service, the largest single tax until the eighteenth century, but it was still not enough to balance the books. In 1665, its deficit was £814,393, rising to £930,516 the following year.[6] These were vast sums, and the shortfalls had a severe impact on the navy. Smaller suppliers went bankrupt, stores became scarce and seamen and dockyard workers disappeared. In his diary, Pepys recorded a typical day at work:

> Did business, though not much, at the office, because of the horrible Crowd and lamentable moan of the poor seamen that lie starving in the streets for lack of money – which doth trouble and perplex me to the heart. And more at noon, when we were to go through them; for then a whole hundred of them fallowed us, some cursing, some swearing, and some praying to us.[7]

Despite the shortfalls, Pepys's Navy Board did make some improvements. In 1664, a commission was appointed for the care of sick and hurt naval seamen. Though it was disbanded in 1674, it provided a model template for the care of sailors.[8] In a similar vein, Pepys investigated the system of provisioning the fleet, proposing a 'Surveyor-General of Victualling' to manage this vital operation. He was himself appointed to this new position in November 1665, and he set about reforming shipboard accounting, providing incentives for pursers to economize and ensuring deterrents were in place to stop them cooking the books. These reforms were not unilaterally successful, but the system was significantly better than in foreign navies.[9]

Operational advantages over foreign navies were important, for Pepys lived through a period of great international tension. His early years in office were marked by hostilities with Holland, which led to the outbreak of the Second Anglo-Dutch War in 1665. Pepys was heavily involved in the preparations for war, but he was all too aware of England's perilous financial position, and its unpreparedness. He feared the coming conflict: 'All the news now is what will become of the Dutch business, whether war or peace. We all seem to desire it, as thinking ourselfs to have advantages at present over them; but for my part I dread it.'[10] Despite his misgivings, the war began well for England: at the Battle of Lowestoft, a fleet commanded by the Duke of York won a crushing victory. The Dutch lost seventeen ships and over 5,000 seamen, and Pepys rejoiced in 'a great victory, never known in the world'. To commemorate the victory, a series of thirteen paintings of his fellow commanders, known as 'The Flagmen of Lowestoft', was commissioned by the Duke of York from Peter Lely. Pepys visited Lely's studio on 18 April 1666 to inspect his progress:

> I to Mr Lillys, the painter's, and there saw the heads, some finished and all begun, of the Flaggmen in the late great fight with the Duke of Yorke against the Dutch. The Duke of Yorke hath them done to hang in his chamber, and very finely they are done endeed.[11]

In the aftermath of the battle, the English attempted to plunder Dutch convoys, with little success, hampered by the navy's poor

Medal commemorating the Battle of Lowestoft Silver, by John Roettier, 1665.

National Maritime Museum, MEC0868.

Dutch Ships in the Medway, June 1667
Oil on canvas, by Willem Schellinks,
late seventeenth century.

National Maritime Museum, BHC0294.

financial position, logistical failures and the outbreak of plague. The Dutch began to commission new ships, and in 1666 they were further boosted when France declared war on England. Pepys remained only too aware of English vulnerability. On 13 May 1666, the Navy Board officers presented a letter to the Duke of York, written by Pepys, bringing attention to 'the badness of our condition in this office for want of money'.[12] At sea, however, the two nations exchanged victories: the Dutch winning the Four Days Battle in June, and the English defeating the Dutch at the St James's Day fight two months later. Charles II, the Duke of York, and Pepys himself gathered in St James's Park to listen to the sound of gunfire, as the war hung in the balance. Following the English victory, amid war-weariness, decaying finances and the devastation of the Great Fire, many looked forward to peace negotiations. Expecting peace, Charles ignored signs of renewed Dutch naval activity, and failed to mobilize the larger naval ships. In June 1667, a Dutch fleet commanded by Admiral Michiel de Ruyter (see 82) sailed up the River Medway, easily breached the haphazard English defences, and attacked the Royal Dockyard at Chatham. A number of English ships were burned, and the fleet's flagship, the *Royal Charles*, was captured and taken back to the Netherlands. It was a humiliating defeat for the navy, and hugely embarrassing for the king. 'I do fear so much that the whole kingdom is undone,' Pepys wrote, with no little hyperbole.[13]

Pepys realized immediately that the navy's administration would come under great scrutiny. He expected 'violence on this office, or perhaps some severity on our persons',[14] and numerous Parliamentary committees were indeed appointed to investigate the harrowing defeat. The unfortunate Master Shipwright Peter Pett, the resident Commissioner at Chatham, became a scapegoat for the disaster. However, accusations continued to fly even after peace was signed in July 1667. Although Pepys was the youngest and least experienced member of the Navy Board, he had earned himself a reputation for technical knowledge and mastery of administration, and he became the navy's chief spokesman against its Parliamentary detractors. On 5 March 1668, Pepys was called to the House of Commons to answer questions regarding the state of the navy, and after liberally fortifying himself with mulled sack and brandy, he stood before Parliament and put in the performance of his life. Following his three-hour speech – delivered 'without any hesitation or losse ... without any interruption from the Speaker' – he was congratulated by his fellow officers, who described it as 'the best thing they ever heard'. Pepys's speech did much to appease the Parliamentarians, and confirmed his position as the spokesman for the navy. 'Everybody says I have got the most honour that any could have had opportunity of getting,' he boasted in his diary.[15]

While Pepys publicly defended his office, in private he followed an instruction from the Duke of York to conduct his own internal investigation into recent failures. Pepys highlighted the want of money, but, rather than defending his colleagues, he turned on them remorselessly. 'Most of the Board's time', he argued, was taken up in 'impertinent talk' and 'confused discourses'. The Treasurer, he charged, was rarely in attendance at meetings, and overlooked contracts and discussions about naval estimates. More seriously, the Comptroller was accused of neglecting his accounts, while the Surveyor had failed to present annual reports. The paper drawn up by Pepys was accepted by the Duke without alteration: this was a severe reprimand, and the accused wrote long and apologetic replies. As the author, Pepys emerged unscathed, indeed, with his reputation further enhanced. In the following years, he continued to defend the navy in Parliament, repeatedly pointing to the lack of money, the pressure of war and the many instances where the Board had punished 'negligences and misdemeanours'.[16]

Pepys's regular Parliamentary appearances demonstrated that the navy gained considerably by having expert representation at Westminster. The Duke of York went to great trouble to ensure Pepys was chosen as a Parliamentary candidate, and in 1673 he was elected to the seat of Castle Rising in Norfolk, defeating a candidate put forward by the mayor and burgesses of the town. The election cost Pepys £700 of his own money, and he later sought and won election at Harwich in Essex, a seaport where he could rely on Admiralty patronage of the electorate rather than his own purse. Throughout the 1670s, Pepys was an active Parliamentarian: he answered the bulk of the questions on naval business and rigorously defended the administration from political attacks. His confidence and knowledge were resented by his critics in the Commons: 'Pepys here speaks more like an admiral than a secretary,' wrote one bitter critic.[17] His entry into Parliament was well timed, for in 1673 the Duke of York was forced to step down as Lord High Admiral following the introduction of the Test Act, which barred Catholics from public office. The office was re-vested in the crown, and Pepys was appointed Secretary to the Board of Admiralty, a position that had been vacant since 1660.[18] It marked a startling rise through the naval hierarchy: Pepys was now the most influential person in the navy, answerable only to the king.

Pepys's promotion came in the middle of another conflict, the Third Anglo-Dutch War, fought from 1672 to 1674. The English had hoped for a speedily decisive campaign, but a number of Dutch naval successes – not least the Battle of Solebay in May 1672 – halted attempts to invade the Netherlands by sea and further reduced the effective strength of the Royal Navy. Once again, the Royal Navy had failed at sea, and Parliament was able to force Charles II to make peace.[19] In the aftermath of the war, it was clear that further reform was much needed. As an MP and Secretary to the Admiralty, Pepys was at the heart of this impulse. He had already overseen the introduction of half-pay for admirals in 1668, but this was extended to captains in 1674 and then masters and commodores in 1675, which ensured the navy maintained a core reserve of trained officers. Pepys also created new positions to spread the Navy Board's workload, and lobbied for further naval spending. In the aftermath of the war, he cleverly used comparisons of national naval strength to argue for further shipbuilding, compiling reports that showed the English navy inferior to the French, and vastly so to the Dutch. This alarming (and largely accurate) picture of continental power was presented to Parliament on 24 April 1675, and sparked months of debate and disagreement. Pepys estimated that over thirty new 'great ships' were needed to match the foreign threat. Pepys's technical knowledge eventually won out, and

on 2 March 1677 the Commons voted over £600,000 for the thirty new vessels. Between 1673 and 1679, the navy increased in size from 144 ships to 172.[20]

Pepys's transformation of the navy did not stop there. Following the Third Anglo-Dutch War, he helped introduce a number of other reforms, despite further naval retrenchment. The dockyard workforce was reduced, and a new victualling contract signed in 1677. Undoubtedly his most lasting legacy was the establishment of the examination for lieutenants. Previously, lieutenants had been appointed without any test of competence, a tradition that favoured the relatively unskilled but high-born 'gentlemen' ahead of more humble but experienced 'tarpaulins'. This preference had excited controversy, for a naval ship was both a complicated and an expensive object. Under Pepys's new scheme, a lieutenant was to have three years' experience and be required to produce certificates that spoke of his 'sobriety, diligence, obedience to order' and his 'application to the study and practice of the art of navigation'. On 22 December 1677, a regular exam was introduced, which tested a potential officer's seamanship and navigational knowledge. Drawn up by Pepys himself, it was adopted without substantial alteration. In one fell swoop, he had created a bar of competence that every officer had to overcome, and created for the first time a truly 'professional' Royal Navy.[21]

During Pepys's tenure as Secretary to the Admiralty, the navy was frequently scrutinized by a more assertive Parliament. Its finance was the state's largest expenditure and in peacetime an obvious place for cuts to be made. Additionally, the navy's close ties with the royal family saw it frequently accused of Catholic sympathies. Much of this centred on the Duke of York, for despite leaving office as Lord High Admiral, he retained a great deal of unofficial influence over naval appointments, some of which were tainted by suspicions of Catholicism. Fears of Catholic subversion came to a head in 1678 when the former naval chaplain Titus Oates went before the Privy Council to reveal a Jesuit plot to kill the king. The Popish Plot, as it became known, was entirely fictitious, but it forced Pepys to launch an extensive enquiry into the religious inclinations of the navy's officers and men. He discovered an overwhelmingly Protestant and loyal force: almost all were ready to sign oaths of allegiance and take the 'test' to affirm their religion, and many did so in the subsequent months. Pepys, however, who had long been seen as the Duke of York's man, was left vulnerable in the face of these attacks. On 20 May 1679, the Commons committee of enquiry into naval miscarriages openly attacked Pepys and accused him of papism: he was dismissed from service and committed to the Tower of London on charges of 'Piracy, Popery and Treachery'.[22] These claims were outlandish, and Pepys was quickly released (though the charges against him were not dropped until June 1680). Yet on his release he was not reinstated, and for the first time in two decades he found himself without employment.

Charles was forced to bring in a new Admiralty commission made up of Parliamentarians who had previously been Pepys's most bitter critics. Determined not to rely on Parliament for money (and thereby repeat the same mistakes as his father), Charles had little choice but to accept a severe retrenchment in the navy's finances. The Treasury was given unprecedented control over all naval expenditure. Pepys was an unabashed critic, though he failed to appreciate the political pressures facing Charles or the financial peril confronting Parliament. 'No king', he wrote:

> ever did so unaccountable a thing to oblige his people by, as to dissolve a commission of the admiralty then in his hand who best understands the business of the sea of any prince the world ever had, and things never better done, and put it into hands which were wholly ignorant thereof, sporting himself with their ignorance.[23]

It soon became clear, however, that the commission was damaging the navy. Though the Admiralty was committed to building thirty new ships, its zeal for economy meant that the new vessels fell into disrepair and essential supplies dried up. Only in 1684 was Charles politically powerful enough to remove the commission and install himself as

The Burning of the *Royal James* at the Battle of Solebay, 28 May 1672
Oil on canvas, by Willem van de Velde, the Younger (1633–1707), late seventeenth century.

National Maritime Museum, Caird Collection, BHC0302.

Full-hull model of a 90-gun warship,
***c.*1675** (and detail opposite)
This may be a preliminary design for the
90-gun vessels in the 1677 'thirty ships'
building programme.

National Maritime Museum, SLR0003.

Lord High Admiral, with the Duke of York as an informal adviser. Pepys was brought back into office, and he became the first holder of a new position: Secretary for the Affairs of the Admiralty of England, an aggrandized version of his previous role. In this new and powerful role, Pepys set up a special 'Navy Commission' in April 1686 to clear the navy's accounts and restore the force to its 1679 levels, with the full support of the new king, James II. Pepys's reforms were so successful that he could declare them completed six months ahead of schedule.[24] It was Pepys's last, and arguably greatest, achievement.

William III's seizure of power in 1688 brought to an end both James II's reign and Pepys's career in naval administration. In the aftermath of the 'Glorious Revolution', he was initially kept on, but following the dismissal of many of James II's other officers he decided to resign on 20 February 1689. True to form, he spent a further two weeks tidying and sorting the files which had served him so well over the previous decades.[25] Pepys intended to use these records to write a comprehensive naval history of England, though this work was never finished. He did, in 1690, publish a shorter book entitled *Memoires Relating to the State of the Royal Navy of England*, which amounted to a forthright defence of his time in office and a violent attack on the commission of 1679–84. For all that Pepys's account was unashamedly self-serving, there was considerable truth to his narrative that the navy had been decimated by the commission, only to be rescued by Pepys. The *Memoires* were subjected to a lengthy Parliamentary investigation in 1691–92, which concluded that Pepys's facts and figures were broadly correct. Though Pepys did not return to naval office, some of his friends did, and many came to dominate naval administration in the subsequent decades.[26] One, Josiah Burchett, later rose to fill Pepys's shoes as Secretary to the Admiralty, and even succeeded in writing the history of which Pepys had so often spoken, in all probability helped by his mentor's vast collection of naval records. In 1720, Burchett published *A Complete History of the Most Remarkable Transactions at Sea*, the first general naval history in the English language.[27]

Pepys's legacy, however, was not as a historian but as the administrator who oversaw the growth and modernization of the Royal Navy. Not all of his reforms were effective, and he struggled to overcome insurmountable financial challenges. Pepys was no stranger to bribes, though it is worth noting that his own standards improved as his career progressed: his naval minutes reveal numerous instances when he detected corrupt practices and suspended and prosecuted those who erred.[28] A century after his death, Pepys was still held up as an exemplar of organizational competence who had helped create the powerful navy of the eighteenth century. In 1803, at the outset of the Napoleonic Wars, the navy once again came under increased political scrutiny. One correspondent to a radical newspaper bewailed the current state of affairs, and looked back fondly on the system of naval administration established by James II 'with the assistance of that able man Pepys, his secretary, a system under which our navy has grown to its present magnitude and celebrity, and has been, and is, the admiration and envy of the world'.[29]

Pepys neither transformed the navy single-handed, nor can we hold him up as a paragon of probity. He was, however, the finest naval administrator of his age, and left behind an institution that was larger, stronger and more professional than any that had come before. Over the course of the eighteenth century, the navy would continue to develop and grow from the foundations that he laid.

Margarette Lincoln

Pepys,
Tangier and
Islam

Pepys is associated with London first and foremost but he is also closely linked to Tangier, an English colony from 1661 to 1683, which he helped to administer. His experience offers opportunities to examine how the Moors of North Africa and the neighbouring Turks of the Ottoman Empire were represented in England. These varied depictions were used to reflect popular attitudes to domestic political upheavals. They also reveal contemporary sensitivities about England's international standing in relation to rival European powers and militant Islam.

England in the second half of the seventeenth century was a small country with colonial and trading ambitions, not only in the Americas and the East but in the Mediterranean, then the world's greatest centre for commerce. The mighty Ottoman Empire, many times more powerful than England in terms of size, population and wealth, loomed large in the English world view. It included the notorious ports of Algiers, Tunis and Tripoli on the North African Barbary Coast (the name derived from the Berbers who lived there). Muslim corsairs sailed from these havens to plunder trade and seize Christians who were put to work as slaves until ransomed. Morocco was never strictly part of the Ottoman Empire but corsairs also set out from Salé on the Atlantic coast and from other Moroccan ports. Of course, some Mediterranean Europeans retaliated by corsairing themselves, but their attacks against Muslims were not so well publicized in England.

Barbary corsairs had stepped up their attacks on English merchant vessels during the reign of Charles I, after his father James I had made peace with Spain, the enemy of the Ottoman Empire. Charles decided to build a navy that would protect English shipping and, in the process, encourage support for the Stuart monarchy. This contributed to his downfall. Short of funds, he extended Ship Money (a medieval coastal tax to cover the cost of fitting out warships and general expenses) to inland counties but he acted without consent of Parliament. The tax was bitterly resented and became one of the causes of the Civil War.

The terror of the Barbary corsairs lessened only gradually as European powers developed navies that could enforce treaties with

Mohammed Ohadu, the Moroccan Ambassador (detail)
Oil on canvas, by Sir Godfrey Kneller
(1646–1723) and Jan Wyck
(c.1640–1702), 1684.

Chiswick House, London, J970154.

the Barbary states. In Pepys's time, when the English considered slavery, 'white slavery' in the Barbary states was uppermost in their minds. Corsairs captured several thousand English sailors each year and even raided coastal villages in Devon and Cornwall. Captains of merchant ships who successfully defended themselves against Barbary pirates were feted in ballads; fundraising by families and church groups to ransom captives was routine; and it was possible to encounter men who had actually been captives of the Moors. Pepys, for example, drank in a tavern with two seamen who had been slaves in Algiers. They described harsh conditions but also explained how those less committed to their Christian faith could live well, receiving lenient treatment from their masters if they earned them a regular income through industry or theft.[1] Captivity narratives about Christian slaves in North Africa were hugely popular. Those read by Pepys and his wife included *The History of Algiers and it's Slavery with many remarkable particularities of Africk. Written by the Sieur Emanuel D'Aranda, sometime a slave there*, translated from the French in 1666.[2]

Yet if corsairs were feared and loathed, the opulence of Ottoman and Moorish palaces was envied. Luxury products from the eastern Mediterranean were much in demand. The English Levant Company enjoyed a monopoly on trade with the Ottoman Empire and provided diplomatic representation in the territories ruled by the sultan. Its merchants sent English cloth, tin and re-exported goods such as cochineal either to Constantinople (Istanbul) or Smyrna (Izmir). In return, they imported currants, indigo, raw silk, carpets, cotton wool, drugs and spices.

In England, exotic luxuries from the eastern Mediterranean such as carpets and toothbrushes became fashionable, and coffeehouses became all the rage. Turkish dress even influenced Western fashion: coats and trousers, essential garments for Ottoman men and women, led to the development of the men's suit of trousers or breeches, shirt, vest or waistcoat, outer coat and cravat. Londoners felt that the licentious behaviour and fashions of the court had helped to provoke God's wrath in the form of the Great Fire. Courtiers, for example, had wantonly exposed their shirts, formerly considered an undergarment, for all to see. After the fire, King Charles announced a new fashion: a 'vest', to be modestly buttoned over the shirt and under the coat. The diaries of Pepys and John Evelyn document the introduction of this notable change in October 1666.

It was in this context of ever-intensifying demand for Eastern goods that Tangier fell into English hands, as part of the dowry of Charles II's Portuguese queen, Catherine of Braganza, in 1661. England did not yet administer Gibraltar and Tangier was in a strategic location, overlooking the entrance to the Mediterranean. The aim was to use Tangier to control the Mediterranean and encourage trade with the Levant. It was hoped that the colony would provide the base for an English fleet in the Mediterranean, allowing it to monitor the rival navies of Spain and France, protect existing trade routes with the southern and eastern Mediterranean, and even open up new routes into Africa. It also offered a stopover for merchant ships trading to the East Indies. Hoping to encourage trade from all nations, Charles proclaimed Tangier a free port. As Pepys cheerfully recorded in his diary, Tangier was 'likely to be the most considerable place the King of England hath in the world'.[3]

Engineers were engaged to build a huge breakwater or 'mole' at Tangier to create a more sheltered harbour. A Tangier Committee was set up in London, responsible for the oversight and supply of the colony's garrison and for the building of the mole. Pepys was appointed to the committee in 1662, thanks to his patron, the Earl of Sandwich. At first, he was responsible for supervising the supply contracts for the new colony. The presents he received from merchants eager to tender for this new business, and from those who had won profitable contracts, immediately and substantially increased his annual income. (It was then routine to reward the official who oversaw the bidding process for government contracts.) In 1665, he took over as Treasurer of the committee. By the end of that year he had raised his estate from £1,300 to £4,400, chiefly through this lucrative employment.

An English Ship in Action with Barbary Corsairs, c.1680
Oil on canvas, by Willem van de Velde, the Younger (1633–1707), c.1685.

National Maritime Museum, BHC0323.

Early descriptions of Tangier painted a rosy picture for those at home but they were unreliable. Pepys's diary entries from 1667 reveal that he and others on the Tangier Committee had realized that the colony was a flawed enterprise.[4] As a crown colony, it was run on a state-controlled model, different to that of England's other burgeoning colonial initiatives in India and North America, which were driven by merchant interest. Tangier was always short of cash and failed to attract trade, perhaps due to the corrupt practices of successive governors. Only the poor and desperate were willing to live there, and it became notorious for drunkenness and immorality. The garrison was under-resourced and barely able to protect the town from encircling Moorish tribes who found a unifying mission in their attempts to eject the foreigners.

Tangier stood as a symbol of English colonial ambition: it was a matter of pride that its garrison should continue to hold the surrounding Moors at bay. Yet Tangier lost high-level support at home. One key issue was the appointment of a succession of Catholic governors to lead a garrison itself largely composed of Irish Catholics. During the Popish Plot (1678–81), false accounts of a Catholic conspiracy to kill the king whipped up intense anti-Catholic feeling. Charles found it impossible to persuade Parliament to vote public funds for Tangier in order to support what was perceived to be a Catholic stronghold.

In 1683, the king therefore appointed the naval commander George Legge, Baron Dartmouth, to evacuate and destroy Tangier and its fortifications. At first this was a secret operation. Pepys was asked to accompany Dartmouth to Tangier with less than forty-eight hours' notice and not told what the mission was before he sailed. He had been out of favour since 1679 when he lost his position as Secretary to the

Prospect of Yorke Castle at Tangier, from ye Strand, and the North-West
Engraving, by Wenceslaus Hollar (1607–77), 1669.

National Maritime Museum, PAD6928.

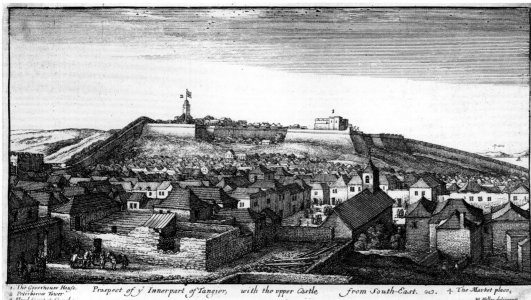

Prospect of ye Innerpart of Tangier, with the upper Castle, from South-East
Engraving, by Wenceslaus Hollar (1607–77), 1669.

National Maritime Museum, PAD6932.

Admiralty during the Popish Plot. His enemies had tried to prove that he favoured Catholics and he was imprisoned in the Tower from May to July that year. Now he saw the dangerous mission to Tangier as a means to win back royal favour. His chief role in the colony was to assess property values so that owners could be compensated when it was abandoned. He kept another brief diary of the experience, known as his Tangier journal.

The English blew up Tangier's fortifications on 5 November 1683 before leaving. This date, the anniversary of the Gunpowder Plot, was probably chosen to ensure that when news that Tangier had been evacuated broke at home it resonated with anti-Catholic feeling (the destruction of Tangier's defences continued beyond this date). Popular prejudice was used to help cover the humiliation of abandoning a failed colony that had cost the exchequer about £2 million. At this time, the Turkish threat to Europe was also hot news, much discussed in coffeehouses and taverns. The Turks had made inroads into the Holy Roman Empire (Germany/Austria), taking advantage of a divided Europe which was already a matter of concern.[5] The Turks laid siege to Vienna but were defeated on 12 September 1683 by a Polish army that arrived to help the beleaguered forces. This reversal was much publicized and is usually regarded as the beginning of the decline of the Ottoman Empire.

Before Pepys went to Tangier, various cultural influences would have informed his view of Islam. Representations of Turks in the theatre or popular literature had become a means of airing contemporary political concerns. William Davenant's musical production, *The Siege of Rhodes*, tells the story of the Ottoman sultan Suleyman the Magnificent's capture of Rhodes from the Christian Knights of St John in 1522, but is full of thinly disguised contemporary references. Apostasy emerges as a strong theme. The work resonated with theatre-goers: Pepys attended eleven performances and bought the text to read with his wife. Pepys also saw *Mustapha*, a rhymed-verse tragedy by Roger Boyle, Earl of Orrery and a former supporter of Cromwell, which similarly explored

George Legge, 1st Baron Dartmouth
Oil on canvas, English school,
seventeenth century.

National Maritime Museum, Greenwich
Hospital Collection, BHC2644.

conflicts of loyalty and expediency in a manner that allowed easy parallels to be drawn with contemporary political concerns. Audiences recognized that they, along with many of their countrymen, had been guilty of switching religious and political loyalties. They had rebelled against their king, had sung the praises of Cromwell during the Protectorate and changed sides again after his death. Islam increasingly came to serve as a metaphor for religious and political turmoil in England. For example, Elkanah Settle's hugely successful play, *The Empress of Morocco* (1673), was an early exploration of the social crisis occasioned by James, Duke of York's, rejection of the Protestant faith, which banned him from holding public office.

Similarly, actual Ottoman history – as opposed to the imaginings of playwrights – was being used as a means to interpret the turbulent domestic events following the execution of Charles I. For example, the anonymous tract, *Learne of A Turk, or Instructions and Advise taken from the Turkish Army at Constantinople to the English Army at London* (1660), pointedly described how the standing army that once defended the Ottoman Empire became a threat to its civil order. The lesson struck home because many English people understood the crucial role that Cromwell's army had played in deciding their country's destiny. They were worried about a standing army's potential to impose its will. Protestant concern about the extent of sovereign power was increased by a distrust of prominent Catholics. More broadly, European debates about legitimate forms of government came to influence the West's stereotypical view of 'despotic' Turks.

After England acquired Tangier, reports of English defeats and the garrison's struggle to hold the town fostered a view of the Moors as a military force to be reckoned with. This changed the stock representation of villainous infidels depicted, for example, in the theatre. In parallel, the English became increasingly apprehensive about 'renegadoes': men who went over to the Moors and converted to Islam. Enslaved seamen, aiming to improve their prospects in captivity, were tempted to 'turn Turk', seduced by a rival doctrine or the prospect of an easier life. Desperate soldiers at Tangier, calculating that conditions were better outside the city walls, did the same. Renegades helped the English to explore the phenomenon of apostasy in their own country, a subject of uneasy satire. For example, the ballad *A Turn-Coat of the Times* (1663), attacking Presbyterians, features 'a turn-coat Knave' who, when aligned with the Roundheads, 'triumphed like the Turk' but after Cromwell's death brazenly wheedled a place at the Restoration court, 'with men of the better sort'.

A more rational curiosity about the Ottoman Empire and knowledge of Muslim society became expected of educated men. Pepys, uneasily aware of the limitations of his geographical knowledge and perhaps judging that he needed a better understanding of Ottoman society to support his work on the Tangier Committee, purchased Paul Rycaut's *The Present State of the Ottoman Empire* in April 1667. He paid an inflated price of 55 shillings for a bound and coloured copy, after most of the stock had been destroyed in the Great Fire, noting in the book itself that it had earlier cost only 20 shillings.

Rycaut had been secretary to the English ambassador to the Ottoman Empire, Sir Heneage Finch, third Earl of Winchilsea. His book was carefully based on eyewitness information and was so well received that it earned him election to the Royal Society. Long considered to be a well-balanced approach, in England it helped to cement scholarly interest in the Ottomans and to place Islam more firmly within a context of international trade. Interestingly, Rycaut, who went on to become the English consul in Smyrna, considered tyrannical rule to be the Ottoman Empire's source of greatness.

Into this milieu, in 1682, came the colourful but urbane Moroccan ambassador, Kaid Mohammed ben Haddu (referred to in English sources as Ben Haddu), sent to negotiate a treaty with England and terms for the release of soldiers captured by the Moors during the recent siege of Tangier. He arrived with a renegade Englishman as translator and an extraordinary present for Charles II of two lions and thirty ostriches. His displays of horsemanship in Hyde Park, when he and his retinue tossed and caught their lances at breakneck speed, were a novel spectacle that attracted crowds. His courtly manners were admired by the well-to-do and he, in turn, appreciated English architecture and the theatre. As the diarist John Evelyn wrote, 'he was the fashion of the season'. The ambassador visited the Royal Society, St Paul's (still re-building after the Great Fire), and the universities of Oxford and Cambridge, where Professors of Arabic were able to converse directly with him in his own tongue. The visit was a striking success in cultural terms: it stimulated interest in Morocco, the Arabic world and Islam. Sadly, hopes for a negotiated treaty with the Moroccans came to nothing thanks to tensions over Tangier, and Charles ignored Ben Haddu's advice to negotiate a deal and yield the colony on good terms, perhaps considering this too humiliating.

So when Pepys sailed to North Africa in 1683, his reading and conversation had given him a cultural framework for thinking about Islam but he had little knowledge based on experience. The colonial community at Tangier had as little to impart: it had only limited contact with the Moors, the walls of the town imprisoning them as much as offering protection from attack. Pepys took personal risks to find out more, getting as close to the Moors outside the walls as he dared, even talking to their sentries.[6] He showed the same curiosity and open-mindedness in matters of faith that he had exhibited in London where, for example, he had purchased and studied a Catholic 'Masse book'. In his Tangier journal he described how he asked a renegade Moor, who had converted to Christianity, to show him the manner in which he prayed. He wrote, 'I never was more taken with any appearance of devotion in my life in any person of any sort or religion'.[7] Certainly the display of piety would have formed a marked contrast to the cynicism and immorality exhibited by the town's Christian inhabitants. In church one Sunday, Pepys was embarrassed for the governor and officers of the garrison when the preacher complained of the vices of the town – until he noticed that the sermon had made no impact on them.[8]

Perhaps Pepys was spurred in his attempt to learn something at first hand about the Moors by England's failure to hold its colony. He was certainly keen to understand more of the history of the conflict between the colonists and indigenous Moroccans. His interest in the renegade Moor may have stemmed from his experience of the effects of religious controversy in England. As a member of the Royal Society, he may also have been drawn to the empirical process of knowing through seeing, which was increasingly gaining ground among those men of learning keen to understand the world through observation and experiment. Furthermore, he was absorbed in the relationship between religion and sovereignty. He went out of his way to secure a copy of the philosopher Thomas Hobbes's study of society and government, *Leviathan*. Hobbes argued that a subject should obey his sovereign whatever his religion and suggested that Islam was as good a religion for civil society as Christianity. (Pepys had to buy a second-hand copy of *Leviathan* since Anglican bishops refused to allow it to be reprinted; he complained that scarcity had pushed up the price.)[9]

The evacuation of Tangier did not end Pepys's preoccupation with the Barbary Coast. His continuing interest in Morocco and the Ottoman Empire is evident from his ownership of Richard Knolles's *The Turkish*

Mohammed Ohadu, the Moroccan Ambassador

Oil on canvas, by Sir Godfrey Kneller (1646–1723) and Jan Wyck (c.1640–1702), 1684.

Chiswick House, London, J970154.

History, from the Original of that Nation to the Growth of the Ottoman Empire, a publication of 1603 updated by Rycaut in 1687. Pepys understood that strategic alliances would be needed to check Turkish advances, and that although England was currently weak, greater power would result from command of the seas and trade protection. He built up a navy equal to that of the Dutch and French, equipping England with a force that would permit a more active foreign policy. A strong navy was needed to thwart the French but also to enforce treaties with the Turks. England had strong rivals in the colonial sphere: in the Americas, South Asia and Africa, but there was growing recognition of the futility of armed intervention on the Continent. Pepys and others understood that conflict with the Turks and Moors was equally undesirable, not least because the Levant trade was particularly important to England: it employed thousands and contributed substantially to government income from customs dues. While the Turks may have been the enemy of Christendom, many English merchants were content to adopt a more pragmatic attitude and seek peaceful trade.

France went further: by the late 1680s, Louis XIV had revived France's old alliance with the Turks and backed their sultan against the Holy Roman Empire. Consequently, in 1689 Louis was vehemently denounced in the House of Commons as 'the most Christian Turk'.[10] The French king was also a correspondent of Moulay Ismaïl, sultan of Morocco from 1672 to 1727. Just as writers used the figure of the Turk to help interpret religious and political conflict in England so, in ballads and other popular works, as fears about Catholic ascendancy increased, they equated French arbitrary rule with Turkish tyranny. Nor were such comparisons unfounded: France remained a great threat to England.

One incident, in June 1687, helps to convey the continuing centrality of the Ottoman Empire to English politics and relations with Europe, while also illuminating ongoing tensions in England between Protestants and Catholics. Pepys, reappointed Secretary to the Admiralty, faced a delicate maritime situation that posed acute political and commercial difficulties. The Dutch, England's rivals, were engaged in a naval war with Algiers whose corsairs now entered the Channel. Their presence off the English coast caused anxiety because England had a treaty with Algiers (the English paid subsidies and their vessels carried passes in the Mediterranean which the Algerines usually respected). The government now feared these corsairs would do something to cause an unfortunate rupture. The situation was also a worry to the Levant Company, who feared loss of trade. A fleet was dispatched to prevent the corsairs from returning home with any English subjects captured from the Dutch. It also had orders to enforce a salute from a French fleet then hovering in the Channel to intercept escaping Huguenots, French Protestants being persecuted by their Catholic king. Skilfully, Pepys managed to resolve all sides of the problem without recourse to fighting. He even managed to secure the release of some Huguenots who had been captured by the Algerines as they tried to escape by sea to Holland, and who could not claim their rights to immunity as French subjects for fear of being sent home to face an even worse fate. Deftly, Pepys managed to persuade the Catholic King James II to secure their release from the Moors as English subjects.[11]

This incident shows continuing anxiety about captivity at the hands of Barbary corsairs. The plight of the Huguenots chimes with another aspect of contemporary thinking, which lumped together concern over the 'tyranny' of the Catholic French king and fear of the Moors. Yet it also shows that ongoing negotiation and dialogue with the Barbary states produced deals in spite of official antagonisms. Just as Pepys, sceptical and broad-minded, took steps to satisfy his own curiosity by testing the popular image of Moors when based in Tangier, so he adopted a pragmatic stance in his later dealings with Ottoman power. In this he was consistent rather than hypocritical. Overall, Pepys's connections with Tangier and Islam illuminate evolving attitudes towards Islamic culture in seventeenth-century England.

Pepys in Greenwich

Pieter van der Merwe

Greenwich in the 1660s was both a country village and a major royal site. Charles II began improving the park, moving on to replace the ruinous riverside Tudor palace, off which he moored his royal yachts: having acquired the Dutch habit of yachting while in exile, he imported both the fashion and the ship-type on his return to England. Thanks to its royal associations, its park (then open only to respectable, privileged visitors), its rural setting, its inns and easy river access from London, Greenwich was becoming an increasingly popular recreational resort.

Its location, between the Royal Dockyards of Deptford (where many of Charles's yachts were built) and Woolwich, meant that Pepys often called there on business, seldom passing up the chance to enjoy some aspect of local pleasures. On rare occasions, he brought his wife there on outings: on 16 June 1662, for example, they came down in a party 'by water', and Pepys 'showed them the King's Yacht, the house [i.e. the palace site], and the parke, all very pleasant; and so to the taverne, and had the Musique of the house, and so merrily home again'.[1]

In autumn 1665, during the plague, the Navy Office also briefly moved to the old palace complex for safety, probably to buildings off the north-west end of modern Park Row (then Back Lane). From October to January, Pepys rented comfortable rooms with a Mrs Clerke in Greenwich, while his wife lodged with William Sheldon, a dockyard official at Woolwich. The couple returned to London early in 1666, but the Second Anglo-Dutch War kept him busy downstream. On 2 June, with the Four Days Battle raging off the Kent coast, Pepys and a naval colleague came on duty to Greenwich, where they

> went on shore ... and into the parke, and there we could hear the guns from the Fleete most plainly. Thence he and I to the King's-head and there bespoke a dish of steaks for our dinner ... While that was doing, we walked to the water-side, and there seeing the King and Duke [of York] come down in their barge to Greenwich-house, I to them and did give them an account [of] what I was doing. They went up to the park to hear the guns of the fleet go off.[2]

If Pepys visited Greenwich today, he would find some things familiar despite the transformation of the town from around 1830 by Greenwich Hospital (still the main landholder), in fine late-Georgian style. The park's form has softened with time but remains largely as he saw it first laid out, with many Spanish chestnuts then planted still standing. It is unclear if or when he visited the Royal Observatory, built in 1675–76, but as Secretary to the Admiralty and a Fellow of the Royal Society he knew its work and the old lodge, called Greenwich Castle, which it replaced. On 11 April 1662, returning from Woolwich with the Commissioner of the Navy Board, Sir William Penn, they strolled 'into the Park, where the King hath planted trees and made steps in the hill up to the Castle, which is very magnificent': a year later he showed his father the same view.[3] The Queen's House, with the walled public highway eastward still running beneath it until shifted north in 1697–99, would also have been familiar to him.

Pepys only lived to see early work on what is now the Old Royal Naval College, built from 1696 to 1751 as the Royal Hospital for Seamen, or 'Greenwich Hospital'. As he later told Evelyn, the scheme had first been suggested by James II; when, after his deposition, his daughter Mary II asked Sir Christopher Wren to produce designs, the latter sought Pepys's advice.[4] Their 1694 site visit was Pepys's last recorded one to Greenwich but he knew well the earlier, uncompleted redevelopment of the old palace complex, which (apart from the Queen's House) was absorbed into the hospital scheme. In 1664, when the foundations of what is now the east range of the King Charles Court were laid, he noted it was intended as 'a very great house for the King, which will cost a great deale of money'.[5] In March 1669, he added that the building 'goes on slow, but is very pretty',[6] though it had by then almost entirely stalled.

Today, Pepys could still disembark at the college water-gate or long-disused Garden Stairs, the old river landing to the town. Walking south, up medieval Church Street, he would still pass a few late 1690s houses (now shops) on his right; while on his left, Turnpin Lane is the last alley of the vanished post-medieval town centre, which obscured today's dramatic westward approach to the parish church of St Alfege. It was also the church's medieval forerunner, not Hawksmoor's present replacement (built in 1718), that Pepys attended on 13 January 1661, approving

London and the River Thames from One Tree Hill, Greenwich Park
Oil on canvas, by Jan Griffier, the Elder (c.1652–1718), c.1690.
The Queen's House is in the centre, with a (largely imagined) garden, in odd perspective, between it and Charles II's new 'King's house' (1664–72). Old St Alfege, Greenwich, is the nearest church, with Deptford beyond. The first four ships from the right are royal yachts.

National Maritime Museum, BHC1833.

The gazebo on the garden wall of Sir William Hooker's house on Crooms Hill

National Maritime Museum, L7526-001.

'a good sermon, a fine church, and a great company of handsome women'.[7] There again at Christmas 1665, he admired the beautiful Mrs Lethieullier, the daughter of his friend Alderman William Hooker.[8] The grand but crumbling Lethieullier family tomb still stands to the south side of the 'new' church.

Past St Alfege's, Crooms Hill still winds up the west side of the park. The oldest of its imposing redbrick residences was finished c.1635;[9] but it was at another house, belonging to the judge Mark Cottle, that Pepys dined on Boxing Day 1665, 'nobly and neatly; with a very pretty house, and a fine Turret at top, with windeing stairs, and the finest prospect I know about all Greenwich, save the top of the hill, and yet in some respects better then that'.[10] A painting by Johannes Vorsterman shows this vanished roof-turreted, tea-caddy mansion, with that of Alderman Hooker to its left.

In 1672, (by then Sir) William Hooker built the fine gazebo, designed by Robert Hooke, that still overlooks Greenwich Park from the garden wall of his former house.[11] Pepys probably knew it, since abandoning his diary in 1669 did not mean he stopped visiting Greenwich. He certainly knew Hooke, who was curator of experiments at the Royal Society, and who helped Wren plan the Royal Observatory three years later. But while one can imagine Pepys sitting there in summer evenings of later years, or dining again with Cottle next door, there is no further record of it. As in other matters, the pages of his diary offer intriguing glimpses of Greenwich in the 1660s, unique in themselves and because nothing similar exists after he abandoned it in 1669.

Samuel Pepys, 'The Right Hand of the Navy'

Pepys was a natural administrator who brought method to all aspects of his employment. This required long hours at his desk. Since he also loved plays and pleasure, he had to force himself to work hard, binding himself by vows and fining himself whenever he broke self-imposed rules. By the mid-1660s, his commitment was recognized: George Monck, Duke of Albemarle, the army and naval officer who had done most to bring about Charles II's restoration, acknowledged Pepys as 'the right hand of the Navy'.[1]

The challenges faced by Pepys were stern. Commercial rivalry with the Dutch – who had gained control over the hugely profitable trade in spices from the East Indies – led Charles II to fight two naval wars against them in 1665–67 and 1672–74. These were years of enormous tension for Pepys, who struggled to prepare the fleet for war with inadequate resources.

While the English obtained some victories, the Dutch gained the upper hand in both wars. The most humiliating episode was the raid on the Medway in June 1667, when the Dutch burned part of the fleet at Chatham Dockyard and captured the flagship, the *Royal Charles*. To add to the disgrace, many of the sailors in the Dutch fleet were Englishmen. They had switched sides because the Dutch paid their seamen promptly and in cash.

Pepys escaped sanction for the Medway disaster, the blame unfairly falling on the Commissioner of Chatham Dockyard, Peter Pett. Although the English managed to beat off subsequent Dutch attacks, the costs of war, in addition to those of the plague and Great Fire, forced Charles to open peace talks, which left him weakened both at home and overseas.

Both the king and the Duke of York retained their confidence in Pepys's ability, even after his imprisonment and loss of office during the political upheavals of 1679. When Charles needed a skilled administrator to help manage the evacuation of the English colony at Tangier in 1683, he once again called on the navy's 'right hand'.

75

Samuel Pepys, aged about fifty-two

*c.*1685
Unknown artist
Oil on canvas, 1097 × 1437
Magdalene College, Cambridge,
College portrait no. 100

For many years, Pepys was a Member of Parliament. He was first elected to the Norfolk seat of Castle Rising in 1673, and subsequently held the seat of the port of Harwich in Essex following the elections of 1679 and 1685. This painting, known as the 'Harwich' portrait, probably dates to around the time of his last electoral victory. Pepys was an active Parliamentarian: he proved an important advocate of the king's naval policies, but also set a precedent by using his influence to further the interests of the town he represented. As late as 1688, with his career nearing its end, he continued to argue for the maritime interests of Harwich. JD

LITERATURE: Ranft.

76

....

Green-tinted spectacles

....

*c.*1650
Glass and leather
College of Optometrists, 1999.1416

Pepys's diary is littered with mentions of eye strain. On 13 December 1666, for example, he wrote that 'I perceive my overworking of my eyes by Candle light doth hurt them ... so that I entend to get some green spectacles'. Later, on 29 December, he noted, 'my left eye still very sore – I write by spectacles all this night'. Pepys recorded purchasing two new pairs of spectacles from the London maker John Turlington in 1667. Less than two years later, incorrectly fearing the onset of blindness, he ceased writing his diary on 31 May 1669. RB

LITERATURE: *Diary*, VII, 406, 424–25; VIII, 486.

77

....

Engrossment as Clerk of the Acts to the Navy Board

....

16 February 1662
Ink on parchment
Ministry of Defence Art Collection, MOD 189

This document is Pepys's patent of office for the position of Clerk of the Acts. In the fraught circumstances of Restoration government, many offices changed hands as royal authority replaced the republican regime in 1660. Pepys gained his appointment through the patronage of the Earl of Sandwich. Nothing was guaranteed, however, and he faced a number of tense days as rivals vied for the clerkship. This engrossment secured the job and marked the beginning of his long career in naval administration. RB

LITERATURE: Bryant, *Pepys: Man in the Making*, pp. 108–18.

78

Full-hull model of the *St Michael*

c.1672
Wood, cotton, brass, mica, paint and gilt
National Maritime Museum, Caird
Collection, SLR0002

The *St Michael* was a 90-gun ship of the
line launched in 1669 but later rebuilt to
add a further eight guns. This model is
particularly important as the *St Michael*
is the earliest English ship whose model
can be identified with any certainty.
It took part in the Battle of Solebay in
1672, the first naval action of the Third
Anglo-Dutch War (1672–74) and a Dutch
strategic victory. The *St Michael* served
for many decades and was renamed the
Marlborough in 1706. JD

79

James, Duke of York (later James II)

1672–73
Henri Gascar (1635–1701)
Oil on canvas, 2286 × 1125
National Maritime Museum, Greenwich
Hospital Collection, BHC2797

James (1633–1701), in recognition of
his role as Lord High Admiral between
1660 and 1673, is portrayed as Mars,
the Roman god of war. Behind, lies the
Royal Prince, the Duke's flagship of 100
guns. James was the last English prince
to command a fleet in battle, defeating
the Dutch off Lowestoft in 1665 and
fighting at Solebay in 1672, which this
portrait may commemorate. He was
a brave soldier by land and sea, and
diligent in the administration of the navy.
He encouraged Pepys in his work as a
naval administrator, becoming his most
important patron (other than Charles II
himself) after the death of Pepys's cousin,
the Earl of Sandwich, at Solebay. PvdM

80

The Sea Triumph of Charles II

c.1674
Antonio Verrio (c.1639–1707)
Oil on canvas, 2245 × 2310
Royal Collection, RCIN 406173

Probably painted for Charles II to commemorate the treaty that ended the Third Anglo-Dutch War in 1674, this allegory glorifies English dominion of the seas, although the war had not been a resounding English victory. Charles wears Roman armour and is driven through the water by Neptune, god of the sea, accompanied by three crowned women embodying his kingdoms of England, Scotland and Ireland. Lightning strikes the figure of Envy in the sky while the goddesses Minerva and Venus look benignly down on the English fleet. Fame holds a scroll inscribed 'IMPERIVM OCEANO FAMAM QVI TERMINET ASTRIS', a quotation from Virgil's *Aeneid* describing Julius Caesar, 'Whose empire ocean, and whose fame the skies / Alone shall bound', and thus comparing Charles to the great Roman conqueror. KB

LITERATURE: Millar, *Tudor, Stuart and Early Georgian Pictures*, cat. 296, p. 133; Sharpe, pp. 106–08.

81

Edward Montagu, 1st Earl of Sandwich ('The Flagmen of Lowestoft')

1666
Sir Peter Lely (1618–80)
Oil on canvas, 1425 × 1200
Inscribed, bottom left: 'The Earle of Sandwich'
National Maritime Museum, Greenwich Hospital Collection, BHC3007

Edward Montagu's astute political manoeuvring enabled his naval career to flourish during both the Commonwealth and Restoration. He was made Earl of Sandwich for commanding the fleet which brought Charles II home from exile in May 1660. He was Admiral of the Blue at the Battle of Lowestoft in 1665, one of the thirteen senior commanders or 'Flagmen' that the victorious James, Duke of York, Lord High Admiral, chose to have commemorated in portraits by Lely.

Sandwich later commanded the fleet at the Battle of Solebay in 1672, when he drowned while trying to escape from his burning flagship, the *Royal James*. KB

LITERATURE: van der Merwe, p. 61.

82

Lieutenant-Admiral Michiel de Ruyter

1667
Ferdinand Bol (1616–80) and Willem van de Velde, the Younger (1633–1707)
Oil on canvas, 1810 × 1635
National Maritime Museum, BHC2997

Michiel de Ruyter (1607–76) remains the most celebrated of all Dutch naval commanders. During the Second Anglo-Dutch War, he inflicted a humiliating defeat on the English in the Four Days Battle (1–4 June 1666). This is one of six near-identical, official portraits of de Ruyter commissioned to commemorate the victory. He is shown holding his commander's baton; the dividers on the table point towards his birthplace on the nearby chart, immortalizing him as local and national hero. The background showing his flagship, the *Zeven Provincien*, among the Dutch fleet, is by the celebrated marine painter Willem van de Velde, the Younger. This unusual collaboration functions as both portrait and history painting. KB

LITERATURE: Blankert, no. 79, pl. 88; Gaschke, pp. 86–87.

83

Dutch attack on the Medway:
the *Royal Charles* carried into Dutch
waters, 12 June 1667

1667
Ludolf Backhuysen
Oil on canvas, 1634 × 2236
National Maritime Museum, BHC0292

The capture of the *Royal Charles* during
the Dutch raid on the Medway in 1667
was embarrassing for both the king and
the English nation. Pepys feared for his
job but Peter Pett, Master Shipwright
and Commissioner of the dockyard at
Chatham, was blamed for not towing
the fleet's capital ships further up river,
though he did not have the resources
to do so and the Dutch would probably
have reached them anyway. He saved
his ship models, believing it impossible
to rebuild the fleet from drawings alone.
This produced much sarcasm in court
circles and he was stripped of office.
By depicting the ship flying a Dutch
ensign (but also Charles's captured royal
standard), Backhuysen underscores the
humbling English defeat. JD

LITERATURE: Gaschke, pp. 18–19.

Control of the Seas

English rulers in the seventeenth century claimed sovereignty over 'the British Seas'. Rather preposterously, these were asserted to include the whole of the English Channel to the shores of France, and the North Sea to the shores of Flanders and Holland. The claim was contested by rival nations, but fiercely upheld at home: foreign vessels were required to strike their flag and lower their topsail on entering these waters as an acknowledgment of England's power and jurisdiction. Sovereigns of England also claimed the power, in common with the rulers of other states, to punish piracy. The need to protect lawful commerce proved a useful justification for England to extend its power at sea.

French, Dutch and English pirates who raided Spanish colonies and Spanish ships in the Caribbean were termed 'buccaneers', from the local practice of smoking meat on a *boucan*, or gridiron, to preserve it. Early French adventurers on Hispaniola (now Haiti and the Dominican Republic) learned this process from the islanders. Later, these hunters turned to piracy. English rulers at first exploited the activities of freebooters and condoned their attacks on Spanish colonies. But when pirates began to damage lucrative trade in the East Indies, they opted for stronger anti-piracy measures.

The English government sent out warships to guard vital trade routes and, occasionally, to hunt down particular pirates. Such efforts remained fairly sporadic until the late 1690s, when it became government policy to maintain a naval presence in colonial waters even in peacetime. Colonial governors, frustrated by the inadequacies of the Royal Navy, sometimes took the initiative, extracted funds from local merchants and equipped their own ships to pursue troublesome pirates near their shores.

Pirate activity was interwoven with England's strategic attempts to advance international trade and open up new markets. This was a period in which long-distance voyages, despite the depredations of pirates, became safer, thanks to improved navigational instruments. Anti-piracy measures became a statement of Britain's ability to exert power over vast tracts of ocean and maintain clear passage over important sea routes.

84

Bucaniers of America: Or, a True Account of the Most Remarkable Assaults Committed of late Years upon the Coasts of The West-Indies

....

By A. O. Exquemelin (London, 1684)
National Maritime Museum, PBB0141

Alexandre Exquemelin's hugely influential book on the Caribbean pirates of the 1660s and 70s immediately gripped the public's imagination. First published in Dutch, in 1678, it was translated into German, Spanish and then (in 1684) into English. Exquemelin (*c.*1645–1707) served alongside Henry Morgan, the notorious buccaneer, probably as a barber-surgeon, until 1674. His narrative firmly associated Morgan with extreme acts of violence and the kinds of ruthless piracy that, by the 1680s, were already being regarded as damaging to the national reputation. ML

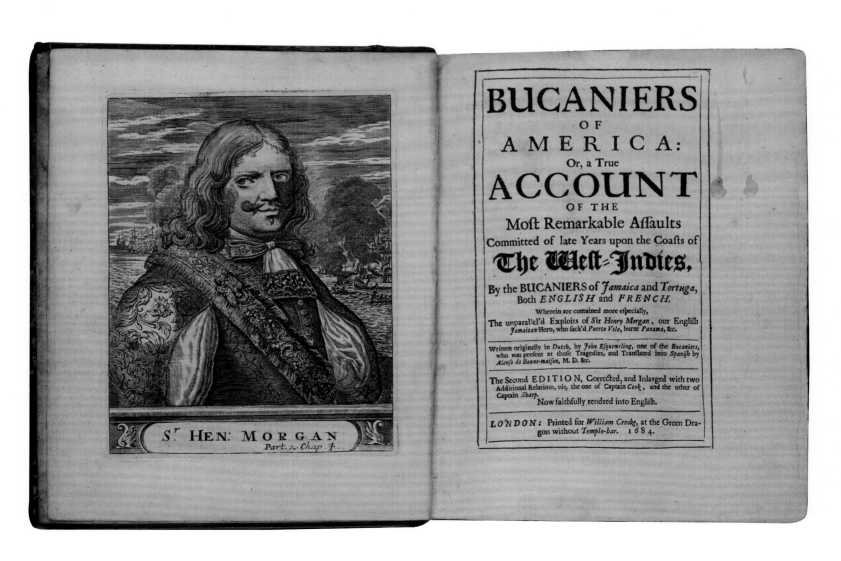

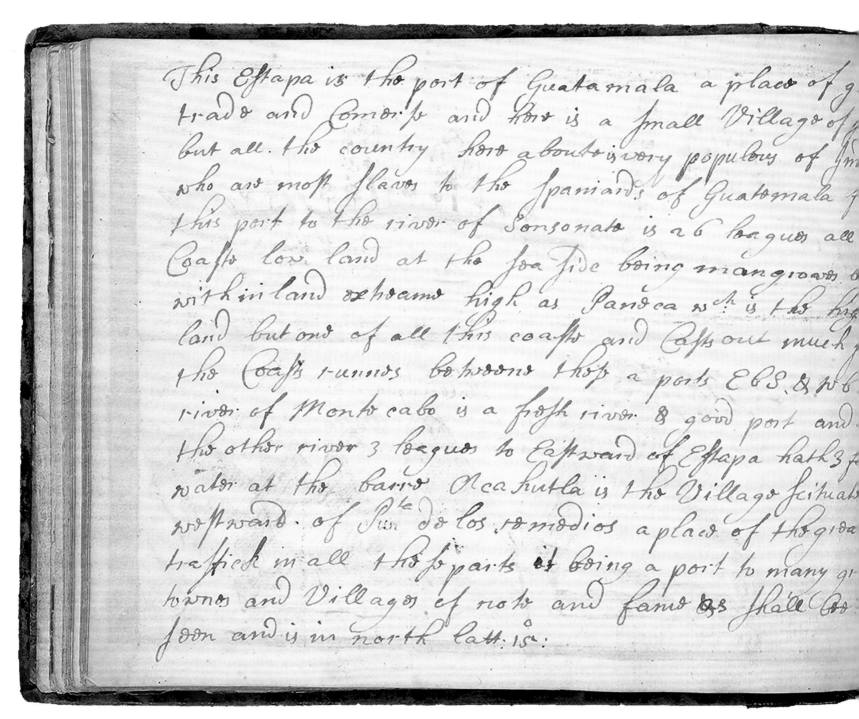

This Estapa is the port of Guatemala a place of g[reat]
trade and comerce and there is a small Village of
but all the country here about is very populous of [Indians]
who are most slaves to the spaniards of Guatemala f[rom]
this port to the river of Sonsonate is 26 leagues all
Coast low land at the sea side being mangroves b[ut]
within land extreame high as Pandea wch is the high[est]
land but one of all this coast and casts out much
the Coast runnes betweene these 2 ports EbS. & WbN
river of Monte cabo is a fresh river & good port and
the other river 3 leagues to Eastward of Estapa hath 3 fa[thom]
water at the barre Acahutla is the Village scituate[d]
westward of Pta de los remedios a place of the great[est]
traffick in all these parts it being a port to many gr[eat]
townes and Villages of note and fame as shall app[ear]
soon and is in north latt. 15°.

85

The South Sea Waggoner, Shewing the making and bearing of all the Coasts from California to the Streights of Le Maire

1682
Basil Ringrose (d. 1686)
Ink on paper
National Maritime Museum, P/32

In 1681, a band of English buccaneers that included the adventurer Basil Ringrose captured a *derrotero*, or book of navigational charts and sailing directions, from a Spanish ship off modern Ecuador. It detailed coasts, hazards and anchorages all the way from California to the Strait of Le Maire at the southern extremity of South America. When the buccaneers returned to England, the Spanish ambassador demanded that they be brought to trial. Charles II appreciated the value of the *derrotero* and acquitted them, to the annoyance of the King of Spain. Translated into English, this book has charts and additional text by Ringrose. The resulting sea atlas is a rich source of geographical and cultural information. ML

LITERATURE: Howse, Thrower and Quinn.

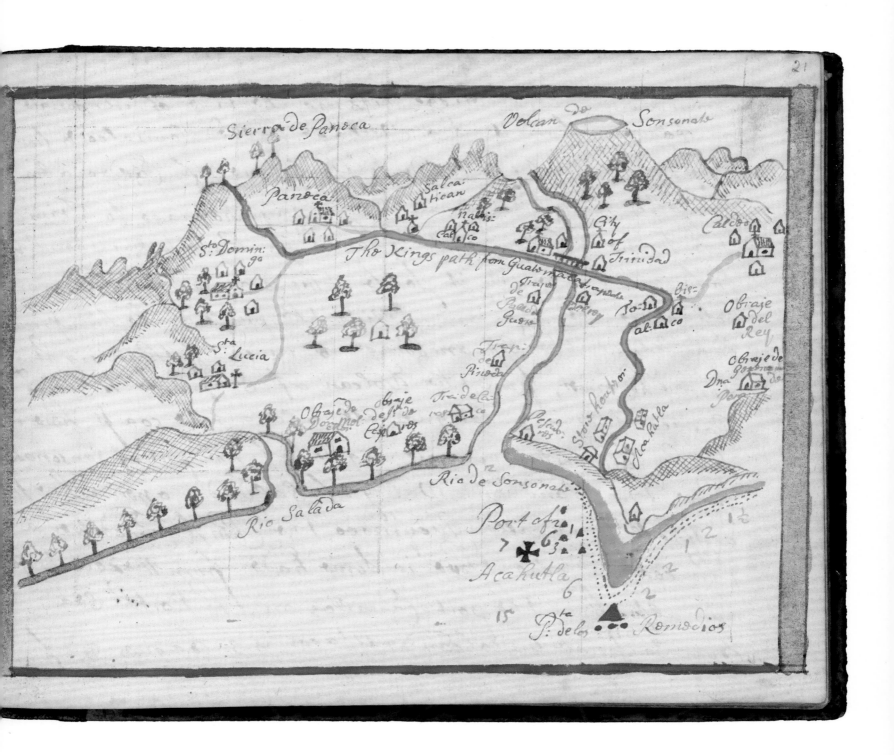

Sierra de Panoca

Volcan de Sonsonate

Panoca

Salca tican

Naris Caleco

City of Trinidad

Caldos

Sto Domingo

The Kings path from Guatemala, &c.

Trapu de Puebo Guare

doroy

Po al: co

Obraje del Rey

Sta Lucia

Trap del Pineda

Tra dela

Stons houpon

Acahutla

Obraje de gosma de Pan

Dna

Obraje de Dora Mol

obraje de St do Esparos

Rio Salada

Rio de Sonsonate

Pesado

Port chr

7 ✠ 6   1
3

Acahutla   6

15   Sta P. de los Remedios

2   1½

2

175

86

Novissima et Accuratissima Insulae Jamaicae Descriptio per Johannem Sellerum, Hydrographum Regium

....

1675
Hand-coloured engraving
National Maritime Museum,
PBE6862(26)

This intricately decorated map of Jamaica, published in John Seller's 1675 *Atlas Maritimus*, shows the parishes of the island as they existed at the time, and lists its principal ports and settlements. Jamaica had been an English colony since Cromwell captured it in 1655. The figure, possibly of Britannia, is shown holding a cornucopia, next to a shield bearing a version of the royal coat of arms. The map also displays the arms of the first five governors of Jamaica, as well as the heraldic insignia of the island itself. JN

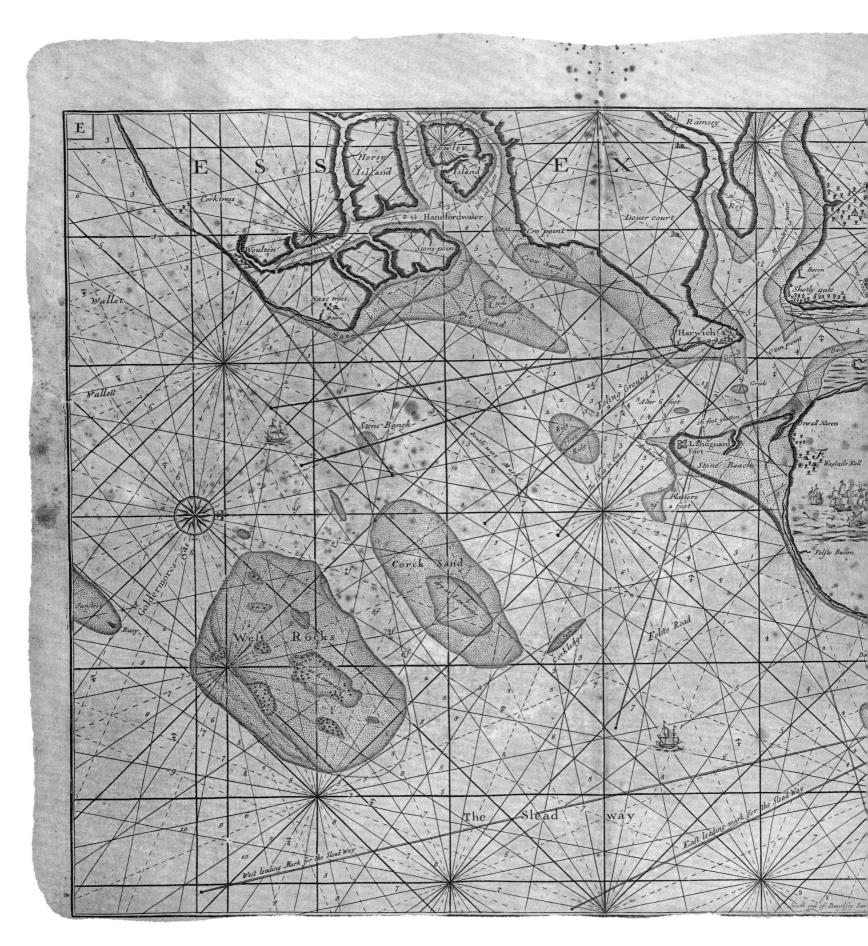

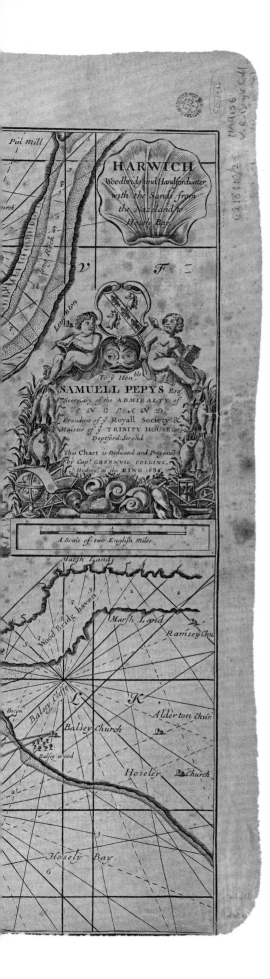

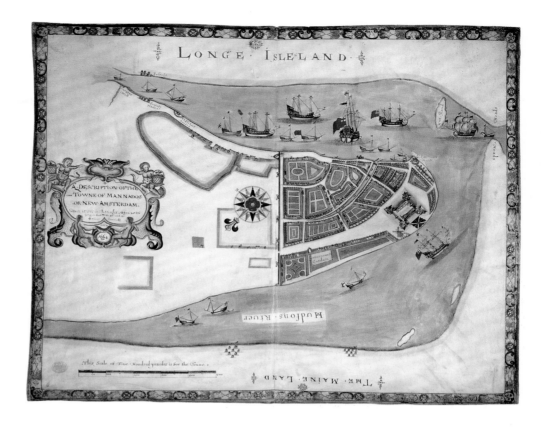

87

Harwich Woodbridg and Handfordwater,
with the Sands from the Nazeland to
Hosely Bay

....

1686
Greenvile Collins (1643–94)
Engraving on paper
National Maritime Museum, G218:11/25

Pepys, as Secretary to the Admiralty, appointed the King's Hydrographer, Captain Collins, to survey the coast of Britain and draw accurate charts. Collins was an experienced navigator who had sailed as master on Sir John Narbrough's voyage to the Pacific (1669–71) and on Captain John Wood's 1676 attempt to find a North-East Passage between the Atlantic and Pacific Oceans. Surveying work began in 1681, using the royal yacht, *Merlin*. This chart was one of the first from the project to be printed, and is dedicated to Pepys. The resulting atlas, *Great Britain's Coasting Pilot*, was published in 1693 and remained on sale without revision for more than a century. GH

88

A Description of the Towne of
Mannados: Or New Amsterdam,
as it was in September 1661

....

1664
Ink on vellum
British Library, Maps.K.Top.121.35

The English seized the Dutch colony of New Amsterdam in 1664, renaming it New York, in honour of James, Duke of York. This map, which belonged to James, is apparently based on a Dutch one of 1661. The colony is shown occupying the southern tip of Manhattan, or 'Mannados'. Prominent features include Fort Amsterdam (near the island's tip), renamed Fort James by the English, along with the governor's house and extensive gardens. Long Island, the Hudson River and Nutt Island (now Governor's Island) are also indicated. The shipping includes four English warships, which probably represent the invasion squadron of the colony's first English governor, Richard Nicolls. JN

179

89

Pocket telescope

*c.*1660
Painted vellum, wood and glass
National Maritime Museum, NAV1553

As Pepys noted, 'the best navigator is the best looker-out', and by his day a good telescope had become an essential aid on all ships. This example is characteristic of telescopes made before about 1660, with a ring around the largest draw tube that has the same diameter as the barrel. The relatively short length (132 mm) suggests that it was for maritime or terrestrial use, rather than for astronomy. RD

LITERATURE: Pepys, *Tangier Papers*, p. 130.

91

Nocturnal

*c.*1650–70
John Brown (*fl.* 1648–95)
Boxwood
National Maritime Museum, AST0133

This instrument was used by mariners to determine the time by the stars, since sea clocks were inaccurate, and to calculate high tide using the phases of the Moon. The tab labelled 'G*B' (the Great Bear constellation) was rotated to the appropriate date on the calendar scale and the instrument was aligned with the Pole Star, visible through the central hole. The long index arm was then rotated until the straight edge was aligned with the two stars at the end of the Great Bear and the time was read off the central hour scale. A combination of the calendar scale and lunar-phase scale (1–29 days) was used with data tables to calculate the time of high tide for specific ports. LD

LITERATURE: Higton, pp. 401, 438; Clifton, p. 40.

90

Hourglass

Seventeenth century
Glass, sand, wood, ivory and wax
National Maritime Museum, AST0073

This is a thirty-minute glass, filled with speckled ochre sand, used for measuring time and speed at sea. Every half hour, the ship's boy would 'turn the glass' as the last few grains of sand passed through, ringing a bell at the same time to alert the crew to the time elapsed. Similarly, a one-minute glass was used in conjunction with a log reel to determine speed. A sailor counted the number of knots passing through his hands as a wooden log attached to a line knotted at regular intervals was cast overboard, hence the derivation of the term 'knots' when referring to speed at sea. LD

LITERATURE: Turner, pp. 68–69.

92

Davis quadrant or backstaff

....

*c.*1700
Thomas Tuttell (*c.*1674–1702)
Ivory and brass
Inscribed: upper arm: 'Thomas Tuttell
Charing X Londini fecit' (Thomas Tuttell
of London Charing Cross made [this]');
back of the 25° arc: 'Fait par Tho:Tuttell
Ingenieur de sa Maiesté Britanique
pour les Instruments Mathematiques,
a Londres'
National Maritime Museum, NAV0040

The backstaff was one of the main
navigational instruments used by English
seamen in the seventeenth century.
It was used to determine latitude from
the Sun. While Pepys was scathing
of navigational practice in the navy,
he noted that celestial observations
improved officers' reckonings of
their location.

Although typical backstaffs were
wooden and fairly plain, this ivory
example is extensively decorated with
scrolling acanthus leaves that mutate
into snakes' heads. It is part of an ivory
presentation set and is unlikely to have

been used at sea. By 1700, Thomas
Tuttell was both instrument maker and
hydrographer to the king. He drowned
while surveying the River Thames in
1702. RD

LITERATURE: Mörzer Bruyns, p. 94.

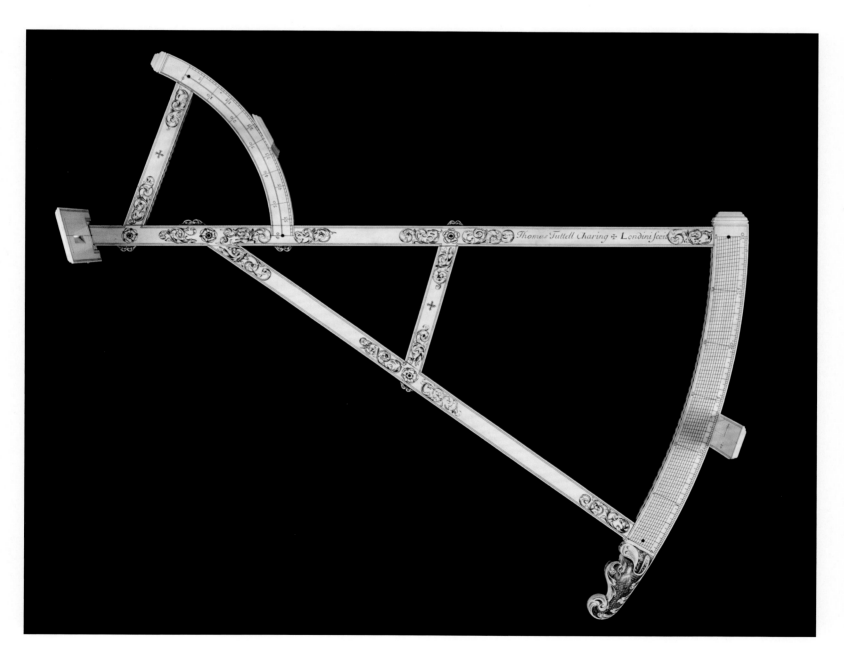

Trade and a Consumer Culture

During Pepys's adult lifetime, England's trading activity underwent dramatic change. Woollen cloth, traditionally sold abroad, still dominated the export market, but England's re-export trade boomed. Merchants imported sugar and tobacco from the West Indies, chintz (or painted cotton), spices and other luxury goods from the East, then exported these to continental Europe. Investment in commerce outstripped that in industry; the merchant class prospered. After Pepys dined with his friend, the merchant James Houblon, in 1690, he told John Evelyn, 'the Meale would have pleas'd you noe lesse than it did mee, as hardly consisting of one dish or glasse (besides bread and beere) of nearer growth than China, Persia and the Cape of Good Hope'.[1]

Overseas trade encouraged a flourishing consumer culture. Coffee, imported from Turkey, became a popular hot drink. Gold, lacquer work and ceramics from Japan and China became fashionable. In 1661, Pepys admired 'two very fine chests covered with gold and Indian varnish' in the Duke of York's closet, a present from the Dutch East India Company.[2] By 1697 the economist John Pollexfen complained, 'From the greatest gallants to the meanest cookmaids nothing was thought so fit to adorn their ... closets like China and lacquered ware.'[3] Then, as now, London had a dominant role in the English economy, and the financial sector was transformed. The Bank of England was founded in 1694, enabling public borrowing by means of the national debt. Government could pay for wars whose costs exceeded tax revenues.

When Charles II married Catherine of Braganza, the inclusion of Tangier and Bombay in her dowry enhanced English trading prospects. Bombay was leased to the East India Company. From the 1660s, the company sent sample patterns for cloth workers in India to copy. Pepys, alert to fashion trends, bought chintz wall hangings and a chintz gown for his wife in 1663. By 1678, Indian chintzes had become so popular they threatened the livelihood of English workers and an Act was passed stipulating that all English corpses had to be buried in local woollen cloth.

93

Chinese teapot or wine vessel

1640–50
Porcelain with gilt metal mounts
Burghley House, CER07499

Chinese hard-paste (or 'true') porcelain was a highly desirable commodity as the secret of making porcelain was not known in seventeenth-century Europe. It was valued particularly for its blue-and-white decoration, which required deft handling of the unstable cobalt pigment. In China, these vessels were used for wine, as tea was brewed in open pans. Until the fashion for tea drinking became relatively widespread in Britain in the late seventeenth century, it is likely that they served the same purpose here as well. AM

94

Pair of Japanese tankards

1660–80
Porcelain with gilt metal mounts
Burghley House, CER0487

These tankards are examples of Japanese Arita-ware. Named for the port from which it was exported, this ware had a distinctive palette of iron-reds and blues. Japanese craftsmen took European vessels as examples in order to create pieces like these for the export market. These examples belonged to John Cecil, the fifth Earl of Exeter, making them among the first Japanese ceramics in a British collection. According to the 1688 inventory of the earl's Lincolnshire home, Burghley House, they were probably prominently displayed above the chimney in the drawing room. AM

95

Chart of the East Indies

....

1665
Nicholas Comberford (1596–1673)
Ink on vellum, pasted on oak boards
National Maritime Museum, G256:1/1

The navigational charts used on English ships for most of the seventeenth century were made to order by chart makers based on the River Thames near the Tower of London. Drawn in ink and decorated in bright colours on sheets of vellum, they were mounted on hinged wooden boards ('platts') for easy use and stowage. Comberford was a leading maker, having completed an apprenticeship with John Daniel in 1620. Daniel (d. 1649) was a key figure in the creation of the English charting tradition. This 1665 East Indies chart is based on earlier ones from Daniel's workshop and omits the north coast of Australia even though it had featured on Dutch charts for many years. GH

LITERATURE: T. R. Smith, pp. 45–96.

96

Cup and cover

1621–22
Mother-of-pearl secured with brass pins,
silver-gilt mounts
Victoria and Albert Museum,
M.18&A-1968

Mother-of-pearl items were made in
Gujarat, in western India, in the sixteenth
and seventeenth centuries, and sold
to Europeans in the ports of Surat and
Cambay. The shell generally came from
Turbo marmoratus – the marbled turban
or great green turban snail, which lives
on tropical reefs. It was used to veneer
caskets and, when held by brass pins,
was strong enough to make cups without
additional support. This example is
made of two shell layers: the petal-
shaped plates on the exterior overlay
longer strips on the inside. The silver-gilt
mounts were added after it arrived in
England. BT

LITERATURE: Jaffer, pp. 96–97.

97

The Bowes Cup

1675–76
Jacob Bodendick (1633–81), London
Gold
Engraved with the arms of William Bowes
and the crest of Elizabeth Blakiston,
and inscribed with the Bowes motto:
'Sans Variance Terme de Vie' ('Steadfast
until the end')
Victoria and Albert Museum, M.63:1,
2-1993

Jacob Bodendick was born in Lüneberg,
in northern Germany, and moved to
London during the late 1650s. He became
one of its most skilled goldsmiths during
the Restoration, when the wealthy liked
to make ostentatious displays of plate.
This covered cup has scrolling handles,
and is embossed with an acanthus leaf
decoration. It also bears the arms of
Sir William Bowes, of Streatlam Castle,
Member of Parliament for County
Durham, and his wife, Elizabeth Blakison
of Gibside. It is made of Guinea gold,
notable for its deep yellow colour. BT

LITERATURE: E. J. G. Smith, pp. 109–22.

98

The Levant Gold Cup

1685
George Garthorne (active 1680–97),
London
Gold
Engraved with the arms of Sir William
Trumbull impaling those of his first wife,
Katherine and, on the other side, the
arms and motto of the Levant Company:
'Deo Repis et Amicis' ('To God, the
Republic [or state] and friends')
British Museum, 2007, 8037. 1

This gold cup was presented by the
Levant Company to Katherine, Lady
Trumbull, the wife of Sir William
Trumbull, the English ambassador to
the Ottoman Empire, on the occasion
of their departure to Constantinople
in 1687. The presentation was made
on board their ship off Greenwich.
Founded in 1581, the Levant Company
regulated English trade with the eastern
Mediterranean under a royal charter.
It was just one of the many trading
companies operating out of London in
the seventeenth century. RB

99

Coffee pot

1681–82
George Garthorne (probably), London
Silver and leather
Engraved with the arms of the Sterne
family, and inscribed: 'The Guift of
Richard Sterne Eq. to yᵉ Honorable East
India Comp[any]'
Victoria and Albert Museum, M.398-1921

This is the earliest known English silver
coffee pot: the shape was introduced
from Turkey during the mid-seventeenth
century, as was the drink itself. The
leather covering of the handle makes
it cooler to hold. Coffeehouses also
became popular at this time as a place of
relatively civilized male political debate,
free from the inflaming influence of
alcohol. The owner of the coffee pot may
have been Richard Sterne (c.1641–1716),
a Yorkshire MP who held considerable
stock in the East India Company. BT

100

Flagon

....

1639–72
Marked 'ELS'
Silver
Portsmouth Cathedral, chu 3/5/2

....

Standing paten

....

1677
Ralph Leeke, London
Silver
Portsmouth Cathedral, chu 3/5/3

....

Communion cup

....

c.1680
Marked 'HC'
Silver
Portsmouth Cathedral, chu 3/5/5

The abandonment of the colony of Tangier in 1683 left the town in ruins. After the fortifications and breakwater, or 'mole', were blown up on 5 November, Lord Dartmouth's expedition took anything of value back to England. Among other things, they brought back the plate of the church of St Charles the Martyr (Charles I), consisting of two flagons, two chalices and two patens, or plates. This silver was presented to the

mayor, aldermen, and burgesses of the borough of Portsmouth by James II in 1687, for use in the parish church there. One of the flagons is inscribed on the base: 'Alderman John McMath his gist [gift] to the Chirrch of Tangier November the 10th 1672'. McMath was a Scottish merchant who had settled in Tangier in the 1660s. JD and RB

LITERATURE: Slight, p. 73.

101

The Demolishing of Tangier, 1683

Seventeenth century
English school
Oil on canvas, 1725 × 2440
Dyrham Park, The Blathwayt Collection
(The National Trust), NT 453737

It is thought that this bird's-eye view
depicts the deliberate destruction of
Tangier's defences on 5 November
1683 by the troops of Lord Dartmouth,
before the town was evacuated and
returned to local rule. Rising smoke can
be seen where explosions demolish its
fortifications, while Moorish tribesmen
observe proceedings from the hills
overlooking the town. Pepys, who
accompanied Dartmouth, took risks
'with no pleasure, but great danger' to
see as much as he could of the colony
despite the encircling Moors outside
the walls. ML

LITERATURE: Pepys, *Tangier Papers*, pp. 18, 40.

102

Tangier in Its Rewings

Before 5 January 1685
Nicholas Yeates and John Collins
Engraving on paper, with inscription
National Maritime Museum, P/43(5)

This is a proof copy of the final image in a series of four views of Tangier, before and after its destruction in 1683. The print was made from original drawings by Thomas Phillips, a military engineer who accompanied Pepys and Lord Dartmouth on the expedition to evacuate the colony. The series was advertised in the *London Gazette*, on 5–8 January 1685,

as available from four dealers in London and Westminster. Each print was engraved on two interlocking plates. Pepys had his own, hand-coloured copy of the series (now in the Pepys Library), which is thought to be the only complete set to survive. ML

LITERATURE: Pepys, *Later Diaries*, p. 133, plates II–V.

103

Portrait medallion of Samuel Pepys

1688
Jean Cavalier
Ivory
Inscribed: 'SAM. PEPYS. CAR. ET.
IAC. ANGL. REGIB. ASECRETIS .
ADMIRALIAE' ('Samuel Pepys, Secretary
to the Admiralty for Charles and James,
Kings of England')
The Clothworkers' Company, ME022

Pepys commissioned this ivory medallion
from the French sculptor Jean Cavalier,
to whom the painter Godfrey Kneller
(a mutual acquaintance) probably
introduced him. It shows Pepys at the
pinnacle of his career as Secretary to the
Admiralty. Kneller also apparently feared
that Cavalier was trying to charge Pepys
too much and suggested he return the
original and keep a wax cast instead.
Despite these 'disingenuous dealings',
Pepys was clearly satisfied with the result
and it remained with the Pepys-Cockerell
family until 1931, when it sold at auction
for £130. RB

LITERATURE: Barber, pp. 7–8; *The Times*,
2 April 1931.

104

Samuel Pepys's Tangier diary

1683
Samuel Pepys
Ink on paper
Bodleian Library, MS Rawlinson C. 859,
f.208r

In 1662, England acquired the North African colony of Tangier, at the entrance to the Mediterranean. The same year, Pepys was appointed to the Tangier Committee, which oversaw the management and supply of this new outpost and put significant effort into developing it for trade and as a naval base. In 1683, amid concerns that the garrison was proving too expensive, he was sent to Tangier to help Lord Dartmouth in its evacuation. During this mission, Pepys began to keep a diary in shorthand again. It offers a remarkable insight into naval life at the time, with accompanying notes of his opinions of the expedition's officers: these were not always complimentary. JD

LITERATURE: Tomalin, pp. 333–37.

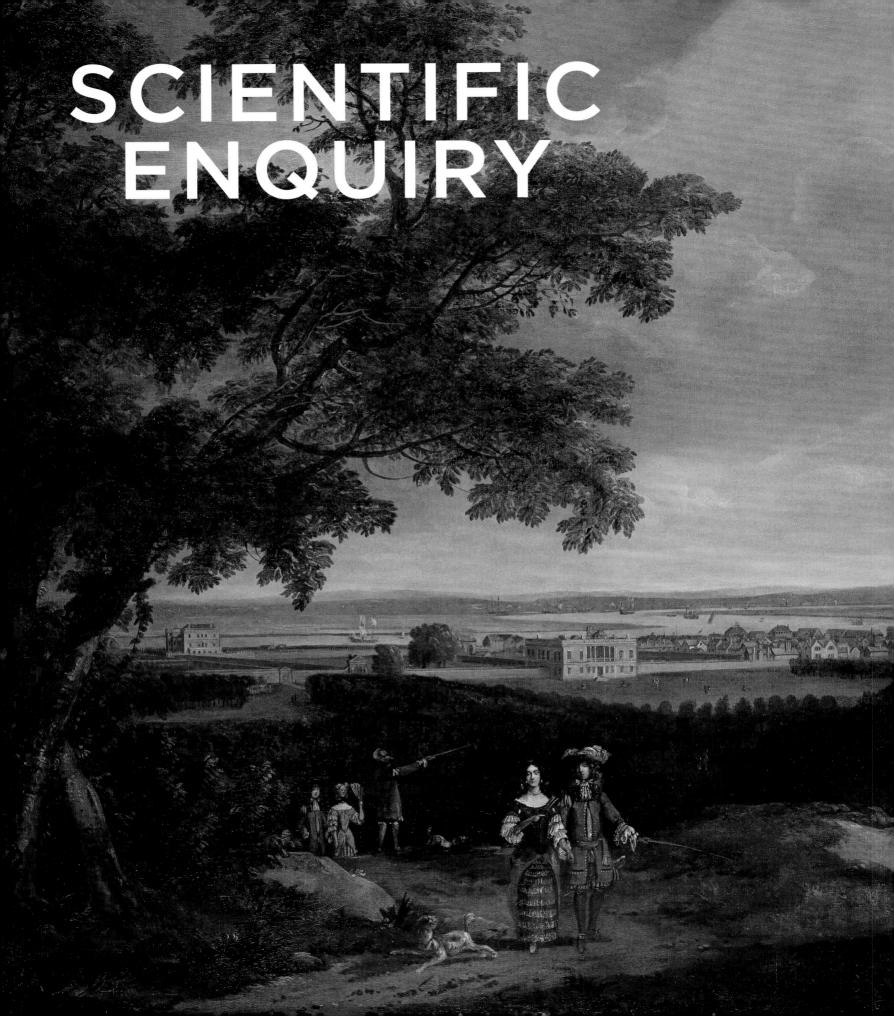

SCIENTIFIC ENQUIRY

Samuel Pepys was fortunate to have worked in London at the very moment when it became the most significant location in the world for scientific activity. Virtuoso natural philosophers such as Robert Hooke, Robert Boyle and Christopher Wren made pioneering contributions to knowledge of the natural world. They were men of learning with the wealth and leisure to pursue knowledge for enjoyment and status rather than material gain. Much of their work was made possible by the presence in the capital of a large number of talented and ambitious instrument makers. The Royal Society, whose members met regularly at Gresham College from November 1660, constituted a forum for proposing, conducting and discussing various experiments. From 1665, its new journal, *The Philosophical Transactions*, became the major vehicle for publishing work in the republic of letters. Soon after the Restoration, 'natural philosophy' – as the sciences were termed – also became a fashionable pursuit of the middle classes. Large numbers of men and women bought and read scientific books, and they also procured telescopes and microscopes to see for themselves what these authors described.

Little is known of Pepys's interest in science before 1660, though references at the start of his diary imply that he already knew some of the best instrument makers in London. As a student at Magdalene College in the early 1650s, he would have received rudimentary instruction in the four subjects of the Quadrivium, namely arithmetic, geometry, astronomy and music. However, his tutor, the mathematician Samuel Morland, who later became 'Master of Mechanicks' to Charles II, does not seem to have inspired his interest in any mathematical or practical subjects, although Pepys was already interested in musical theory and practice. He never found the time to understand the discoveries of Boyle and others, but he did come to comprehend the activities of sailors, victuallers and major officers of the Navy Board, especially those of the Surveyor, who was responsible for the design, construction and repair of vessels.

Over the course of his career, Pepys obtained many models of ships that served as objects of delight as well as demonstration devices. In 1662,

Robert Iliffe

Pepys and the New Science

Sʳ William Petty. Kⁿᵗ. (detail)
Mezzotint, by John Smith after
John Closterman, 1696.

National Maritime Museum, PBE9953/2.

he received lectures from the sailing master Richard Cooper, who made use of ship models to teach Pepys about the anatomy of sailing vessels. In the spring and summer of 1663, the master shipbuilder Anthony Deane continued instructing Pepys where Cooper had left off. Deane composed a large work on shipbuilding for him in 1670, and thereafter their careers rose and fell together. In 1679 and 1685 both were briefly Members of Parliament for Harwich, while Pepys supported Deane's appointment as a member of the Navy Board in the later 1680s.

By the mid-1660s, Pepys was regularly attending meetings of the Royal Society. His first visit had taken place on 23 January 1661, in the company of the instrument maker and inventor Ralph Greatorex. He evidently appreciated the opportunity to discuss scientific topics (which included rare 'curiosities') and to see the latest instruments and experiments. As he confessed, it also offered him the chance to mix with 'persons of honour', though his position as Clerk of the Acts to the Navy Board already gave him ready access to the most powerful figures in the land. One of these was Lord Brouncker, whom Pepys met at the society in late April 1662. Brouncker, who was President of the institution from 1663 to 1677, would be close to Pepys following his own appointment in 1664 as Commissioner of the Navy, and no doubt helped Pepys achieve his goal of mixing with persons of quality.

In 1664, Pepys became a supporter of William Petty, a brilliant polymath, statistician and inventor whom he described as one of the most rational men he had ever met. Petty had made a number of trials with a 'double-bottomed' boat, and Pepys recorded on 1 February 1664 that Charles II had spent an hour or two mocking the invention. He lamented Petty's discomfort at the 'unreasonable follies' of Charles and his cronies but also noted that Peter Pett, the Naval Commissioner and Master Shipwright, thought it was the most dangerous invention in the world, since whoever had such a vessel would be master of the ocean. Pepys, who was in his element when surrounded by talkative virtuosi, left a tantalizingly brief account of an encounter on 11 January, when Petty was joined by the other great population statistician of the age,

John Graunt. They talked of many things, such as music, a universal language, forgery and memory techniques, and Pepys extolled their 'excellent discourses'.

Pepys was proposed as a Fellow of the Royal Society on 8 February 1665 by Thomas Povey, his colleague on the Tangier Committee.[1] A week later, he was accompanied to his inauguration as a Fellow by John Creed, his close colleague and rival at the Navy Office. Creed, a Fellow since 1663, was another client of Pepys's patron, the Earl of Sandwich, and in mid-April 1664 he had spoken to Pepys about a series of air-pump experiments at the Royal Society on the effects of heating and cooling. Pepys picked a good meeting for his inauguration, for Boyle and Hooke were present, and he was treated to another air-pump experiment, this time involving combustion. Pepys thought Hooke 'the most, and promises the least, of any man in the world that ever I saw', and he would be an unwavering admirer for the rest of his life. After the meeting, as he did on so many other occasions, Pepys went to the Crown Tavern with 'most of the company', where he continued to enjoy their 'excellent discourse' until 10 p.m.

Pepys's diary offers a fascinating window into his brief obsessions (such as musical theory, which captivated him in March and April 1668), and gives a unique insight into the content and context of Restoration scientific debate. Part of the richness of the diary comes from the way that these discussions – in lecture theatres, workshops and coffeehouses – appear part of the fabric of everyday life. On 28 July 1666, for example, Pepys had lunch with Brouncker (accompanied by his mistress), Peter Pett, the naval contractor William Warren and the virtuoso Walter Charleton. Charleton argued that the teeth of different species had been fashioned for certain types of food, and he added that human teeth had been designed for fruit and not for meat. His comments on human dentition were made while the group was treated to Pepys's favourite dish of venison pasty. Later the same day, Pepys heard Brouncker discourse at length on the basic rules of refraction and reflection, followed by supper with 'some Scotch people ... pretty odd

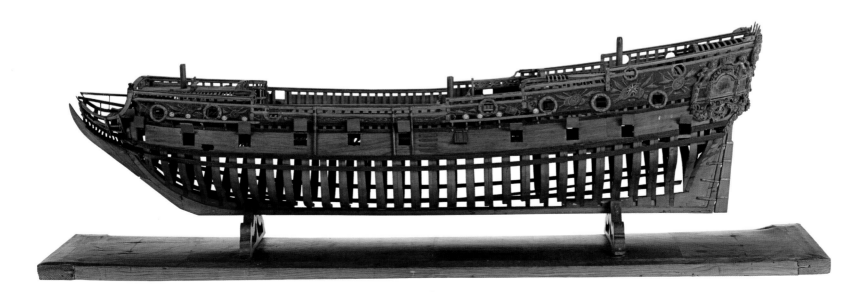

Sr William Petty. K^{nt}.
Mezzotint, by John Smith after
John Closterman, 1696.

National Maritime Museum, PBE9953/2.

**Full-hull model of a ship of the line,
36–40 guns**
c.1680.
Models were made to show the design
of a ship, as a normal part of the
commissioning process.

National Maritime Museum, SLR0368.

company', where a Scottish violinist played 'the strangest air that ever I heard in my life'.

The diary also reveals Pepys's great penchant for acquiring mechanical toys and scientific instruments. His addiction to such gadgets was in fact lifelong: when he was attacked by highwaymen in September 1693, their ill-gotten gains included a silver ruler, a magnifying glass and five mathematical instruments.[2] In the 1660s, Pepys spent a great deal of time with makers of these devices, such as Greatorex, John Spong and Richard Reeve, and he continued to be a regular customer at similar haunts after the diary ended. Of these men, the most important was Reeve, whom Pepys rated the best maker of microscopes in the world. Pepys recorded a number of purchases from Reeve's shop in Covent Garden, and Reeve often visited Pepys at his home and stayed the night. He bought a pocket 'perspective' (a type of early spy glass) from Reeve on 23 March 1660, using the instrument both for serious purposes and for more frivolous activities, such as looking at attractive women in his local church.[3]

Reeve came to Pepys's office on 13 August to sell him a microscope for £5 10s ('a great price, but a most curious bauble it is') and added a scotoscope (a globe filled with brine that focused the light from a lamp) as a gift. In the evening, Pepys read Henry Power's recently published *Experimental Philosophy*, the first English book on the microscope, which appealed to a broad audience that was enthralled by his account of the latest scientific experiments. On the following day, Pepys read Power's work with his wife, Elizabeth, though both struggled to see anything at all through the microscope. They eventually succeeded but Pepys noted that they would see even more when he had a better understanding of the device. On 29 July 1666, Spong and Reeve dined with Pepys, and he spent the entire afternoon with them in a dark room in the Navy Office, receiving detailed instructions on how to look through his telescope and his various microscopes. 'Most excellently', Pepys recorded of his microscopic enquiries, 'things appeared beyond imagination'. He was similarly captivated by Hooke's *Micrographia* (see 122).

Reeve visited Pepys at his office again on 7 August 1666, bringing a 12-foot (3.66 m) refractor, and they went up on to the roof of Pepys's house to look at Saturn and Jupiter. Having spent a long time setting up the instrument, they found that the night sky was too cloudy for them to see anything. The following morning, they met Hooke, who told them of his theory concerning the relationship between the pitch of a note and the rate at which the strings of an instrument vibrated. As a result, he claimed, he could deduce the rate at which a fly's wings beat by determining the musical note they made. That evening, Reeve and Pepys used 12-foot and 6-foot (1.83 m) refractors to look at Jupiter and the Moon, and Pepys promised to buy a telescope, justifying the purchase (during a period of self-imposed restraint) by noting that it would be 'very usefull'. On 19 August, Reeve came to Pepys's house laden with scientific equipment. Pepys spent the whole day with Reeve and Spong 'upon opticke enquiries', and they did various experiments involving the intersection of rays of light. Reeve brought a magic lantern, which projected images on to a wall, and in the evening they saw Jupiter and its satellites through the 12-foot telescope, which Pepys now claimed as his own.

The ingenious craftsmen satisfied Pepys with their working knowledge of the equipment he bought from them, and collectively they spent many happy hours performing experiments and making observations. However, the artisans were unable to enlighten him about the principles that governed the operation of the instruments. Pepys spent some time with Spong discussing the nature and use of globes, but neither could work out why the stars did not rise and set at the same times throughout the year. Similarly, Reeve was unable to explain the basic theory of refraction that underlay the optical phenomena they saw. Pepys also wanted to be *au fait* with the latest discoveries in natural philosophy, but he was irritated by his own ignorance. He could be momentarily satisfied by going to Gresham College or by talking to people like Hooke, Brouncker and Petty, but, as he perceptively noted after a Royal Society meeting on 1 March 1665, he lacked sufficient 'philosophy' to understand the 'fine discourses and experiments ... and so cannot remember them'.

Pepys's attempts with his wife to look through a microscope were not the only moments when the couple studied or discussed scientific or mathematical topics. Pepys claimed that he taught Elizabeth some astronomy in February 1663, and at the start of September he noted that he had been to the shop of Joseph Moxon to buy a pair of globes for his wife, 'who has a mind to understand them, and I shall take pleasure to teach her'. On 21 October, he began to teach her arithmetic which, he hoped, would 'bring her to understand many fine things'. This extraordinary course of study, which Elizabeth (whose father was a frustrated inventor)[4] apparently received with 'great ease and pleasure', was carried out assiduously over the following months, sometimes with more than one session on the same day. On 1 December, Pepys intimated that these occasions were a source of great joy to him. Five days later, as he played with his slide rule and mathematical books, he decided that Elizabeth had progressed well enough in arithmetic (though division could wait until a later date), and that it was time to go on to study the globe. When his eyes failed him towards the end of the decade, Elizabeth read him scientific works. Although Pepys must have learned a great deal from their joint sessions, he was also committed to the idea that those in possession of useful or interesting knowledge had an obligation to impart it to the curious. His conviction that such instruction could form the basis of a good relationship lasted into the late 1690s, when he wrote down a list of activities to be performed by his long-time partner, Mary Skinner. These included visiting Gresham College and touring various workshops.[5]

Although Pepys enjoyed working with his wife, he expressed nothing but scorn for the accomplishments of Margaret Cavendish, Duchess of Newcastle. By the mid-1660s, she had published a number of works, including poems, plays and tracts on various subjects such as natural philosophy. In the spring of 1667, following the publication the previous year of her *Observations upon Experimental Philosophy*, she and

her husband, William Cavendish, made a celebrated visit to London, where her accomplishments, dress sense and behaviour made her a social phenomenon. Pepys was immediately obsessed with her and went to see the play *The Humorous Lovers* on 30 March, believing it to be by her (though in fact it was written by her husband). It was, he wrote, 'the most silly thing that ever come upon a stage [but] I was sick to see it, yet would not but have seen it, that I might the better understand her'. With his usual disarming frankness, Pepys recorded his many futile efforts to see her in person in late April and May, but he finally set eyes on her on 30 May at Arundel House, the temporary location for meetings of the Royal Society. Hooke and Boyle showed a number of experiments with lenses, magnets and an air-pump, and the duchess looked at specimens through a microscope. She also saw what Pepys called a 'very rare' experiment in which a piece of mutton was reduced to blood with sulphuric acid. Now able to see her close-up for the first time, Pepys was dismissive, sneering at the eccentricity of her dress and the ordinariness of her 'deportment'. She said nothing worth hearing, he complained, merely repeating that she was 'full of admiration, all admiration'.[6]

Pepys was also engrossed by the most famous experiments carried out under the auspices of the Royal Society in its first decade. During these trials, the blood of a lamb was transfused into the veins of a human subject, with a view to seeing whether the injected blood would improve his health. There had been previous transfusion experiments on dogs, which Pepys had recorded in November 1666, and prior to this he had been witness to, or had been told about, a number of efforts to inject poisons into canine subjects. By 1667, French researchers had already performed a number of blood transfusions between humans, and the Royal Society felt obliged to follow. Following the meeting of the society on 21 November, Pepys and Creed went to a tavern in St Clement Churchyard. Here, the eminent natural philosopher John Wilkins told them that a 'poor and debauched man' called Arthur Coga, who was one of his parishioners, had agreed to accept £1 in payment

Celestial and terrestrial table globes
By Matthew Greuter, 1632–36.

National Maritime Museum, GLB0143 and GLB0082.

for having 12 ounces (340 ml) of sheep's blood let into his body. The society concluded that Coga, who had serious mental health problems, could nevertheless give a good account of his experiences, and, indeed, that the treatment might cure him. At the society's meeting on 30 November, Coga gave a discourse in Latin on his experience following the transfusion (which had taken place a week earlier). Pepys noted that Coga was 'cracked a little in his head', and that he had agreed (as a good experimental subject) to undergo the same procedure all over again. There is no more discussion of Coga in the diary but the trials were soon stopped, for fear that the animal–human transfusion caused more harm than benefit.

Pepys's professed inability to follow the details of the work of major scientists has led some historians to conclude that he was a mere dilettante, while the fact that the diary ends in 1669 has led others to assume that his interest in science diminished rapidly thereafter. However, he remained closely concerned with scientific developments until his death, and as a senior naval administrator he made unrivalled efforts to ensure that recruits and officers received the best technical training available. And at the height of his career, he combined the most powerful administrative position in the navy with the Presidency of the Royal Society.

As early as 1671, Pepys had approached Sandwich with the idea of creating a school for children where future naval officers could receive high-level training in scientific, mathematical and technical methods and theory. Christ's Hospital Mathematical School was set up two years later, and Pepys was involved with that establishment for the last three decades of his life. Towards the end of 1677, he gave a thorough assessment of the extent to which the school had achieved the aims of its founders. He was critical of many aspects of the ways

in which boys had been taught by its first Headmaster, claiming that their Latin, arithmetic and draughtsmanship (as well as their general discipline) were poor. Finding a suitable master was almost impossible: as Pepys saw it, the role required scholarly learning, mathematical expertise and experience at sea. He convinced the mathematician Sir Jonas Moore to write a new textbook for the school, but the project was halted by Moore's death in 1679. Pepys then wrote to a number of major figures, including Hooke, Isaac Newton and the Astronomer Royal, John Flamsteed (to whom he had sent some boys for lessons), both for advice on what the curriculum should contain and on candidates for the vacant position. In time, Pepys would grudgingly concede that Latin was not essential for young seamen, but he always maintained that a strong navy required recruits who were adept in both the theory and the practice of navigation, who could instruct and correct those around them, and who could keep good records.

In tandem with his efforts at Christ's Hospital School, from 1676 Pepys used his joint positions as Master of Trinity House and Secretary to the Admiralty to push hard for 'reformadoes' (gentleman volunteers), prospective lieutenants and captains of sixth-rate warships, which encompassed ships with up to 30 guns, to be subject to the existing test of competence administered by Trinity House, the body responsible for pilotage in the Thames and the safety of shipping. Pepys had long held the view, promoted early in his career by people such as Sandwich and William Coventry (Secretary to the Duke of York, who was then Lord High Admiral), that the Restoration navy suffered from a surfeit of inexperienced and technically deficient gentlemen seamen, who had been commissioned as officers because of their political connections. At the end of 1676, Pepys convened a committee

Mariner's quadrant
c.1725.
This instrument was used for determining latitude at sea.

National Maritime Museum, NAV1062.

to add more mathematical and technical content to the Trinity House examination, and within a year there were new regulations detailing the expertise that each of these categories of seaman was supposed to have. This involved a combination of skills in astronomy and navigation with evidence of experience and practical competence at sea.

Pepys often tried to identify problems in various organizations by understanding their historical development. In the 1670s he compiled a dossier relating to the long-term mismanagement of Christ's Hospital Mathematical School, while in the early 1680s, he tried to compose a monumental history of the Royal Navy, an undertaking that included an account of improvements in navigation and naval architecture. Pepys built on a work composed by his friend John Evelyn, and drew from his own substantial and historically significant collection of books and manuscripts. His papers attest to the amount of time he spent talking to master shipbuilders about the principles of their craft. His extensive notes of these discussions show that he despaired that the knowledge of many of the best shipwrights lay 'in their hands so confusedly, so as they were not able themselves to render it intelligible to anyone else'. As a result, he noted in the 1690s, not one Englishman had ever written a work on naval architecture 'like a philosopher or a mathematician'.[7]

Beyond Pepys's efforts to improve the scientific and technical skills of naval personnel, his most conspicuous contribution to late-seventeenth-century science was also as an administrator. Seldom lacking in ambition, he stood for a position on the council of the Royal Society as early as 1666, donated £40 for the purposes of constructing a new building to house the society two years later, and finally served on the council in 1672. He was elected President in December 1684, and served for two years. He made some efforts to put the organization of the society and its haphazard record-keeping practices on a sounder footing, though his commitments as James II's senior naval official made it difficult for him to attend as many meetings as he would have liked. He was President of the Society in 1686 when Newton presented it with the first of the three books that made up the *Principia Mathematica*, and his name took up the same space as Newton's on the title page when it was published the following year. Pepys renewed his acquaintance with Newton in the early 1690s, but their generally harmonious relationship was rocked by Newton's paranoid remark in a letter to Pepys of September 1693 that he himself had never gained anything by James II's favour. Pepys was too civil, and had suffered far worse barbs, to be affronted by this (in any case, the implication that he had benefited substantially from his relationship with James was true). Instead, he rose above these insinuations to express his concern to friends about Newton's sanity, and soon began a fascinating exchange with him on the topic of probability theory.

Pepys remained absorbed by scientific matters up to his death, and his papers constitute a lasting testament to the vitality of late-seventeenth-century scientific activity. Because the diary presents an image of a man who took great delight in the pleasures of scientific activity, he has been dismissed by some historians as nothing more than a scientific dilettante. However, both his success as a scientific administrator, and his efforts to ensure that sailors had a satisfactory level of technical competence, show that he was deadly serious about the proper organization of science and about the central place of technical expertise in a modern navy. Far from being a mere amateur of early English science, Pepys was perhaps its first professional.

Dividers
*c.*1680.
Using dividers and a chart, navigators could work out the distance between two points in nautical miles.

National Maritime Museum, NAV0524.

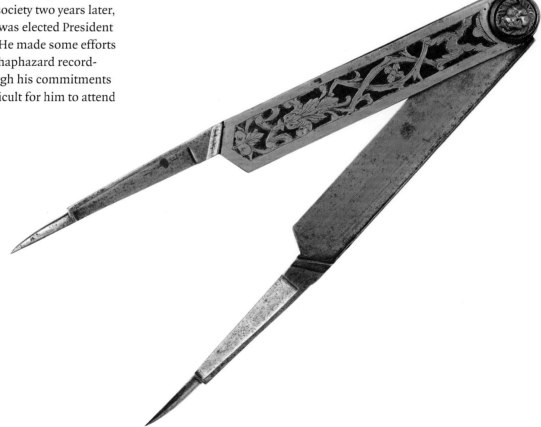

A New Visible World

Richard Dunn

View from One Tree Hill:
The Queen's House and the
Royal Observatory, Greenwich
**Oil on canvas, by Jan Griffier, the Elder,
late seventeenth century.**

National Maritime Museum, BHC1817.

By the time Pepys was penning his diary in the 1660s, telescopes and microscopes were bringing previously unknown worlds, big and small, to light. Invented around 1600, the two instruments were by then familiar research tools and, increasingly, personal accessories. Pepys himself purchased several, and was as fascinated as his contemporaries by their extraordinary revelations.

The telescope already had a substantial pedigree as an aid for revealing the very distant, whether on Earth or in the heavens. In 1610, Galileo Galilei's *Sidereus Nuncius* ('Starry Messenger') made shocking claims from his telescopic observations: the Moon had mountains; Jupiter had moons of its own; and there were stars invisible to the naked eye. Thereafter, the new device rapidly established itself in astronomy. As the century wore on, ever longer telescopes were made in the hope of observing the stars and planets in greater detail. Pepys observed the heavens with 6- and 12-foot (3.66 m) telescopes, not to mention using smaller ones for more earthly pursuits. Serious observers went to greater lengths. While a 60-foot (18.3 m) telescope installed at the Royal Observatory in Greenwich proved unstable, the frontispiece to Thomas Sprat's *History of the Royal-Society of London* (1667) celebrated as an icon of the new science a more successful one of the same size used by Robert Hooke. Hooke also helped Christopher Wren design the Monument to the Great Fire of London as a giant telescope to prove the Earth's motion around the Sun. It failed in this task, but remains as a potent symbol of the scientific ambitions of the age.[1]

Building bigger telescopes was about overcoming the limitations of lenses. Drawing on his optical investigations of the 1660s, Isaac Newton (incorrectly) concluded that a lens-based telescope could never produce a perfect image and turned his expertise to making a curved mirror that could bring light to a sharper focus. The resulting instrument was impressive enough to earn him election to the Royal Society in 1671 (see 125), although reflecting telescopes would only become widespread in the following century.[2]

The microscope was also beginning to have an impact on science, an area in which the Royal Society took a lead through the work of Hooke and others. As curator of experiments, Hooke introduced microscope demonstrations to the society's gatherings and was charged with preparing at least one for each meeting.[3] However, it was the publication of his *Micrographia* in 1665 (see 122) that forever linked Hooke's name to the microscope. The meticulous illustrations caught readers' imaginations, revealing the world of the very small in fascinatingly horrible detail. In the first, Hooke showed that even the simplest manmade things were manifestly imperfect, a printed full stop appearing like a 'great splatch of London dirt'.[4] Turning to nature, he showed that, 'the more we magnify the object, the more excellencies and mysteries do appear'.[5] *Micrographia* astonished readers with its grossly magnified images of the flea, louse, bee's sting, fly's head, ice crystals, plant cells and other tiny wonders. Pepys also took to the microscope with enthusiasm, purchasing a fine example that he considered 'a most curious bauble'.[6] A few months later, he was awake until two in the morning with *Micrographia*, 'the most ingenious book that ever I read in my life'.[7]

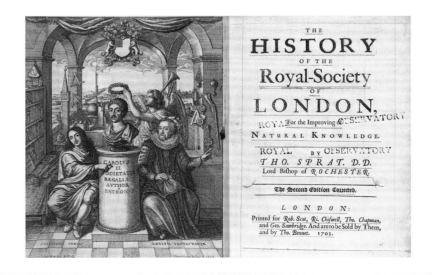

The Monument

From *A Survey of the Cities of London and Westminster* by John Stow [1598], revised by John Strype (London, 1720).

National Maritime Museum, PBD7598.

Frontispiece to Thomas Sprat's *History of the Royal-Society of London* (London, 1667)

Hooke's 60-foot telescope is in the background, visible through the central archway to the left of the bust. Two telescopic instruments for navigation hang from a pillar to the left of the telescope.

National Maritime Museum, PBG0382.

Louse viewed under the microscope

From *Micrographia* by Robert Hooke (London, 1665).

Hooke did the drawings and oversaw the engraving of the plates.

British Library 435.e.19.

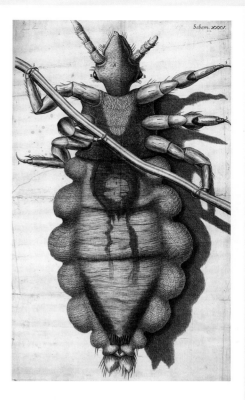

For some authors, the invention of the microscope and telescope proved the superiority of the 'moderns' over the 'ancients'. 'Antiquity gives us not the least hint' of such things, Henry Power noted in *Experimental Philosophy* in 1664.[8] Hooke anticipated further wondrous revelations:

> By the means of Telescopes, there is nothing so far distant but may be represented to our view; and by the help of Microscopes, there is nothing so small, as to escape our enquiry; hence there is a new visible World discovered to the understanding.[9]

Others were more uncertain. By the 1670s, both devices were bound up with satirical swipes at the natural philosophers of the Royal Society. Cast as 'virtuosi' (here used pejoratively), they became foolish knowledge-seekers, obsessed with their instruments, yet oblivious to the real world under their noses. Those who used these optical distractions, satirists suggested, were gullible and prone to wild and useless speculation. Samuel Butler's satirical poem, 'The Elephant in the Moon' (1676), ridiculed its virtuosi as stupid and morally bankrupt, interested only in a hypothetical lunar elephant and the fame it might bring, not the mundane mouse it turns out to be. Theatrical telescopes were long and cumbersome, capitalizing on the way the technology was developing: the stage directions for Aphra Behn's *The Emperor of the Moon* (1687) call for a telescope of 20 feet (6.1 m) or more. Behn's short-sighted Dr Baliardo is so caught up in his observations that he is easily persuaded that the Moon's emperor has come to take his daughter as a bride.[10]

The microscope suffered a similar fate. Sir Nicholas Gimcrack, the butt of Thomas Shadwell's comedy *The Virtuoso* (1676), not only devotes his time to mapping the Moon (which also has elephants) but has 'spent two thousand pounds in microscopes to find out the nature of eels in vinegar, mites in a cheese, and the blue of plums'.[11] Gimcrack's researches explicitly drew on those described in Hooke's *Micrographia*, Sprat's *History* and the Royal Society's *Philosophical Transactions*.[12] Audiences cannot have doubted where Shadwell's attack was aimed. Indeed, by the time *The Virtuoso* was playing, the microscope was losing its scientific mystique. By the century's end, Hooke regretted that it was more a tool for personal amusement than an instrument for serious research.[13]

Curious Mr Pepys

When Pepys died, John Evelyn wrote a generous yet candid tribute to his friend in his diary on 26 May 1703, justly praising him as a 'very worthy, Industrious & curious person'. Pepys had never been able to understand people who showed no curiosity. When a dull country acquaintance, William Stanks, came to London on 30 April 1663, he marvelled at the man's apathy:

> but, Lord! what a stir Stankes makes with his being crowded in the streets and wearied in walking in London, and would not be wooed by my wife … to go to a play nor to white-Hall, or to see the lyons [in the Tower menagerie], though he was carried in a coach.

Pepys's own innate curiosity was central to his career success – it impelled him to find out all he could about the navy and dockyard administration in order to do his job well. He was similarly inquisitive about his own person, his feelings and emotions, which is in large part why his diary is such a vital and enduringly interesting work.

Pepys instinctively made sure that he was part of a creative community: he played music with others, he was highly convivial, and he frequented coffeehouses, taverns and other locations in the City where he could pick up gossip and learn the latest news. He was absorbed in the general flow of ideas and enjoyed the company of men from all walks of life with new knowledge to impart. And his inherent eye for detail meant that he found the contemporary spirit of enquiry – based as it was on experimentation, precise observation and careful measurement – simply intoxicating.

105

Samuel Pepys, aged about forty

c.1673
Unknown artist
Oil on canvas, 296 × 247 (approx.)
Private collection

This portrait, presenting Pepys as a quieter, more studious man than the famous Hayls image, was chosen as the frontispiece for Braybrooke's 1825 edition of the diary. It was then attributed to Godfrey Kneller. Pepys probably chose his accompanying objects himself, displaying his eclectic interests. The scientific instruments were all recorded in his diary as they joined his collection. He bought the pair of Joseph Moxon globes to teach his wife geography. The dividers and slide rule remained the tools of his trade when he became Secretary to the Board of Admiralty. KB

LITERATURE: Barber, pp. 3–4, 6.

106

Morland's calculating machine

....

1670–95
Brass, silver, velvet, satin and leather
Inscribed: 'Samuel Morland Inventor 1666'
Science Museum, 1876-538t

With a particular interest in mathematics, Samuel Morland, Pepys's tutor at Magdalene, created a series of calculating machines: this example is used for the addition of pounds, shillings, pence and farthings (a quarter of a penny). Pepys was rather underwhelmed by the device: 'very pretty, but not very useful'. Nonetheless, Morland advertised it in the *London Gazette* for the princely sum of £3 10s. and tapped into the market of young, fashionable gentlemen who sought to improve themselves through mathematics. Afterwards, he continued to apply his innovative ideas to the fields of cryptography, acoustics, hydraulics and letter-copying machines. LD

LITERATURE: *ODNB*; *Diary*, IX, 116–17; Ratcliff.

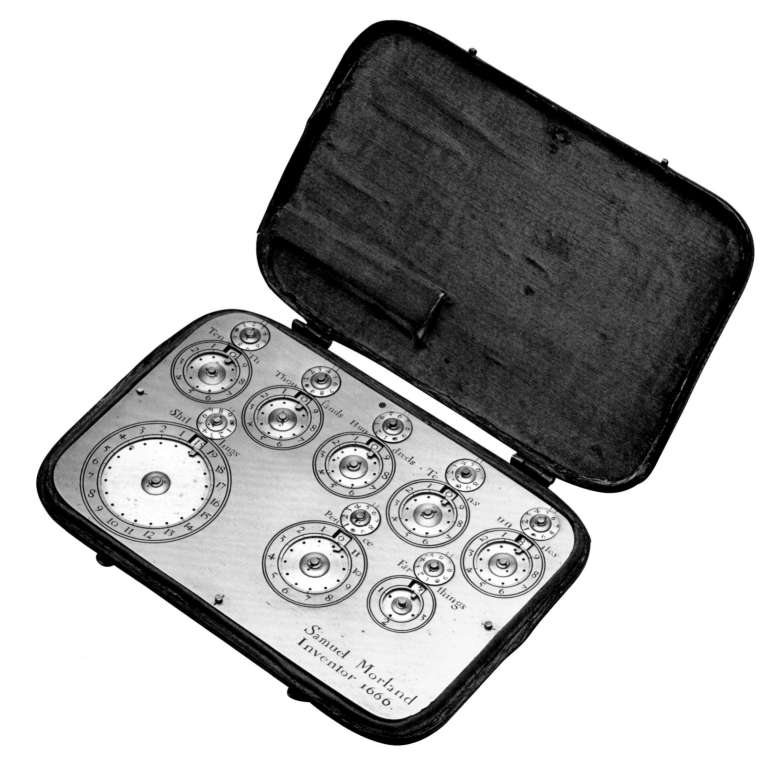

107

Miniature of Sir Samuel Morland

....

1660–61
Samuel Cooper (1609–72)
Watercolour on vellum, 60 × 48
Victoria and Albert Museum, 481-1903

Samuel Morland (1625–95) and Pepys remained lifelong acquaintances after Cambridge. Morland, who became a diplomat, was notoriously improvident, spending lavishly on wine, costly houses and expensive experiments. His reputation at court was never assured and Pepys noted he was 'looked upon by … all men as a knave'. Nevertheless, he was also an innovator and an accomplished engineer. Morland clearly thought well of Pepys: he asked him to be godfather to his daughter in 1677. RB

LITERATURE: *ODNB*; *Diary*, I, 141; Tomalin, p. 304.

108

Napier's bones

....

*c.*1679
Boxwood
National Maritime Museum, NAV0126

This early form of calculator was devised by the mathematician John Napier (1550–1617) in 1617 as a practical tool to facilitate speedy and accurate calculations. Pepys was already interested in mathematics and rules of mensuration when the mathematician Jonas Moore introduced him to the use of Napier's bones in 1667. Pepys found it a valuable device for helping with his accounts and for teaching his wife simple arithmetical operations such as addition, subtraction, division and multiplication. LD

LITERATURE: *Diary*, IV, 357; VIII, 450–51.

109

Analemmatic dial (horizontal sundial)

c.1697
Thomas Tuttell (c.1674–1702)
Brass and steel
Inscribed: 'Tho. Tuttell Charing Londini
Fecit' ('Thomas Tuttell of London Charing
Cross made [this]')
National Maritime Museum, AST0216

Pepys is known to have purchased a double horizontal sundial similar to this one, specifically constructed for the latitude of London (51°30' N), with a black shark-skin case lined with silk and velvet. Most sundials are orientated with a magnetic compass, but here a clever combination of dials makes this unnecessary. With the dial level, the pin-shaped gnomon (shadow caster) is first moved along the slit to the corresponding month. The whole instrument is then rotated until the shadows cast by the triangular gnomon and pin gnomon both read the same hour. The reverse side features a perpetual calendar for the period 1697–1758 and a scale to show the times of sunrise and sunset throughout the year. LD

LITERATURE: *Diary*, IV, 171–72; Tuttell; Higton, pp. 230–32; *ODNB*.

110

Armillary sphere

1624
Johannes Paolo Ferreri (*fl.* 1600–25)
Brass and wood
National Maritime Museum, AST0634

An armillary sphere is a skeleton model of the cosmos: the Earth, at its centre, is surrounded by rings (*armillae*) that can be used to measure the celestial coordinates of the Sun, Moon and stars. This particular example features a horizon ring with a calendar scale and flame-like star pointers, which enables the time when certain prominent stars will appear throughout the year to be calculated. In January 1660, Pepys chatted with the London instrument maker, Ralph Greatorex, and recalled that 'at an alehouse he showed me the first sphere of wire that ever he made, and indeed it was very pleasant'. LD

LITERATURE: Clifton, p. 118; Dekker, pp. 157–58; *Diary*, I, 14.

111

Portable telescope

1661
Jacob Cunigham
Wood, marbled vellum, gold-tooled
leather, glass and brass
Inscribed: 'IACOB CVNIGHAM 1661'
National Maritime Museum, NAV1547

One of the oldest dated telescopes
in Britain, this instrument is typical of
portable examples produced during the
mid-seventeenth century, often for use at
sea. Pepys had a keen interest in optical
devices and was well acquainted with
the instrument maker Richard Reeve,
who frequently came for dinner and
brought along his new microscopes and
telescopes for Pepys to inspect, enjoy and
occasionally purchase. The curious shape
of the barrel is designed to accommodate
a large lens, which was easier to grind at
this date than a small one. LD

LITERATURE: *Diary*, VII, 226, 238.

112

**Horary quadrant with Gunter projection
scales**

*c.*1680
John Marke (*fl.* 1665–79), based on a
design by Edmund Gunter (1581–1626)
Brass and string
Inscribed in centre section: 'J. Marke fecit'
National Maritime Museum, NAV1061

With his fascination for mathematical
instruments, Pepys would have probably
owned an horary quadrant like this. It is
marked with a scale invented by the Revd
Edmund Gunter (1581–1626), Professor of
Astronomy at Gresham College, London.
Frequently used by sundial makers, it
can be employed to tell the time from
the Sun. An observer would move a
small bead (now missing) on the string
to set the date, and hold the quadrant
vertically so a beam of sunlight passes
through both sighting vanes along the top
(the right-hand edge as illustrated). The
hour is indicated by the crossing point
of the bead as the string falls across the
hour lines when the instrument is tilted
vertically towards the Sun. LD

LITERATURE: Clifton, p. 179; Higton,
pp. 344–45.

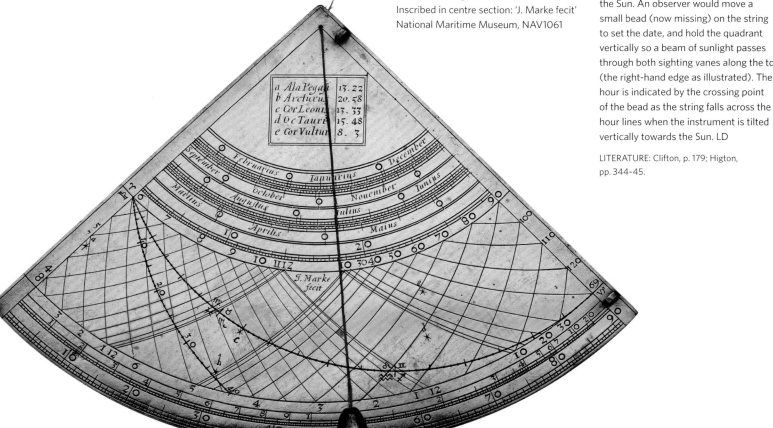

Pepys the Public Man

Pepys's good fortune and innate qualities enabled him to enjoy a place within the brilliant network of scholarly and talented men that comprised the fellowship of the Royal Society. Founded in 1660 – and granted a royal charter in 1662 – this was a wholly new type of institution, unprecedented in England or anywhere else. Its purpose was to break new ground in the field of scientific research, rather than unquestioningly disseminating received opinion.

To outsiders, the society's deliberations often seemed ludicrous. Charles II laughed himself speechless when he heard that members had spent a whole meeting discussing the weight of air. But its discoveries and methodologies – in particular its emphasis on controlled experimentation – had enormous significance for the progress of science. Furthermore, the 'close, naked, natural way of speaking' adopted by members, and preserved in the pages of the society's *Philosophical Transactions*, had an enduring effect on English prose style.

Pepys was elected a Fellow of the Royal Society in 1665, and rose to be President in 1684–86. As his career at the Navy Board then at the Admiralty blossomed, he was also elected to a number of other prestigious public offices, including Master of Trinity House in 1676 and Master of the Clothworkers' Company in 1677. By now a rich man, he honoured various institutions, notably the Clothworkers' Company, with gifts such as expensive plate (see 129). This public display of wealth both advertised his success and indicated the respect that he expected in return, as his due. It was a way of announcing that Pepys, self-made man, son of a tailor and a laundress, had achieved honourable status.

JOANNES EVELYN ARMIG.
REG. SOCIETATIS SOC.

113

John Evelyn

*c.*1687
Sir Godfrey Kneller (1646–1723)
Oil on canvas, 765 × 635
Inscribed: 'JOANNES EVELYN ARMIG.
REG. SOCIETATIS. SOC.' ('John Evelyn
Esq., Fellow of the Royal Society')
Royal Society, RS.9268

On Pepys's death, John Evelyn
(1620–1706), the historian, gardener
and diarist, mourned him as 'for neere
40 years ... my particular Friend'. Evelyn,
unlike Pepys, was a wealthy landed
gentleman. He possessed unusually wide
cultural and scientific interests, and was
recognized as an influential 'virtuoso' and
writer. In this portrait of him as one of the
founding members of the Royal Society,
he holds his most famous work, *Sylva*,

a famous study of trees. Evelyn's sense
of duty led him to serve many good
causes and refuse public honours.
He was on the naval 'sick and hurt'
board in both the Second and Third
Anglo-Dutch Wars, and was a key figure
in the creation of the Royal Hospital
for Seamen at Greenwich. PvdM

LITERATURE: de la Bédoyère, p. 11.

114

Sylva, Or A Discourse of Forest-Trees, and the Propagation of Timber in His Majesties Dominions ...

By John Evelyn (London, 1664)
British Library, 447.i.9

In England, by the mid-seventeenth century, there were widespread shortages of wood. The Royal Society worked for the navy on how to ensure a constant supply of timber in order to maintain the fleet. It commissioned this report from John Evelyn, one of its members. Evelyn first delivered the work as a lecture to the Society in 1662. He blamed the glass and iron industries for excessive use of charcoal, and farmers for extending agricultural land into forests. His book also recommends methods for planting, gardening, designing parks and managing forests. At the core of his argument for sustainability is a concern that the environment should be left in a fit state for future generations. ML

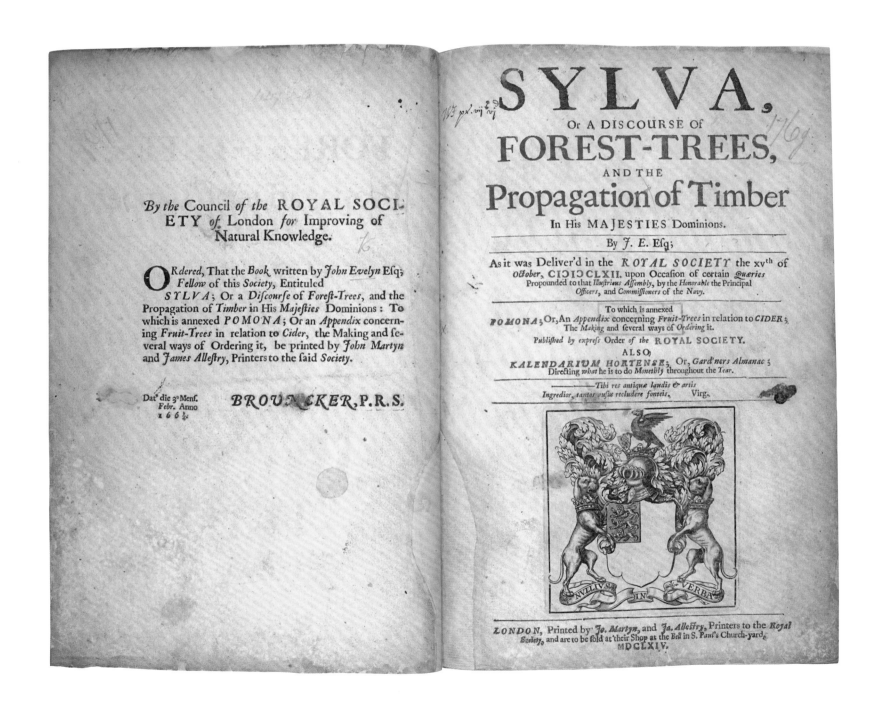

115

A Plan of the City of London, after the Great Fire in the year of our Lord 1666, according to the design & proposal of Sir Christopher Wren, Kᵗ. for rebuilding it ...

Engraved for Walter Harrison, *A New and Universal History, Description and Survey of the Cities of London and Westminster ...* (London, 1776)
Ink on paper
National Maritime Museum, G297:20/16

There were many schemes to rebuild London after the Great Fire. Although different in detail, those suggested by Evelyn and Wren each sought to bring order to the crowded clutter of the fire-ravaged City. Where winding streets and narrow lanes had gone before, broad boulevards and neatly arranged squares and piazzas were proposed. Some wider thoroughfares were built, but the new London – reconfigured in stone and brick, rather than the timber used before – followed much of its old, tangled topography. Idealistic, rational visions for a grand, planned capital were replaced by quick and practical responses to an urgent urban crisis: within three years, nearly 3,000 houses were constructed, although over 13,000 had been lost. RB

LITERATURE: Ackroyd, pp. 238–40.

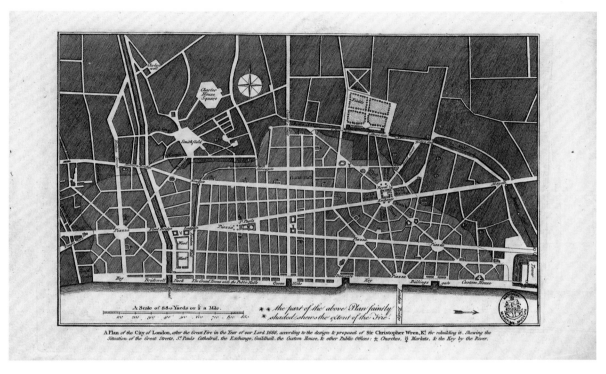

A Plan of the City of London, after the Great Fire in the Year of our Lord 1666, according to the design & proposal of Sir Christopher Wren, Kᵗ. for rebuilding it: Shewing the Situation of the Great Streets, Sᵗ Pauls Cathedral, the Exchange, Guildhall, the Custom House, & other Public Offices: ✱ Churches, ☐ Markets, & the Key by the River.

116

Sir John Evelyn's Plan for Rebuilding the City of London after the Great Fire in 1666

c.1666
Ink on paper
National Maritime Museum, G297:20/15

In the weeks following the fire, John Evelyn assembled various plans for the redevelopment of London into a published report, *Londinium Redivivum* (London Revived). It set out proposals for planning guidelines and building regulations akin to modern-day standards. Evelyn's rebuilding scheme was ambitious, imposing a gridiron of principal streets to replace the medieval jumble. His aim was to make London 'far superior to any other city in the habitable world for beauty, commodiousness, and magnificence'. RB

LITERATURE: Darley, p. 219.

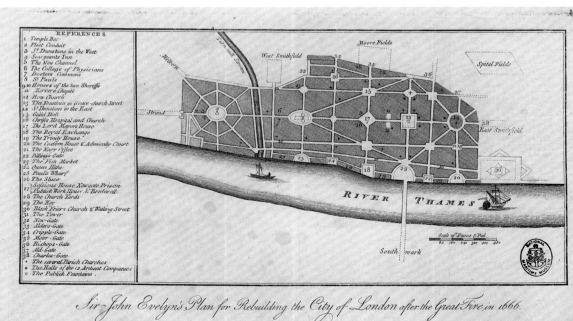

Sir John Evelyn's Plan for Rebuilding the City of London after the Great Fire in 1666.

118

Sir Hans Sloane

1716
Sir Godfrey Kneller (1646–1723)
Oil on canvas, 762 × 629
Royal Society, RS.9723

A polymath with eclectic interests and wide connections, Hans Sloane (1660–1753) is most famous for creating the founding collection of the British Museum and for introducing drinking chocolate to England (as a medicine). He followed in Pepys's footsteps as President of the Royal Society in 1727, presenting this portrait in 1716. Sloane was Pepys's physician in later years, and the two men enjoyed each other's conversation and shared their books. Pepys once wrote to Sloane how he was 'almost wishing myself sick, that I might have a pretence to invite you for an hour or two to another [visit]'. Sloane was one of the doctors who performed the autopsy on Pepys's body, a controversial procedure, but one that Pepys would have generally approved, as furthering medical knowledge. KB

LITERATURE: Tomalin, p. 363.

117

Sir Christopher Wren

c.1690
John Closterman (1660–1711)
Oil on canvas, 1433 × 1214
Royal Society, RS.9545

Although chiefly remembered now for his achievements in architecture, Wren (1632–1723) was a distinguished scholar of mathematics, astronomy, mechanics and optics. As Professor of Astronomy at Gresham College, he was one of the founders of the Royal Society (and its third President). He turned to architecture in the early 1660s, while Savilian Professor of Astronomy at Oxford, establishing his reputation with buildings in Oxford and Cambridge. Although his proposals for rebuilding London after the Great Fire were never implemented, he was appointed King's Surveyor by Charles II in 1669. As such, he masterminded the design and construction of St Paul's Cathedral (seen here), which was finally declared finished in 1711, as well as building over fifty other new churches in the City. His later secular work began with the design of the Royal Hospital, Chelsea, in the 1680s; and Pepys's last recorded visit to Greenwich, in 1694, was to meet Wren and discuss his plans for the Royal Hospital for Seamen. Wren remained Surveyor at Greenwich until 1716 and of Westminster Abbey until his death in 1723, aged ninety. PvdM

119

....

Mace of the Royal Society

....

c.1663
Silver-gilt
Royal Society, RS.8467

Charles II presented this elaborate
mace to the Royal Society in 1663.
No formal meeting of the Society
can be held without it being present.
Made from more than 150 ounces
(4.25 kilogrammes) of gilded silver, it
consists of a stem, chased with a thistle
pattern, terminating in an urn-shaped
head, surmounted by a crown and orb.
The head has embossed figures of a
rose, thistle, harp and fleur-de-lys,
representing England, Scotland, Ireland
and France. (Kings and queens of England
echoed Edward III's claim to France until
it became a republic in 1801). The royal
cipher, 'CR', and coat of arms complete
the decorative scheme. The mace was
a familiar object to Pepys, especially
during his term as President of the
Royal Society. RB

LITERATURE: Weld.

120

....

De Historia Piscium ...

....

By Francis Willughby (London, 1686)
British Library, 457.e.10

During Pepys's presidency, the Royal
Society oversaw publication of Francis
Willughby's natural history of fish.
Willughby died in 1672 and the project
was completed by his collaborator, the
distinguished naturalist John Ray. The
book was large and lavishly illustrated,
requiring considerable financial support
in the form of subscriptions. Pepys
contributed the substantial sum of £63
for illustrations to be engraved. The work
proved very costly to produce and was
a commercial failure. RB

LITERATURE: Kusukawa.

121

Compound microscope

1671–1700
Designed by Robert Hooke (1635–1703)
Iron, copper alloy, rosewood, mahogany,
boxwood, glass and gold-tooled leather
Science Museum, 1928-786

Robert Hooke, the curator of experiments
at the newly founded Royal Society,
was an Oxford-educated man who had
practical expertise in many areas of
natural philosophy, including acoustics,
astronomy, optics and meteorology. His
most famous publication, *Micrographia*
(1665), was a meticulous description
of his use of the microscope to observe
insects, fossils and crystals, accompanied
by detailed drawings. Pepys was
enthralled by Hooke's work. LD

LITERATURE: Andrade, pp. 82–87; Hooke;
Diary, VI, 18.

122

*Micrographia: Or Some Physiological
Descriptions of Minute Bodies Made By
Magnifying Glasses With Observations
and Inquiries thereupon*

By Robert Hooke (London, 1665)
British Library, 435.e.19

Published by order of the Royal Society,
Hooke's *Micrographia* was an immediate
sensation, which showed readers a
world never seen before. Its popularity
was undoubtedly helped by its arresting
illustrations of the tiniest creatures,
most famously the flea. It was also the
work in which the word 'cell' was first
used in its biological sense. On seeing a
copy in a London bookshop, Pepys found
Micrographia 'so pretty that I presently
bespoke it'. Having taken it home,
he became engrossed into the early
hours of the morning. It was, he wrote,
'a most excellent piece'. RD

LITERATURE: *Diary*, VI, 2, 17.

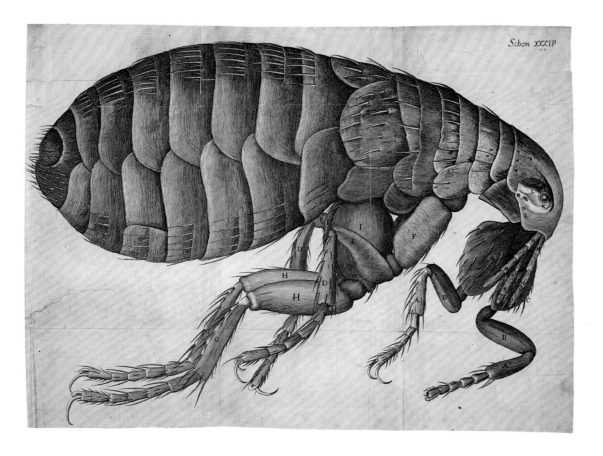

123

Sir Isaac Newton

*c.*1731
Louis-François Roubiliac (1702/05–1762)
Terracotta
National Maritime Museum, ZBA1640

Isaac Newton (1642–1727) was the greatest scientist of his or most other ages in terms of his original contributions to mathematics, physics, astronomy, optics and other fields. He was Lucasian Professor of Mathematics at Cambridge for over thirty years, and President of the Royal Society for more than twenty. He was also Master of the Royal Mint from 1699. His most important work, *Principia Mathematica* (1687), laid the basis of classical mechanics by formulating the laws of motion and the theory of universal gravitation. This bust is based on casts of Newton's face made at his death. It was originally commissioned by Newton's nephew, and then bequeathed to the Royal Society by a later owner, the surgeon John Belchier, a Fellow of the society. His will asserted that it was 'esteemed more like than anything extant of Sir Isaac', and instructed that it be placed in the Royal Observatory at Greenwich. PvdM

124

Philosophiæ Naturalis Principia Mathematica

By Sir Isaac Newton (London, 1687)
Royal Society, Newton 6

It was during Pepys's term as President of the Royal Society (1684–86) that the society agreed to publish this remarkable scientific treatise. The society was under financial strain owing to its support for Francis Willughby's *De Historia Piscium*, so Newton's friend, the well-off astronomer, Edmond Halley, covered the cost of publishing the *Principia* himself. His reward was payment in unsold copies of the Willughby tomes. Composed of three sections, the *Principia* contains Newton's innovative laws of motion and universal gravitation which, for the first time, were based on mathematical principles rather than philosophical arguments. This edition belonged to the first Astronomer Royal, John Flamsteed. LD

LITERATURE: Andrade; *ODNB*.

125

Sir Isaac Newton's reflecting telescope

c.1671, with later modifications
Sir Isaac Newton (1643–1727)
Paper, vellum, wood, metal and cork
Royal Society, RS.8462

This telescope is one of the oldest surviving examples of a revolutionary design which emerged in the late seventeenth century and remains the basis for astronomical telescopes today. Previously, telescopes had been composed of a series of lenses mounted within long and unwieldy tubes. Using mirrors instead of lenses to collect light enabled instrument makers to create shorter telescopes that were easier to use and less affected by colour distortion. Newton presented an example of this reflecting telescope to the Royal Society in 1671, and he was elected a Fellow on the success of this design. LD

LITERATURE: Hall and Simpson.

126

Edmond Halley, second Astronomer Royal

Before 1721
Sir Godfrey Kneller (1646–1723)
Oil on canvas, 535 × 430 (cut down)
National Maritime Museum, BHC2734

Best known for the comet bearing his name, the regular return of which he predicted in 1705, Edmond Halley (1656–1742) worked on many scientific problems. His contributions to navigation included compiling a 341-star catalogue of the southern skies from the Atlantic island of St Helena and making scientific voyages in command of a small naval vessel, the *Paramore*, between 1698 and 1703. First he undertook (unsuccessful) longitude research, sailing south as far as 52° into the ice field; then he investigated tides in the English Channel. He became Professor of Geometry at Oxford in 1703, the year Pepys died, and in 1720 succeeded John Flamsteed as the Astronomer Royal at Greenwich. It was Halley who, in 1684, persuaded Isaac Newton finally to publish his epoch-making *Principia*, which appeared in 1687. Halley is buried in St Margaret's Churchyard, Lee, near Greenwich, but his original tombstone (which had to be replaced) is today set in a wall at the Royal Observatory. PvdM

127

The Royal Observatory at Greenwich from Crooms Hill

*c.*1696
English school
Oil on canvas, 1016 × 1676
National Maritime Museum, BHC1812

Pepys would have known this view well, although there is no record of him visiting the observatory. It was built in 1675–76 on the foundations of Greenwich Castle, an old residential lodge in Greenwich Park, which Pepys mentions in his diary. In the middle distance, the walled Greenwich to Woolwich road is shown running under Inigo Jones's Queen's House (as last adapted in 1662). Beyond, to the left, is the former garden of the Tudor palace, and across a further wall is the site of the palace itself. The unfinished wing of what is now the King Charles Court of the Old Royal Naval College is on the far left. Beyond the road, right of the Queen's House, is the former palace tiltyard: the ruinous brickwork just projecting above its roof is one of two remaining Tudor towers on the yard's west side that were only demolished about 1699. The group of buildings immediately behind the house, which includes part of the old palace chapel, is probably where Pepys ran the Navy Office late in the plague year (1665). PvdM

128

Samuel Pepys, aged about fifty

c.1680–85
Attributed to John Riley (1646–91)
Oil on canvas, 775 × 667
The Clothworkers' Company,
GLC/PO/P008

In middle age, Pepys was prosperous and well connected at court, in the City of London and beyond. He could afford to commission portraits from fashionable painters like John Riley. This shows a serious and thoughtful, if perhaps a slightly weary, Pepys. Between June 1684 and February 1689, he was at the height of his career as Secretary to the Admiralty, an important and time-consuming role. But he was preoccupied with other duties too. In 1685, for example, he was also, simultaneously, MP for Harwich, Master of Trinity House, President of the Royal Society and the Deputy Lieutenant for Huntingdonshire. RB

129

Cup and cover

....

*c.*1677
Gerard Cooques, London
Silver-gilt
The Clothworkers' Company, W15

....

Ewer

....

*c.*1677
John Sutton, London
Silver-gilt
The Clothworkers' Company, W16

....

Rosewater dish

....

*c.*1677
John Sutton, London
Silver-gilt
Inscribed: 'SAMVEL PEPYS / Admiralitati
Angl : a Secretis / & Societ : Pannif :
Lond : Mag' / An MDCLXXVII / D.'
('Samuel Pepys Secretary to the
Admiralty of England and Master of the
Clothworkers Company, London')
The Clothworkers' Company, W17

It is not altogether clear why Samuel
Pepys was appointed Master of the
Clothworkers' Company. He was not
a member of this livery company; but,
through his father's profession as a tailor,
he did have a loose connection with
textiles. It is more likely that his social
circles and administrative skills secured
the position, which he held in 1677–78.
Ever busy, Pepys was hardly assiduous
in his duties as Master, but he did present
the company with this magnificent suite
of plate, testament to his growing wealth.
The pieces bear the Clothworkers' arms
and Pepys's own. RB

130

James II receiving the Mathematical Scholars of Christ's Hospital

....

After 1685
Studio of Antonio Verrio (c.1639–1707)
Gouache on paper laid down on canvas,
459 × 2356
Yale Center for British Art, Paul Mellon
Collection, B1977.14.6307

At the end of 1681, Pepys sought to commemorate Charles II's benevolence to Christ's Hospital by commissioning a painting for its Great Hall. The Mathematical Committee agreed, and in January 1682, accompanied by his secretary, Will Hewer, he discussed the scheme with Antonio Verrio. Pepys then borrowed a City alderman's red gown for his inclusion in the painting: he can be seen close to the central throne, gesturing towards the kneeling schoolboys. This is a study. The finished work is a vast and imposing panorama, 16 feet (4.9 metres) high and 87 feet (26.5 metres) across. James II occupies the throne, Charles having died before the painting's completion. This version belonged to Pepys. RB

LITERATURE: Bryant, *Pepys: Years of Peril*, p. 356; Sotheby, p. 9 (lot 10).

131

....

Foundation medal of the Mathematical School of Christ's Hospital

....

1673
John Roettier (1631–1703), London
Silver
Inscribed: 'INSTITVTOR AVGVSTVS.
1673' ('The King is the Founder')
National Maritime Museum, MEC0878

This 'glorious medal' (as John Evelyn called it) has a portrait bust of Charles II in profile, looking right, on the obverse. The design of the reverse consists of a figurative group (which can be seen on the badge to the right). A schoolboy in the distinctive long, blue coat of Christ's Hospital stands in the centre; to the left is Arithmetic, her right hand holding a tablet inscribed 1 to 10, her left on the boy's head. Behind and to the right are Mathematics, holding a triangle and dividers, Mercury, bearing a caduceus, signifying genius, and Astronomy, carrying an armillary sphere and a cross-staff. In the clouds above, two cherubs support a cornucopia and a third, in the guise of Fame, sounds a trumpet. To the left, Zephyrs blow a favourable wind, filling the sails of ships in the distance below. Pepys visited the Royal Mint at the Tower of London in 1666 to commission John Roettier, joint chief engraver there, 'to grave a seal' for the Navy Board. He described his work as 'some of the finest pieces ... that ever I did see in my life'. RB

LITERATURE: Evelyn, *Discourse*, p. 140; *Diary*, VII, 82–83.

132

....

Badge of the Mathematical Scholars of Christ's Hospital

....

Late seventeenth or early eighteenth century
John Roettier, London
Silver
Inscribed: 'AVSPICIO CAROL SECVNDI . REGIS . 1673.' ('Under the auspice of King Charles II')
National Maritime Museum, MEC0879

This single-sided badge, adapted from the design of Roettier's foundation medal, was worn by the Mathematical Scholars of Christ's Hospital. These scholarships, the result of Charles II's endowment of 1672, allowed forty poor boys to be taught mathematics in preparation for a career at sea. The rim of the badge (although not this example) was normally pierced for sewing on to the school's distinctive blue coat. Pepys, appointed as a school governor in 1675, was granted the freedom of the City of London in 1699 for his services to Christ's Hospital. RB

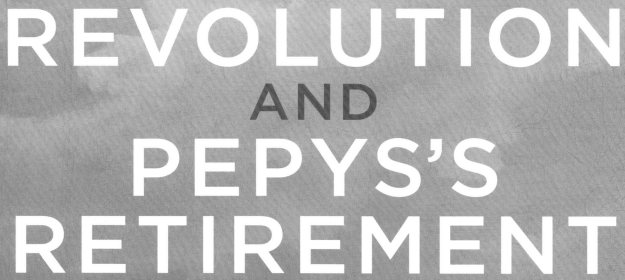

REVOLUTION
AND
PEPYS'S
RETIREMENT

The start of Pepys's diary coincided not only with the restoration of the Stuart monarchy, but also the accompanying re-establishment of the Episcopalian Church of England and reintroduction of the traditional Book of Common Prayer. Although Pepys's frequent attendance at Anglican services supplied a regular rhythm to his life during the 1660s, his diary is as far from a typical seventeenth-century spiritual journal – usually describing an individual's moral struggles and surrender to God's will – as it is possible to imagine. Accordingly, his personal religiosity needs to be reconstructed from implicit assumptions and tangential observations. Pepys's support for Anglicanism's re-establishment was primarily predicated on what is termed the 'Erastian' belief that the nation's peace was best secured by entrusting decisions about forms of church government to secular authority. As a keen and critical theatre-goer, Pepys also clearly appreciated the ritualistic aspects of public religion and often commented on pulpit oratory and ceremonial observance, while characteristic inquisitiveness informed much of his private reading on theological matters.

Though born an Anglican, the youthful Pepys had inclined to Puritan republicanism. When he observed Charles I's execution as a teenager in 1649, he had imagined himself, on a future anniversary of the regicide, preaching on the Scriptural text: 'The memory of the wicked shall rot'.[1] By the time of Charles II's restoration in May 1660, however, Pepys had started to attend services, conducted according to the banned Book of Common Prayer, which had evidently provoked maternal dismay. In March, Pepys recorded a conversation in which he and his mother, Margaret, 'talked very high about Religion, I in defence of the Religion I was born in', and his mother presumably defending what soon became illegal nonconformity after the Restoration.[2] In 1662, the Act of Uniformity enshrined a narrowly exclusive version of Anglicanism that established the Book of Common Prayer as the only legal form of worship and thereby risked perpetuating mid-century sectarian divisions. As nonconformist agitation later escalated, Pepys's instinctive sympathy for freedom of conscience undermined his earlier

Clare Jackson

Pepys and Religion

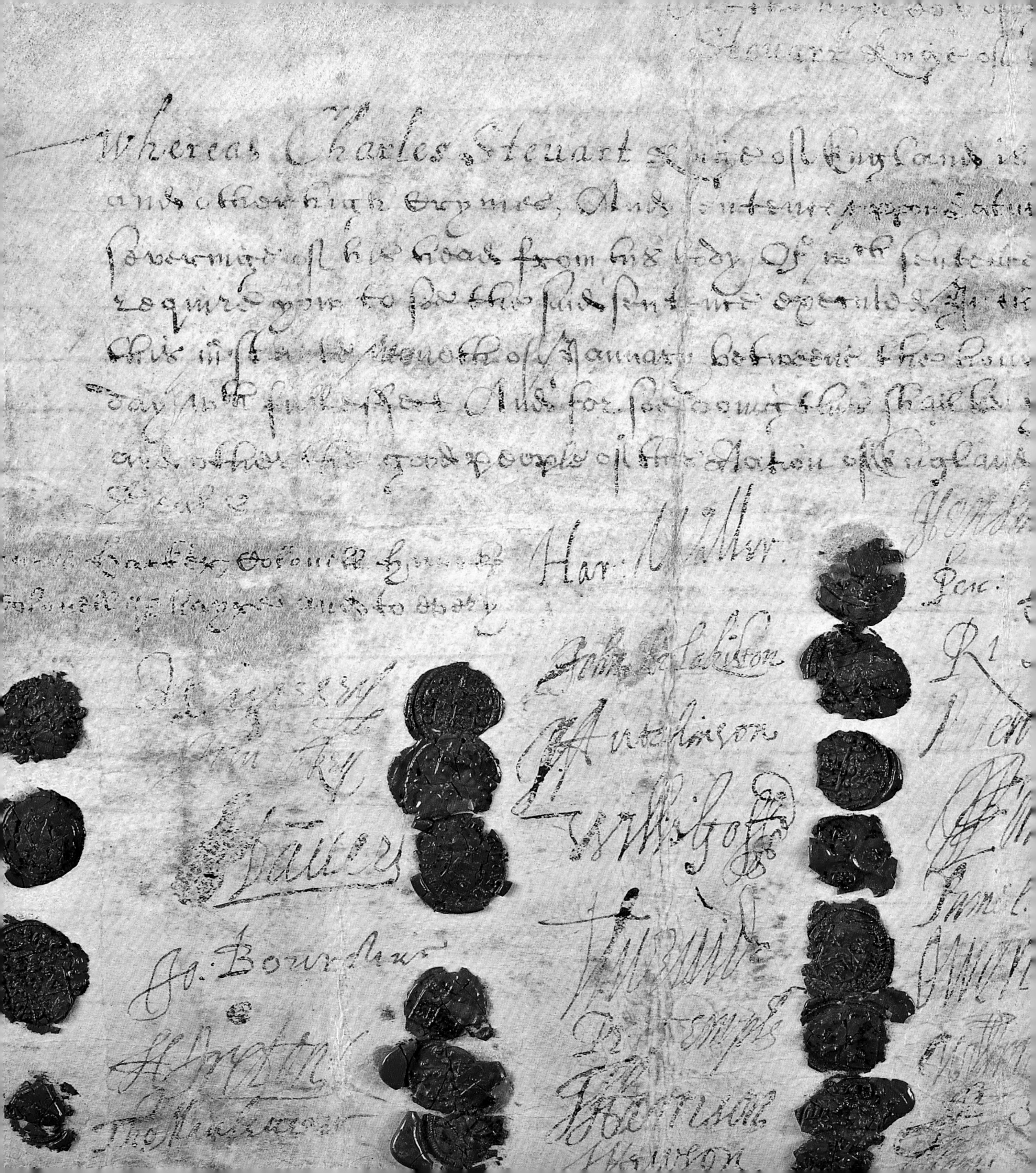

Whereas Charles Steuart Kinge of England is
and other high Crymes, And sentence uppon...
overninge of his head from his body Of w[hi]ch sentence
required you to see the said sentence executed In the
this instante moneth of January betweene the houres
day w[i]th full effect And for soe doeing this Sh[all] be
and other the good people of the Nation of England

...soldier, officer, and others... whom it may concerne to be herein ayding...

Har: Walter

J. Bourchier

Tho. ...

John Blakiston
J. Hutchinson
Gr. Millington
J. Wayte
Tho. ...
... Mauleverer

support for the state's right to enforce conformity. Observing several Quakers arrested for attending an illegal meeting-house in 1664, for instance, Pepys wished 'to God they would either conform, or be more wise' and avoid detection. Instead, he was left to marvel as, being pacifists, they were led away 'like lambs, without any resistance'.[3]

For his part, Pepys regularly attended his local Anglican church, St Olave's, in Hart Street in the City of London, which was also the church of the Clothworkers' Company, of which he became Master in 1677. In his diary, Pepys referred to St Olave's as 'our own church', and Daniel Mills, who served as its vicar from 1659 to 1689, as 'our minister'. Even after moving to Will Hewer's house in Clapham in 1701, Pepys returned to worship at St Olave's, where he was eventually buried on 4 June 1703. Although Pepys usually attended St Olave's with his wife, Elizabeth, on Sunday mornings, on Sunday afternoons and weekdays he visited other churches across London, sometimes staying only momentarily. On 8 December 1661, for example, after dining with Lady Sandwich at her house near the Temple, Pepys 'went away, up and down into all the churches almost between that place and my house' in Seething Lane. The following March, he likewise spent a Sunday morning 'going from one church to another hearing a bit here and a bit there'.[4]

Through regular attendance at St Olave's, Pepys witnessed the gradual reimposition of traditional forms of Anglican worship that accompanied the Restoration, including revival of a set liturgy or pattern of worship. On 4 November 1660, for instance, he remarked that Daniel Mills 'did begin to nibble at', or slip in, forms prescribed in the Book of Common Prayer by offering short expressions of praise to God, known as doxologies, 'though the people have beene so little used to it that they could not tell what to answer'. The following month, Pepys found his pew covered with rosemary and baize for Christmas, as decorations reappeared after a decade of Puritan proscription of seasonal festivities. As ecclesiastical vestments also became more popular, Pepys observed Mills wearing a surplice for the first time in October 1662, but deemed it 'absurd for him to pull it over his eares

in the reading-pew', watched by the congregation, in order to set it aside before preaching.[5] Two months earlier, Pepys had objected to Mills publicly inveighing against private confession to a priest, while simultaneously 'advising people to come to him to confess their sins when they had any weight upon their consciences, as much as is possible'.[6] He was equally unimpressed, in February 1667, when Mills preached on the much-debated theological subject of Original Sin, which Pepys deemed 'an unnecessary sermon ... neither understood by himself nor the people'.[7]

Indeed, it was as a sermon critic that Pepys's religious preferences emerge most vividly from his diary. While published sermons were commercial best-sellers during the Restoration, pulpit addresses in all churches offered daily opportunities to engage in religious controversy, transmit news, shape public opinion and take part in rhetorical persuasion. Pepys's often pithy verdicts on ministers' oratory vividly reveal his preferences for incisive prose, the informed exposition and application of relevant Scriptural texts, well-judged length and the emotional capacity to inspire a congregation. In April 1665, for example, Pepys attended the Chapel Royal at Whitehall specifically to hear Edward Stillingfleet, whom he had known as a student at Cambridge. Now, aged thirty, Stillingfleet was recognized as 'the ablest young man to preach the gospel of any since the Apostles'. Pepys was appropriately impressed by his delivery of 'the most plain, honest, good, grave sermon, in the most unconcerned and easy yet substantial manner, that ever I heard in my life'.[8] Occasionally, however, the qualities of an accomplished preacher could be deemed inappropriate. Visiting family and friends in Huntingdonshire in 1668, for example, Pepys heard an address by Jervas Fulwood, the Sandwiches' chaplain, which he judged 'a very good and seraphic kind of sermon, too good for an ordinary congregation'.[9]

As Restoration religion and politics became inextricably fused, Pepys was particularly impressed by the controversial audacity of preachers willing to apply insights from Scriptural texts to contemporary events. In March 1662, for instance, he judged the Dean of Wells, Robert

Death Warrant of King Charles I, 29 January 1649

Parliamentary Archives, HL/PO/ JO/10/1/297A.

The Holy Bible
This was probably bound for the Chapel
Royal at Whitehall, 1659–60.

Royal Collection, RCIN 1142247.

Creighton, 'the most comicall man that ever I heard in my life' for applying Micah's injunction to 'Instead, roll in the dust' to erstwhile Royalists denied compensation for their Civil War sufferings. Creighton claimed that recalcitrant republicans were 'better treated nowadays in newgate [prison] then a poor Royalist, that hath suffered all his life for the King, is at Whitehall among his friends'.[10] The following April, Pepys heard Creighton preach 'a most admirable, good, learned, honest and most severe Sermon, yet Comicall' at Whitehall, which incorporated a witty aside about breast-feeding – 'Blessed is the womb that bore thee [Christ] and the paps that gave thee suck' – within a bitter denunciation of Protestant nonconformity. Recalling Charles II's undertaking in the Declaration of Breda (1660) to allow all his subjects to worship peaceably according to their consciences, Creighton 'railed bitterly ever and anon against John Calvin and his brood, the presbyterians, and against the present terme now in use of "Tender consciences"'.[11] As Charles's government struggled to contain dissent, in 1664 Creighton again let rip in Whitehall, insisting that 'the greatest part of the Lay-Magistrates in England were puritans and would not do justice', while sanctions formerly available to the Church of England's bishops had been so diluted 'that they could not exercise the power they ought'.[12] Three years later, Charles himself became the target of Creighton's invective, when Pepys received reports of a 'strange bold sermon' preached before the king 'against the sins of the Court, and particularly against adultery', invoking 'over and over' the widely perceived parallels between Charles II and the infidelities of the biblical King David to demonstrate 'how for that single sin ... the whole nation was undone'.[13]

In contrast to the most daring and eloquent examples of Restoration pulpit oratory, Pepys regularly denounced other ministers for preaching sermons that were 'dull', 'lazy', 'drowsy' or full of technical errors. Aboard a naval ketch at Portsmouth in April 1662, for example, he heard the dockyard chaplain 'preach a sad sermon, full of nonsense and false Latin'.[14] Away again on naval business the following year, Pepys attended church in Chatham, where he heard 'a poor sermon, with a great deal of false Greek in it'.[15] On other occasions, it was the sheer tone of a minister's delivery that Pepys deemed insufferable. Throughout 1663, he endured various addresses by an unidentified Scots minister visiting St Olave's, initially reporting 'a pitiful sermon' in January, then describing the cleric as 'a simple bawling young Scot' in April, before eventually, in June and for the rest of the year, opting simply to sleep through sermons by the same 'Scot, to whose voice I am not to be reconciled'.[16]

Pepys's sermon preferences were neither narrowly traditional nor exclusively Anglican. While being rowed to Gravesend on 'a fine day' in September 1668, he compared different examples of pulpit oratory presented in Abraham Wright's *Five Sermons, in Five several Styles; or Waies of Preaching ...* (1656). Although Wright had sought to counter the popularity of prophetic and inspirational preaching during the Interregnum by showcasing the best of traditional Anglican eloquence, Pepys evidently preferred the newer styles, concluding that 'the Presbyterian style and the Independent are the best'.[17] Moreover,

THE SOUTH-EAST PROSPECT OF THE CHURCH OF ALHALLOWS BARKING.

as an avid and perceptive playgoer, Pepys relished the general theatricality of daily worship and the capacity for a minister's tone of delivery, carriage in the pulpit and general demeanour to transform a sermon's content. Indeed, part of Wright's aim in the *Five Sermons* had been to confirm the potential for talented Anglican preachers to 'change the *Theatre* into a *Church*; having a greater power over the passions of their *Auditorie*, than the *Actor* hath upon the *Stage*'.[18] Yet there was a risk that spiritual edification could become confused with dramatic entertainment. In May 1669, for instance, Pepys dined at Lambeth Palace with the Archbishop of Canterbury, Gilbert Sheldon, an invitation he had 'long longed for'. After dinner, he expected a 'serious' sermon. Instead, he was treated to 'a mockery': a man named Cornet Bolton substituted a chair for a pulpit, behind which he 'did pray and preach like a presbyter-Scot that ever I heard in my life, with all the possible imitation in grimaces and voice ... till it made us all burst'. Confessing himself startled by the archbishop's choice of post-prandial amusement, Pepys observed that Sheldon 'took care to have the room-door shut' and Bolton's performance restricted to the twenty or so select guests.[19]

Pepys's surprise reflected broader anxieties regarding the spiritual dilution of national life and the alarmingly low esteem in which many clergy were held. In July 1662, he witheringly described his local minister, Daniel Mills, as 'a cunning fellow', whose social visits at least showed he 'knows where the good victualls is and the good drink'.[20] That Christmas, Pepys attended the Chapel Royal at Whitehall, where he heard Bishop George Morley of Winchester preach a long sermon 'reprehending the mistaken jollity of the Court', especially 'their excess in playes and gameing'. Pepys was, however, disconcerted to see courtiers so unmoved by Morley's tirade 'that they all laugh in the chapel when he reflected on their ill actions and courses'.[21] A year later, Pepys was dolefully observing that 'the present clergy will never heartily go down with the generality' of English people, since parishioners had become 'so used to liberty and freedom' in earlier decades and

were also 'so acquainted with the pride and debauchery of the present clergy'.[22] Remarking on 'the posture of the Church' in 1668, Pepys confirmed that 'things of it were managed with the same self-interest and design that every other thing is'.[23]

Pepys's verdict on a service at St Alfege's Church in Greenwich in January 1661 summarized, in characteristically trenchant style, the fulfilment he derived as a young man from Anglican worship: 'a good sermon, a fine church, and a great company of handsome women'.[24] Regular church attendance also offered Pepys and his wife opportunities for gossip and people-watching. In November 1663, Pepys was surprised that his arrival at St Olave's 'in a perriwig did not prove so strange to the world as I was afeared it would'; having assumed that 'all the church would presently have cast their eye all upon me ... I found no such thing'.[25] Even in the privacy of his own home, religious observance could be diverted by less elevated concerns: in June 1666, when 'in the middle of my grace, and praying for a blessing' on a meal with his brother-in-law, Pepys suddenly exclaimed 'Cuds zookes!' as he realized he had left recently purchased lobsters behind in a hackney coach.[26] The following month, again at dinner, Pepys found himself – in candidly material terms – 'reflecting upon the ease and plenty that I live in, of money, goods, servants, honour, everything', for which he privately offered thanks to God.[27] Yet after the disruption of the Civil Wars and Interregnum, Pepys's attachment to Anglican traditions also provided nostalgic security and comfortable reassurance. Walking in the Surrey countryside in July 1667, he observed a shepherd reading the Bible to 'his little boy ... far from any houses or sight of people' and judged this halcyon vision of rustic piety 'the most pleasant and innocent sight that ever I saw in my life'.[28]

In November 1673, Pepys achieved his long-term ambition to enter Parliament when he successfully contested a by-election at Castle Rising in Norfolk, winning by twenty-nine votes to six. Pepys's candidacy had been supported by a member of England's leading Catholic dynasty, Henry Howard, Earl of Norwich and also Baron

The South-East Prospect of the Church of Alhallows Barking
Engraving, by R. West and W. H. Toms, 1736.
In his diary, Pepys mentions hearing the bells of All Hallows. Famously, he climbed its tower to watch the Great Fire.

National Maritime Museum, PBE9953/1.

Howard of Castle Rising. Politically motivated allegations quickly emerged that Pepys had cynically aligned himself with Catholicism to get elected. Earlier that year, Charles II's brother and heir, James, Duke of York, had been obliged to resign as Lord High Admiral on account of his Roman Catholicism following the introduction of a Test Act. The Act barred Catholics from public office by requiring all civil and military office-holders to swear oaths of allegiance to the monarch as supreme governor of the Church of England, deny the Catholic doctrine of transubstantiation and provide proof of having received Anglican communion. Following the Duke of York's resignation, Pepys's subsequent promotion to Secretary to the Admiralty provoked further suspicion among those who inferred (correctly) that the duke's influence in naval affairs might thereby continue.

Pepys's political detractors persisted. In the spring of 1674, the newly elected Pepys was confronted by rumours in the House of Commons that the prominent Whig peer, Anthony Ashley Cooper, Earl of Shaftesbury, had seen a Catholic altar and crucifix at Pepys's house, although Shaftesbury prevaricated when asked to substantiate the charge. After the earl refused an interview in person, Pepys wrote to him on 15 February 1674, denouncing 'the injurious consequence of that ambiguity' and demanding that he provide 'a categorical answer

The Right Hon[ble]: Anthony Earle
of Shaftesbury
Engraving, by Robert White (1645–1703),
1680.

National Maritime Museum, PBE9953/1.

one way or t'other'.[29] The following day, Pepys defended himself before a House of Commons committee, strenuously insisting that he had always been 'a good Protestant and a good Churchman, and the best sort of Protestant', and the damaging allegations were set aside.[30]

Similar accusations of covert Catholicism nevertheless resurfaced when Pepys was elected MP for Harwich five years later, obliging him to reassure the town's mayor that anyone doubting his religious orthodoxy would find such 'proof of my Protestancy as I doubt no private man in England can show but myself upon record in Parliament'.[31] Two months afterwards, Pepys wrote to the Duke of York, grimly acknowledging that, whether or not such rumours were proved false, 'a Papist I must be, because favoured by your Royal Highness'.[32] At this time, York was in voluntary exile in Brussels, having left the English court in 1678 amid mounting paranoia regarding a 'Popish Plot' – an alleged conspiracy, fomented by Jesuits, to assassinate Charles II – that had led to all Catholics being banned from coming within 20 miles (32 km) of London. As anti-popish hysteria increased, a parallel 'Sea-Plot' was suspected, in which Pepys and a colleague, the shipbuilder Sir Anthony Deane, were rumoured to have supplied Louis XIV's administration with strategic information to facilitate a French-sponsored Catholic invasion. Formally accused of 'Piracy, Popery and Treachery', Pepys was forced to resign as Secretary to the Admiralty and Treasurer of the Tangier Committee, and imprisoned in the Tower of London on 20 May 1679. Although freed on bail for £30,000 – the equivalent of several million pounds today – Pepys remained accused of capital offences and, in assembling his defence, regretted having to exclude any testimony from Catholic witnesses, 'such is the captiousness of our age against anything that is not Protestant'.[33]

Although the capital charges against Pepys were later dropped, his harrowing experience of imprisonment and prosecution underscored the highly politicized character of seventeenth-century religion. Indeed, political implications pervaded all forms of Restoration

Earthenware tiles, 1679–80
These depict scenes from the Popish
Plot, based on designs from a pack
of playing cards printed at the time.

Victoria and Albert Museum,
414:823/1-9-1885.

The Plot first hatcht at Rome by the Pope and Cardinalls &c.

The Conspirators Signeing ye Resolve for killing the King.

Father Connyers Preaching against ye Oathes of Alejance & Supremacy.

Dr Oates discovereth ye Plot to ye king and Councell.

Ct bedlow discoverer of the plott.

Capt bedlow examind by ye secret Comitee of the house of Commons.

Pickerin attempts to kill ye K. in St Iames Park.

Pickerin Executed.

Sr William waller burning Popish books Images and Reliques.

religious observance. When accused of being a closet Catholic in 1674, Pepys insisted to a House of Commons investigating committee that he had 'received the Communion seven or eight times, and not less than six times a year, in twenty years'.[34] Several years later, amid the frenzy of the Popish Plot, the minister of St Olave's formally certified – to a formula supplied by Pepys – that Pepys had been a constant communicant at the church between June 1660 and Whitsunday, or the seventh Sunday after Easter, 1681.[35] But Pepys's own account belies such faithful observance: he confessed in March 1662 that taking communion was something he had 'hitherto neglected all my life', except 'once or twice' as a student in Cambridge; and no mention of his receiving the sacrament appears in his diary. Rather, Pepys remained content to watch others, such as Charles II, taking the sacrament, observing on Easter Sunday 1666, 'very little difference' between the Anglican service attended by the king in the Chapel Royal at Whitehall and Catholic Mass in the Queen's Chapel in St James's Palace, except that the former 'was not so fine, nor the manner of doing it so glorious'.[36]

It was, indeed, the same aspects of Anglican worship – good music, well-dressed women and ritual ceremony – that also attracted him to Catholic services. On Easter Sunday 1668, he was overwhelmed by the singing of the Italian choir in Catherine of Braganza's Chapel, which 'did appear most admirable to me, beyond anything of ours – I was never so well satisfied in my life with it'.[37] Several months previously, he had attended Christmas Eve Mass in the same chapel, marvelling at finding himself amid such 'a crowd of people, here a footman, there a beggar, here a fine lady, there a zealous poor papist, and here a Protestant, two or three together, come to see the show'. Having been 'afeared of my pocket being picked very much', Pepys distracted himself by enjoying the sacred music and indulging in successful masturbatory fantasies 'with my eyes open, which I never did before – and God forgive me for it, it being in the chapel'.[38] Ironically, it was the discovery in October 1668

Sereniss Regina Catharina
[Catherine of Braganza]
Engraving, by William Faithorne
(1616–91) after Dirck Stoop, 1662.

National Maritime Museum, PBE9953/1.

of Pepys's recurrent extramarital liaisons that provoked Elizabeth Pepys furiously to announce 'as a great secret that she was a Roman Catholique and had received the Holy Sacrament'. Pepys, however, 'took no notice' of it in the context of a tempestuous marital argument. Yet just as Charles II's Catholic wife and his heir provided ammunition for his political enemies in the late 1670s, similar anxieties evidently prompted Pepys to obtain written confirmation from Mills shortly before his wife's death in 1669 that she had received Anglican communion.[39]

Pepys survived attempts to discredit him during the Popish Plot, while his patron, the Duke of York, withstood repeated attempts during the ensuing 'Exclusion Crisis' to prevent him, as a Catholic, from succeeding to the throne. James's accession after Charles II's sudden death in February 1685 was followed by speedy evidence of the new king's determination to remove the penal laws and Test Act that had been designed to promote conformity to the Church of England by excluding non-Anglicans from public office. According to Pepys's friend and fellow diarist, John Evelyn, Pepys asked James in the autumn of 1685 about the veracity of the rumours alleging Charles II's deathbed conversion to Catholicism, prompting the king to show him two manuscripts ostensibly penned by his brother. Published in 1686 as *Two Papers written by the late King Charles II*, these tracts purportedly confirmed Charles's conviction not only that the Catholic church was the true church of Christ, but that divinely ordained monarchs were entitled to recast the national church as they pleased.

Yet under a proselytizing Catholic monarch like James, such an unremittingly Erastian view of royal supremacy boded ill for Protestantism's survival. State office-holders, like Pepys, came under increasing political pressure either to accede to James's plans for full religious toleration – which proved unacceptable for most in extending to Catholics – or face dismissal. Insights into how Pepys responded to this dilemma are found in a draft 'Discourses touching Religion' which Pepys penned between 1685 and 1687, reflecting on church–state relations and the relative authority of the Protestant and Catholic churches. After a generation of enforced religious conformity had failed to contain religious pluralism, Pepys's 'Discourses' acknowledged that state sanctions inevitably compromised the sincerity with which individuals swore religious oaths and recognized a clear difference 'between a man's private Religion' and a more 'Publick' version required by law, which could 'extend only to an Outward profession'.[40] Echoing arguments notoriously advanced by writers such as Thomas Hobbes and Samuel Parker (later Bishop of Oxford) – in works owned by Pepys – this defence of the difference between internal religious belief and external observance effectively justified the gap between Pepys's formal insistence, under political pressure, that he had regularly taken Anglican Communion and his frank acknowledgments otherwise in his diary.

Following James's dramatic flight to France in December 1688 and the ensuing 'Glorious Revolution', however, Pepys eschewed pragmatism and remained quietly loyal to James II, enduring another brief period of imprisonment in 1690 as a suspected Jacobite sympathizer. As a confirmed 'nonjuror', Pepys was subjected to additional taxation during the 1690s for refusing to swear the new oath of allegiance to William and Mary. Yet his political loyalty to James, and his characteristically inquisitive interest in competing theologies, did not erode his lifelong attachment to the Church of England. Among his friends were prominent Anglican nonjurors such as Dr George Hickes, who visited the exiled Jacobite court in France and underwent a clandestine consecration as a nonjuring bishop in 1694. In May 1703, Hickes attended Pepys on his deathbed and conducted his funeral service. A few days later, he paid tribute to Pepys, writing that he had 'never attended any sick or dying person that died with so much Christian greatness of mind, or a more lively sense of immortality, or so much fortitude and patience'.[41]

Kate Loveman

~

Pepys's 'Retirement'

Shortly after James II was driven out of England by William of Orange in 1688, Samuel Pepys was forced to resign from the Admiralty. His retirement, which lasted until his death in May 1703, was not a quiet one. In part, this was because the ministers in charge of William and Mary's new government had trouble believing he would peaceably accept the change of regime. In May 1689, Pepys was arrested on suspicion of treason – but was released a few weeks later. The next year, he was detained again for conspiring to bring about 'a general insurrection' (as one enraged pamphleteer put it).[1] As in 1689, the charges were unfounded. Pepys had other outlets for his organizational talents than plotting treason. For the rest of his life, he threw much of his energy and resources into assembling one of the most admired private libraries in England. His collection of books and manuscripts helped to maintain his reputation among university scholars, natural philosophers and naval men. He also turned to print publication for the first time in order to make his views known, publishing his *Memoires Relating to the State of the Royal Navy of England* in 1690, and later conducting an audacious one-man pamphlet campaign against corrupt London officials. Pepys's naval career may have ended in 1689, but his reputation as a man of influence, and his efforts to serve his country, did not.

Pepys's work for the Admiralty meant he retired a wealthy man. Initially, he lived in some luxury in a house overlooking the Thames at York Buildings, Westminster. As Secretary to the Admiralty, Pepys's patronage network had stretched well beyond England's shores and so the contents of his house included many gifts from merchants, diplomats and naval officials stationed abroad who had sought his favour. During the 1670s and 1680s, presents had poured in: musical instruments and scores had come from Italy; a desk, velvet carpet and fifteen fine birds in a cage from India. Visitors admired Pepys's and his partner Mary Skinner's taste in furnishings and the imported luxuries on display.

The room of which Pepys was most proud – for he commissioned the artist Sutton Nicholls to record it – was his library. Pepys's delight

Mary II
Oil on canvas, by Sir Godfrey Kneller
(1646–1723).

National Maritime Museum, Greenwich
Hospital Collection BHC2853.

William III
Oil on canvas, by Sir Godfrey Kneller
(1646–1723).
In this portrait and the one of Mary,
the monarchs are in coronation robes.

National Maritime Museum, Greenwich
Hospital Collection BHC3094.

in book-collecting went back to the 1660s, when he had made regular raids on London's bookshops and piled his purchases around his study in Seething Lane. To solve the problem of book storage, in 1666 he had two specially designed bookcases made. These remained a source of pride for they were to his own design, and purpose-built bookcases were unusual in private homes. By the mid-1690s, there were seven cases, since Pepys no longer had to be so cautious in his spending and had found many reasons to invest in his collections.

During the 1690s, Pepys made several attempts at drafting a paper on the rationale for a 'Private Library' such as his. It should, he felt, contain 'the greatest diversity of Subjects & Stiles (from the most solemn & polite down to the most Vulgar) & in such variety of Languages as the Owner's Reading will bear'. This was to be done 'in fewest Books & least Room'. In a later draft he also stressed that the collection should reflect the 'particular Genius' of its owner (by 'genius' he meant spirit or character, rather than dazzling intelligence).[2] Pepys's 'particular Genius', of course, was applied to the sea and to the navy, so his manuscript holdings and print collections on these subjects were especially impressive. He gathered medieval naval records, journals of recent sea voyages, illustrated accounts of foreign lands and a host of other works. It would, he told his friend Dr Arthur Charlett, be a source of reproach if there was 'one Hole found unsearcht by mee' in the hunt for material on nautical topics.[3]

Pepys's emphasis on the diversity of a library's holdings meant that it was not enough for him to preserve maritime works alone. Nor was he content to purchase only expensive, elite works: cheap and popular publications also deserved shelf space. When Pepys wrote of collecting the 'most Vulgar' books, he meant the ballads and short chapbooks (offering religious instruction, songs or stories) that sold in great numbers to less affluent readers. Pepys often found ballads and chapbooks entertaining, and he recognized them as valuable sources on social history and popular taste. His pursuit of diversity also meant owning texts from across the broadest possible timespan. In 1701,

he realized that his oldest manuscript was 900 years old – but that a thousand-year-old one would be even better. He therefore asked the young scholar Humfrey Wanley to find a suitably venerable manuscript (of whatever kind), since 'I should thinke it a great Addition to my little Collection, to bee able to close it with something that might bring it up to 1000 yeares or neere it'.[4]

Wanley was one of many people who aided Pepys's collecting, for it was not usually Pepys himself who hunted in 'Holes' for desirable items. He was helped by expert booksellers and professional agents who attended auctions of libraries on his behalf. Friends and kin were also recruited to the cause. In 1699, Pepys's nephew John Jackson was sent off on a literary tour of Europe armed with lists of items that Pepys desired for his collection. He brought back with him many boxes of material from Rome and other publishing centres, which Pepys spent happy months sorting and binding together to suit his taste. Pepys's principle of 'fewest Books & least Room' meant he was as meticulous in deciding which works to retain in his collection as he was in hunting down particular items to add to it. For Pepys, as for many other library owners of his period, possessing the most up-to-date and comprehensive edition often took priority over preserving a rare edition. Some of the items Pepys decided not to keep therefore make today's collectors of rare books wince: after purchasing a third edition of Shakespeare's collected works in 1664, he dispensed with it in favour of the more common fourth edition of 1685. Pepys's policy of avoiding multiple copies also led to some brutal decisions. He ejected a copy of a nautical almanac said to have been owned by Henry VIII in favour of one he believed had belonged to Sir Francis Drake. Pepys's collecting priorities meant a monarch could be outranked by a mariner.

For Pepys, a library reflected the self and might be a place for self-reflection, but it was also a space for socializing. His friends in the 1690s included clergymen, scholars and natural philosophers, many of whom were members of the Royal Society: the privilege of inspecting Pepys's library was part of the hospitality he provided to guests. He hosted regular Saturday night gatherings there, which offered good food, good books and the chance to talk over the latest ideas in science, history and religion. His friends jokingly called these gatherings 'the Club in York buildings', 'Saturday's table' and 'the Round Table'.[5] Among those who attended were Pepys's close friends John Evelyn and Thomas Gale (the High Master of St Paul's School), as well as Richard Bentley (a noted classical scholar), Thomas Smith (who was keeper of the famous Cotton Library), and John Arbuthnot (who would later make his name as a great satirist). Isaac Newton also visited Pepys's home. Many of Pepys's friends – Evelyn, Gale, Bentley and Newton among them – had written works that circulated in print or manuscript; when

visiting the library, these men would have been surrounded by their own publications.

Some visitors also found themselves under the gaze of their own portraits. Soon after his retirement, Pepys came up with a plan to 'adorn [his] Library with the pictures of Men Illustrious for their parts and Erudition'.[6] This, at least, was how Evelyn characterized the scheme, in the process of expressing his surprise that he was one of Pepys's first targets. Pepys commissioned Godfrey Kneller to paint his friend's portrait. In order to celebrate Evelyn's scholarship, he was shown holding his book *Sylva*, a work on timber-growing first published in 1664. A version of this portrait was later given to

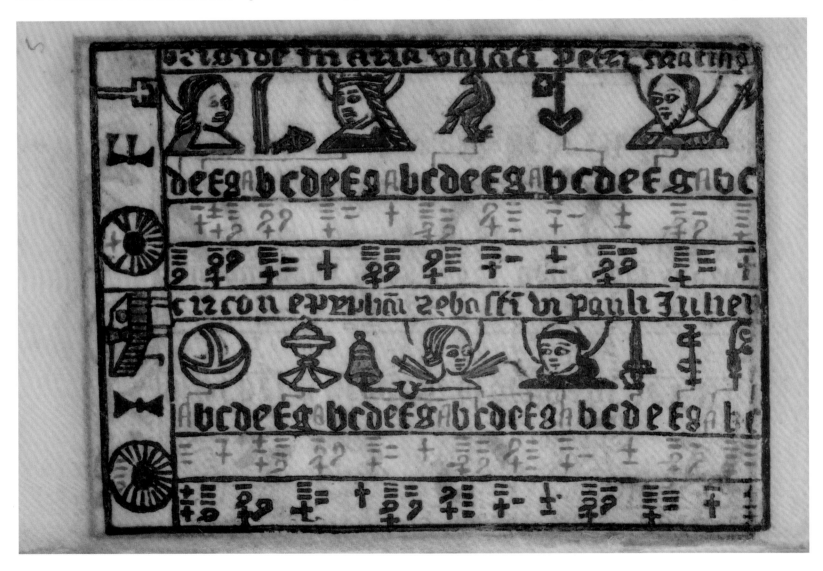

Xylographic nautical almanac
By Guillaume Brouscon (*fl*. 1543–48), *c*.1546.
Compiled in signs and signals, such an almanac could be understood by unlettered seamen, but this copy was reputedly owned by Henry VIII.

National Maritime Museum, NVT/40.

the Royal Society (see 113). Among the other faces displayed on the library walls were Thomas Gale and Isaac Newton. Pepys chose to commemorate men who had contributed to learning directly through their publications, but certain friends also earned their places by aiding his collecting: both Gale and Evelyn, for example, had offered advice on what to purchase and how to obtain rare works. Pepys also acknowledged his patrons. Portraits of the Earl of Sandwich and James II were on display, with James's image prominently placed over the fireplace. In Pepys's 'private' library – which was open only to a select few – he could honour his debt to James and make manifest his Jacobite convictions. Thus the library was intended not just to project Pepys's character, but also to display the network of friendships and allegiances that had shaped both his character and his collections.

As a repository of information, Pepys's library was a source of power, particularly after 1688 when many other means of influence were lost to him. If Pepys no longer held naval office, he did hold a lot of valuable manuscripts and books on naval affairs in his collections. During his years at the Admiralty, for example, Pepys had kept copies of letters sent from his office. When he resigned, he took these letterbooks with him, and refused to hand all of them over to his successors, regarding them as his private property rather than official records. He remained a gatekeeper to rare materials, withholding or granting access. Favoured individuals were allowed to see and copy his manuscript holdings, and might even be allowed to print certain of them. For instance, he used his papers to supply nautical information for a revised edition of *Britannia* (1695), a history of Britain originally written by William Camden, and he was gratefully credited by the editor for this service. In fact, Pepys himself had long cherished the ambition to write a great history of the navy, and he saw his holdings on maritime affairs as the research material for this. The project, however, got out of hand. It had begun in the 1660s, with Pepys considering writing a short piece on recent naval history; by the 1680s, the notes for his history reached back to ancient Greek and Roman authors, and even

to the description of the ark in the Old Testament. As his collection of potential materials grew so too did his reluctance to actually get down to writing his book.

Although Pepys never managed to produce his history of the navy, the 1690s did see him appear as an author in print for the first time. Before his retirement, Pepys had no need to resort to print in order make his presence felt. As Secretary to the Admiralty, he had the ear of powerful courtiers and the king himself. If he wanted to contribute to policy or spread an idea through writing, his normal method was to send proposals in manuscript to influential men. Once out of office, though, print became a more attractive medium: it offered the possibility of wider circulation than manuscript and gave his writing an air of permanence and authority.

Pepys published his *Memoires Relating to the State of the Royal Navy of England* in the winter of 1690. The work was a defence of the management of the navy during the 1680s when Pepys, working under James II, had overseen a programme of shipbuilding. It was intended to ward off allegations of neglect by his enemies in the new administration. Pepys was fastidious about the appearance of the books in his collection and was similarly demanding when it came to his own print publications. Careful use was made of different types and inks, and mistakes in the text were hand-corrected before the work was distributed. Pepys's name did not appear on the title page itself, but it was inscribed on the fine portrait engraved as the frontispiece, which depicted the author as a man of high standing (see 153).

Pepys's writing style was similarly elevated: this was not the informal, energetic prose of his private diary, but the kind of elaborate, Latinate language which he employed in public, especially when he was on the defensive. For example, when discussing the good condition of the navy before 1679, Pepys wrote:

> Though I am one, who could never think any room left for a *Subject's* Supererogating in the honest *Service* of his *Prince*; yet cannot I but own

so much content in the contemplation of that little *Part* I had born in the rendring it such, as may reasonably arise from the not being conscious of any one *Instance* to be shewn me through the whole *Marine History of England*, of a time wherein its *Navy* had been ever before recorded in a better.[7]

Or, in other words, 'I don't believe a man can ever do too much in the service of his prince, but (though I'm really modest about this) when I look back on my achievements, I'm pleased to think that history shows England's navy was never in a better state than when I was running it.' Pepys supported his version of events with copious letters, reports and official orders culled from his records. His intent in going into print was to create a kind of surrogate public record – one which appeared authoritative and relatively impartial, but which was in fact highly selective and skewed in its author's favour.[8] He was worried about the reception of his book, so he circulated it in stages: first he showed friends the manuscript version, then he handed out specially printed copies to allies and men of influence. As these copies were not intended for sale, they had no bookseller's address on the title page, but simply gave the year of publication. By spring 1691, another issue of the book, designed for public sale, was available on London's bookstalls. While Pepys's book did not win him widespread acclaim or a return to office, it did provide Jacobite authors with ammunition to defend James's record of care for the national interest.

The *Memoires* was not the last of Pepys's sorties into print. In 1698, he began a remarkable pamphlet campaign to stamp out corruption at Christ's Hospital, a charitable institution charged with educating children selected from London's poor. In the early 1670s, Pepys had helped set up a Royal Mathematical School at the hospital in order to supply the navy with boys trained in navigation. He became a member of the hospital's governing body, but his growing frustration at the mismanagement of the institution led him to retreat from close involvement. During his retirement, with more time on his hands, he went back to investigating the running of the hospital. Pepys's enquiries persuaded him that the hospital officials were at best incompetent and at worst grossly corrupt; moreover, their mismanagement had led to the moral corruption of the children. 'Lewd Visitors', he informed the hospital's President, had recently started a 'Riot' in the girls' quarters. Even worse, two boys from the Mathematical School had been found 'Dead-Drunk' in the City and been paraded back to the hospital by a London mob. The incident was all the more shocking because the angry citizens had been able to identify the pupils by 'the Badge of their Royal Founder', Charles II, sewn on to their clothes (see 132).[9] This mark of honour had become a badge of shame.

When Pepys's warnings were ignored by the hospital's President and governors, he turned to the Lord Mayor of London. The Lord Mayor had power over the governors as the hospital was overseen by the Corporation of London. However, the Lord Mayor, Sir Humphrey Edwin, felt that he could safely ignore the elderly and ailing Pepys. This was a grave mistake. Pepys decided that the Lord Mayor, too, was corrupt and involved in supressing his report. With conventional channels exhausted, Pepys resorted to unconventional ones. He had his warning letters to the Lord Mayor printed. The pamphlet was issued in a small print run, for Pepys had a very specific target audience in mind: the aldermen of London from whose body the Lord Mayor was elected. Pepys addressed a copy of his pamphlet to each of the twenty-six aldermen and sent it to them. To have circulated these letters in manuscript would have been bad enough, but to distribute them in print was a complete violation of gentlemanly decorum – a move from a polite tap on the shoulder to a declaration of war. Despite his professed care to ensure the pamphlet's limited circulation, Pepys's use of print signalled an appeal to a wider audience: the London public. Sure enough, Pepys informed readers of a second pamphlet that its predecessor was the talk of coffeehouses and that the incensed Lord Mayor had declared it to be libellous.[10] At least Pepys was no longer being ignored.

Pepys's creative whistle-blowing scheme continued until there were six pamphlets in all. Each contained letters addressed to the Lord Mayor, the aldermen, or the governors of Christ's Hospital. It became,

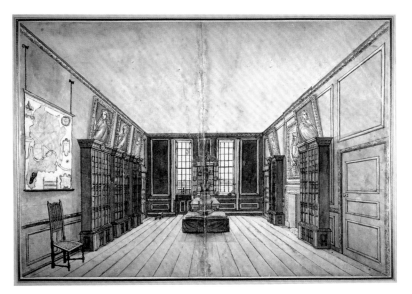

Pepys's Library, York Buildings
By Sutton Nicholls, c.1693.

Pepys Library, Magdalene College,
Cambridge, PL Catalogue and Alphabet.

in effect, a semi-public blackmail campaign by instalments, with Pepys threatening to print his full report if the Corporation of London did not succeed in bringing the President and governors of the hospital to heel. Pepys came close to outright insults in this campaign and seems to have taken his share of insults in return. In May 1699, his friend Thomas Gale wrote to him to sympathize: 'you have mett with what was to be expected from men whose education is vile', adding for good measure that they were a 'generation of caterpillars!'[11]

Despite considerable opposition, Pepys triumphed. The aldermen and a new Lord Mayor took steps to reform the hospital, including ordering the appointment of one Samuel Pepys as its Vice-President. This new position was something of a poisoned chalice – a lot of labour for an ill man. Yet it did have one gratifying consequence: such a post could only be held by a freeman of the City of London, and Pepys (despite having lived in London almost his entire life) did not have this status. Therefore, as an enticement to accept a difficult role, the aldermen granted him the freedom of the City, explaining that this was 'in acknowledgement of the great zeal and concern for the interest of *Christ's* Hospital, manifested upon all occasions by *Samuel Pepys*, esquire'.[12] Surprisingly, Pepys's Christ's Hospital pamphlets did not earn a place in his library. Perhaps he felt the whole affair (and the methods he had used) did not reflect well on anyone involved. He was too unwell, and the hospital's problems too entrenched, for him to long pursue his efforts there.

In the last few years of his life, Pepys turned his attention to the final organization of his library. He had always been mindful of how his library and the room that held it might be interpreted, but he was now thinking increasingly about future users of his collection and imagining posterity as his audience. In 1700, he set about a major review of the library and oversaw the compilation of a new catalogue. To save space, Pepys organized his books by size, not by subject or author, so finding aids were particularly important for navigating the library. Pepys's unusually elaborate, three-part catalogue had headings specially devised to suit his lifetime of interests. For example, Robert Boyle was one of only three writers to have a section all to himself in the subject catalogue, thereby highlighting his contributions to natural philosophy and Pepys's interest in his works. 'Sea, & Navy' of course had their own section, as did 'Vulgaria' (Pepys's chapbooks).[13] In its final form, Pepys's library had almost 3,000 volumes, with the volumes often containing many publications bound up together. This made it one of the largest private libraries owned by a gentleman in England at the time.

For Pepys, the library had become the sum of his achievements, an image of himself that he wanted to pass down to his heir and to future scholars. He therefore added a codicil to his will which instructed his nephew John Jackson on how to complete and preserve the library. Jackson was to make a few final additions to the collection, update the catalogue, and then ensure that it 'would remaine unalterable and forever accompany the said Library'.[14] Pepys wanted his library to be passed to a Cambridge college, preferably Magdalene where both Pepys and Jackson had studied. He directed that it should be kept in a separate room known as the 'Bibliotheca Pepysiana' – since Pepys had no children, the library was one means of passing on his name.

Jackson was a conscientious heir and, in 1724, Pepys got his wish. The Pepys Library is today in Magdalene College, Cambridge, with its fine furniture and gilded bindings very much as Pepys left them. Among its books and manuscripts was one particular treasure: Pepys's diary of the 1660s, its full riches masked by shorthand. The reason behind Pepys's decision to preserve his diary on his library shelves can be traced to the rationale for the library itself: this 'Private Library' was designed to reflect the 'particular Genius' of its owner, and Pepys must have realized that no writing better captured this than his diary. Having carefully crafted his public image for posterity, Pepys ultimately decided that his diary – with all its lively, intimate, embarrassing detail – deserved to be part of his library and his legacy.

Pepys's Library today

Magdalene College, Cambridge.

Religious Tension

The course of Pepys's career, as well as his personal safety, were both threatened by the fierce religious controversies of the age. During the period of the supposed Popish Plot, attempts were made to implicate Pepys in the murder of the London magistrate Sir Edmund Berry Godfrey. Then, unfounded allegations that he had sold naval secrets to the French, at a time when anti-Catholic feeling was still running high, cost him his job in the Navy Office and almost his life.

After the Exclusion Crisis of 1679–81, when the Whig opposition had tried to disbar the Catholic James, Duke of York, from ever inheriting the throne, the crown attempted to root out prominent Whigs from their positions of power. The final years of Charles's reign were to see the most sustained period of religious persecution ever known in Britain. Heavy fines were imposed on nonconformist worshippers. From late 1684, in Scotland, suspected Presbyterians who refused to take an oath to prove their loyalty could be summarily shot without trial (unless they were women, in which case they were drowned). The period was subsequently given the name of 'the Killing Times'. It was a far cry from the optimism that had greeted Charles on his restoration a generation before.

When James came to the throne in 1685, he tried to calm fears about his Catholicism, pledging to uphold the established church. Yet he soon began to repeal laws that prevented Catholics and nonconformists from taking public office. His actions posed difficulties for loyal officials like Pepys: their allegiance to the king was in conflict with their religious beliefs, reopening questions about the extent of sovereign power and the relationship of church and state.

133

'Godfrey' dagger

1678
Wood, steel, leather and gold
Inscribed: 'MEMENTO GODFREY
CÆSUS OCTO: 12 1678: PRO RELIGIONE
PROTESTANTIVM' ('In memory of
Godfrey killed on the 12 October 1678
for the Protestant religion')
Lambeth Palace Library

One of the strangest events associated
with the Popish Plot is the death of a
magistrate, Sir Edmund Berry Godfrey,
whose body was discovered, five days
after his disappearance, in a ditch on
Primrose Hill outside London on 17
October 1678. He had been run through
the chest by a sword, which remained in
place; strangulation marks were visible
on his neck. A shoddy inquest concluded
that he had been murdered, and theories
abounded that he was a victim of a
Catholic conspiracy. Daggers like this
one were produced as grisly reminders
of the event and as protection against
the militant Roman Catholics alleged
to be at large. His death – the reason
for which is still unknown – fuelled
anti-Catholic sentiments. The blade
is inscribed with a skull and motto. RB

LITERATURE: *ODNB*.

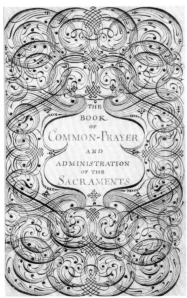

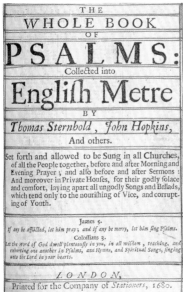

134

The Book of Common-Prayer and Administration of the Sacraments, bound with *The Whole Book of Psalms: Collected into English Metre*

By Thomas Sternhold, John Hopkins, and others ... (London, 1680)
St Olave, London

Following his release from the Tower of London in July 1679 and the collapse of allegations made against him as part of the Popish Plot, Pepys, perhaps wisely, either belatedly bought or was given this copy of the Book of Common Prayer. Pepys embellished the volume by adding engravings of biblical scenes. The book's pages are, as was his standard practice, ruled neatly around the margins in red ink. RB

LITERATURE: Sotheby, p. 11 (lot 13).

135

Charles II

c.1680–85
Studio of John Riley (1646–91)
Oil on canvas, 724 × 578
National Portrait Gallery, NPG 3798

This portrait of Charles, towards the end of his life, shows a sombre and careworn 'merry monarch' – a term mockingly applied to him by the Earl of Rochester. Riley's original portrait displeased the king but, despite this upset, he was appointed 'Painter and Picture Drawer in Ordinary' to the monarch in 1681. Charles died after a short illness on 6 February 1685. He was fifty-four and had fathered no legitimate heir, although his mistresses produced fourteen acknowledged children. The crown passed to his brother, James, a practising Roman Catholic. RB

LITERATURE: *ODNB.*

136

Wedding suit worn by James,
Duke of York

1673
Wool, embroidered with silver and
silver-gilt thread and lined with
red silk Victoria and Albert Museum,
T.117:1–2-1995

The Duke of York's first wife, Anne Hyde, mother to his daughters, Mary and Anne, died in 1671. He married his second wife, the Italian noblewoman Mary of Modena, by proxy in September 1673. The fifteen-year-old had been reluctant to marry James, almost twenty-five years her senior, and only agreed when the Pope himself wrote explaining it was the greatest thing she could do for the Catholic faith. The marriage contract was confirmed when she arrived at Dover on 21 November, when James wore this suit of a coat and breeches. The fine wool suit is embroidered with silver and silver-gilt thread, giving it a glistening effect in the light; the associated waistcoat is now lost. RB

137

Miniature of James Scott,
Duke of Monmouth

c.1667
Samuel Cooper (1609–72)
Watercolour on vellum, 83 × 66
Royal Collection, RCIN 420087

James (1649–85), the illegitimate son of Charles II and Lucy Walter, was born in The Hague in 1649, during the king's exile. In 1662, he was made Duke of Monmouth. The following year, upon his marriage to Lady Anne Scott, whose name he adopted, he was granted the additional title of Duke of Buccleuch. On the occasion of a royal visit to Greenwich on 26 July 1665, Pepys observed the teenaged Monmouth to be 'the most skittish, leaping gallant that ever I saw, alway[s] in action, vaulting or leaping or clambering'. Monmouth was put forward as leader of the Protestant cause and attempted to take the throne from Catholic James II after his father's death. His rebels were easily defeated by James II's forces at the Battle of Sedgemoor in July 1685. Monmouth was captured, tried for treason and beheaded. RB

LITERATURE: *Diary*, VI, 170.

138

The History of the Coronation of the Most High, Most Mighty, and Most Excellent Monarch, James II ... And of His Royal Consort Queen Mary ...

....

By Francis Sandford (London, 1687)
British Library, 141.h.1

Sandford and his fellow herald Gregory King worked for two years on this sumptuously produced history of James's coronation in April 1685. Twenty-seven engraved prints follow its ceremonial progress, with details of the regalia worn and plans of the major buildings involved. It depicts the host of individuals, including Pepys, participating in the great event. It was this group that Sandford hoped would buy the costly folio, but the king was already unpopular by the time it was published. Sandford struggled to cover his costs, despite a gift of £300 from James himself. RB

LITERATURE: *ODNB*; Sharpe, pp. 259–60, 275–76, 290–91.

139

....

Coronation cup and cover

....

*c.*1685
Silver-gilt
Inscribed: 'Hoc obtinui / Ex in Aug: lac: 2. D /Et Mar: Ap: 23.85' ('I obtained this from the Coronation of James II and Mary, April 23 1685')
Victoria and Albert Museum, M.34.1-2-2008

At Charles II's coronation in 1661, Pepys had merely been part of the crowd in Westminster Abbey, arriving early in the morning in order to obtain a seat. In 1685, however, as senior Baron of the Cinque Ports, he was integral to the great pageant, bearing the front left-hand pole of James II's royal canopy. The occasion was not without incident: the crown slipped on James's head, later interpreted as a bad omen; the royal canopy broke; and a gust of wind tore the royal standard flown at the Tower of London as guns sounded a salute to the king. This commemorative cup is made from the bells and staves of the canopy and the front is engraved with an image of the four bearers. RB

LITERATURE: Bryant, *Pepys: Saviour of the Navy*, p. 114.

140

Alms dish

1683, with later additions
Francis Leake, London
Silver-gilt
Burghley House, SIL04924

This is one of a pair of silver-gilt dishes decorated for use at James II's coronation. In the central roundel, a rose, with crown above, is flanked by the royal cipher, 'JR'; the border consists of a scrolling acanthus leaf pattern. The dishes were given to John Cecil, Earl of Exeter, as a perquisite of his appointment as Hereditary Grand Almoner of England, a post created at the time of the coronation. Exeter declined to serve at the coronation of William and Mary in 1689. RB

141

Mary of Modena's crown frame

1685 (with later additions)
Sir Robert Vyner (1631–88)
Gilt copper alloy, paste diamonds, imitation pearls and velvet
Museum of London, 56.11

James II's queen, Mary of Modena, wore this crown as she entered Westminster Abbey in 1685. It was then worn at three further coronations: by Queen Mary II in 1689; by George II, as Prince of Wales, at the coronation of George I in 1714; and by Caroline of Ansbach at that of her husband George II in 1727. As was common practice, the original precious stones were subsequently incorporated into other pieces of jewellery and replaced with paste replicas. RB

Regime Change and Pepys's Legacy

The birth of a Catholic heir to the throne in June 1688 precipitated James II's fall. Seven prominent Whig nobles wrote to the Protestant William of Orange, husband of James's elder daughter, Mary, inviting him to intervene. Whatever they thought would happen, William always meant to seize the throne. He landed in November, taking a risk by embarking late in the year. Yet the same 'Protestant' wind that sped him across the Channel kept the English fleet from sailing out to intercept him. James seems to have suffered a complete mental collapse. In England his forces never met William's in battle. Queen Mary, disguised as a laundress, escaped to France with her son on 10 December 1688, and James soon followed.

Pepys remained at his post during the revolution, but James's flight delivered the country into William's hands. Just one week after the accession of William III and Mary II in April 1689, Pepys resigned from the Admiralty. He had received no encouraging sign from either monarch, and it was clear that his career was at an end. He did contest his Parliamentary seat of Harwich, but old accusations of connections with Catholicism were raked up and he was heavily defeated. In the summer of that year, he was briefly imprisoned by the new regime, and again in 1690. On both occasions, he was bailed by friends.

Pepys was never an active Jacobite. Even so, in 1695 he interviewed a certain Mrs Dawson, present at the birth of James II's son and 'the best living evidence' he could find to assure himself that the child was legitimate.[1] It is typical of Pepys that he would want to settle this question himself, to his own satisfaction. After a retirement spent perfecting his library, he died on 26 May 1703 and was buried at St Olave's, Hart Street. At his funeral 123 mourning rings were handed out, an unusually large number and testimony to the respect in which he was still held.

142

Sir Edward Petre, Mary of Modena and Prince James Francis Edward Stuart

c.1688
Attributed to Pieter Schenck (1660–1711)
Mezzotint
National Portrait Gallery, NPG D10694

It was widely assumed that Mary of Modena would not produce a healthy heir. The queen's many pregnancies had ended either in miscarriage or with the children dying in infancy. In late November 1687, rumours abounded that she was expecting a child again. In the charged anti-Catholic atmosphere of the time, unfounded theories spread that the pregnancy was a sham and an illegitimate baby would be substituted and made James's heir. Mary duly gave birth to a healthy boy, named James, on 10 June 1688. This Dutch print shows Sir Edward Petre, a Jesuit and dean of the new Chapel Royal at St James's, fondling the queen, clearly implying a Catholic conspiracy. As Petre had been embroiled in the Popish Plot, he was a recognizable figure who would help to underscore the engraving's point. RB

Biegtvader peters, met de rykxvorstin en zoon,
staan, buiten londen, hier voor't oog van elk, ten toon.
merkuur paap peters, puik knaphandig in't bedriegen,

weet vorst, vorstin, en volk, wel diep in slaap te wiegen.
de prins van wallis knikt, het molentje hout stant,
maalt koning, koningin, en pop uit engelant.

143

Resolution of the Convention Parliament

28 January 1689
Ink on paper
Parliamentary Archives, HL/PO/
JO/10/1/403A

The Convention Parliament, established
to deal with the crisis, was deeply divided
after James's flight into exile in December
1688, with major divisions between
the Tory supporters of James and their
Whig opponents. The Commons finally
resolved on 28 January 1689 that James
had abdicated and the throne was vacant.
The Lords replaced the word 'abdicated'
with 'deserted'. This Whig victory cleared
the way for William and Mary to be
offered the crown, but it took a great deal
of further debate and popular pressure
before the House of Lords fell into line on
6 February. RB

LITERATURE: Pincus, pp. 282–86.

144

Letter to the Prince of Orange

30 June 1688
Ink on paper
The National Archives, SP 8/1/pt 2, ff.
224–27

As opposition to James grew after
the birth of his Catholic male heir, a
Protestant opposition faction gained
in strength and confidence. On 30
June 1688, seven leading politicians
put their ciphers to a letter inviting
William of Orange, as the husband of
James's eldest, Protestant daughter, to
intervene. The carefully worded invitation
was composed by Henry Sidney and
signed by him and the Earls of Danby,
Devonshire and Shrewsbury, Viscount
Lumley, Admiral Edward Russell and
Henry Compton, the Bishop of London.
The letter was taken to The Hague by
Rear-Admiral Arthur Herbert, who
adopted the disguise of a common sailor.
RB

145

William of Orange landing at Brixham, Torbay, 5 November 1688

....

1688

Jan Wyck (c.1640–1702)
Oil on canvas, 1575 × 1321
National Maritime Museum, BHC3095

Domination is the central theme of this equestrian portrait of William (1650–1702). Although he was usually mounted on a roan, the future king is depicted on a white horse (a symbol of kingship and of the House of Orange) shown out of scale with the surrounding composition. Even the Dutch fleet and the invasion force on the shore are rendered insignificant by comparison. William's spurred, black boot in its glinting stirrup is poised above English soil, ready to lay claim to crown and country. His outstretched marshal's baton points the way forward to Protestant victory and a 'Glorious Revolution'. RB

QUEEN MARY.   WISSING.

146

Queen Mary II as Princess of Orange

c.1686–87
William Wissing (1656–87)
Oil on canvas, 1258 × 1053
Royal Collection, RCIN 405643

James II commissioned this portrait of his elder daughter, conceived as one of a pair with that of William of Orange, in 1685. Mary (1662–94), a devout adherent of the Church of England, resisted her father's attempts to convert her to Catholicism. In 1688, she was deeply suspicious of the legitimacy of the royal heir born to her stepmother and supported William's invasion. Mary followed her husband to Britain on 12 February 1689 and, after they jointly accepted the throne next day, they reigned as co-monarchs until her death from smallpox in 1694. RB

LITERATURE: *ODNB*; Millar, *Tudor, Stuart and Early Georgian Pictures*, cat. 323, p. 139.

147

Draft of the Declaration of Rights

12 February 1689
Ink on paper
Parliamentary Archives, HL/PO/JO/10/1/403D

The Declaration of Rights was created by the Convention Parliament, the body established to deal with the crisis caused by James's flight and William's invasion. It encapsulated the Parliamentary and Protestant principles of the 'Glorious Revolution' and invited William and Mary to become joint monarchs. The Declaration formed the essential basis of the Bill of Rights, which remains a cornerstone of the British constitution. RB

148

....

James II's harquebusier's armour

....

1686
Richard Holden, Royal Armourer, London
Steel plate, leather
Royal Armouries, II.123

James II owned this set of light cavalry
armour, consisting of a helmet (or 'pot'),
breastplate, backplate and long elbow
gauntlet. The faceguard is fretted in
the form of the royal coat of arms with
supporting lion and unicorn; the initials
'IR' (for Iacobus Rex – King James) form
part of the decorative scheme. The
breastplate, which bears a proof-mark, is
also elaborately decorated with punched
and engraved designs, and bears the
royal cipher. This was the last suit of
armour made for a British monarch. RB

149

Medal commemorating the
Battle of La Hogue

1692
Philipp Heinrich Müller and F. Kleinert,
Nuremberg
Bronze-gilt
Inscribed, obverse: 'NON ILLI IMPERIVM:
SED MIHI SORTE DATVM' and
'GUILIELMO . III . M . BRIT . R . OB
IMPERIUM MARIS ASSERT' ('To William
III King of Great Britain upon his asserting
this Dominion of the Sea' and 'Not to him
but to me was the empire allotted')
National Maritime Museum, MEC0306

The obverse of this medal shows
Neptune with his trident raised driving
back Louis XIV as battle rages. The
inscription is an adaptation of Virgil's
Aeneid, I, l.138. On the reverse, a winged
figure of Victory, carrying a palm frond
and laurel wreath, stands in a stylized
galley with cherubs bearing the royal
arms of Britain and Holland. In the
distance to the left, the French fleet is
shown scattered and sinking (see 150).
RB

150

**Destruction of the *Soleil Royal* at the
Battle of La Hogue, 23 May 1692**

*c.*1700
Adriaen van Diest (1655–1704)
Oil on canvas, 915 × 1510
National Maritime Museum, BHC0338

After the accession of William III, he led
a European-wide coalition to contain the
power of Louis XIV of France and secure
his throne. The Battle of La Hogue was
part of a series of actions fought over six
days off the Normandy coast between
the French and an Anglo-Dutch fleet.
Following an inconclusive engagement off
Barfleur, the French force tried to escape
its numerically superior foe. Three French
ships, including the flagship the *Soleil
Royal*, were beached near Cherbourg
and burned in the fighting that followed.
A further twelve French ships sought
protection at Saint-Vaast-la-Hogue,
but in the ensuing battle they too were
destroyed. RB

LITERATURE: Rodger, pp. 149–50.

151

Samuel Pepys, aged 56

1689
Sir Godfrey Kneller (1646–1723)
Oil on canvas, 760 × 635
National Maritime Museum, Caird
Collection, BHC2947

Following the trend in portrait fashion,
Pepys moved to Kneller towards the
end of his life, commissioning this as
one of a trio of portraits, the others
being of his nephew John Jackson (now
lost) and his long-term friend, by now
a businessman, William Hewer. This
is Pepys's most dignified and solemn
portrait, showing him as both intellectual
and administrator, after he retired from
office in 1689. It appears to have been
Pepys's favourite: three further versions
exist, including one presented to the
Royal Society to commemorate his
presidency. KB

LITERATURE: Barber, pp. 3, 7.

152

William Hewer

1689
Sir Godfrey Kneller (1646–1723)
Oil on canvas, 762 × 635
National Maritime Museum, Caird
Collection, BHC2765

As Pepys's personal secretary and
clerk at the Navy Board, Will Hewer
(1642–1715) became a lifelong friend.
He saw the highs and lows of Pepys's
life and moved with Pepys and his wife
to the Admiralty, living with them in
York Buildings and acting as go-between
during their estrangement after Pepys
was caught philandering. Hewer made
his career as Governor of the East India
Company after Pepys's retirement
in 1689, and Pepys lived with him in
Clapham from 1701 until his death. He
acted as executor of Pepys's will with
Pepys's nephew and main heir John
Jackson. KB

LITERATURE: Barber, pp. 9–10.

153

*Memoires Relating to the State of the
Royal Navy of England …*

By Samuel Pepys (London, 1690)
National Maritime Museum, PBE9929

In his *Memoires … of the Royal Navy*,
Pepys analysed the management of
the navy from 1679 to 1688. Derived
from the records he kept throughout his
career, it is more a defence of his time in
office than a work of history. It made an
important contribution to the partisan
battles in 1689–90 over the navy's prior
management. Pepys manipulated many
statistics for his own ends, but most of
the book's charges were accepted by a
subsequent Parliamentary investigation.
There is also a private edition ('Printed
Anno MDCXC'). JD

LITERATURE: Pepys, *Memoires*, pp. v–xv.

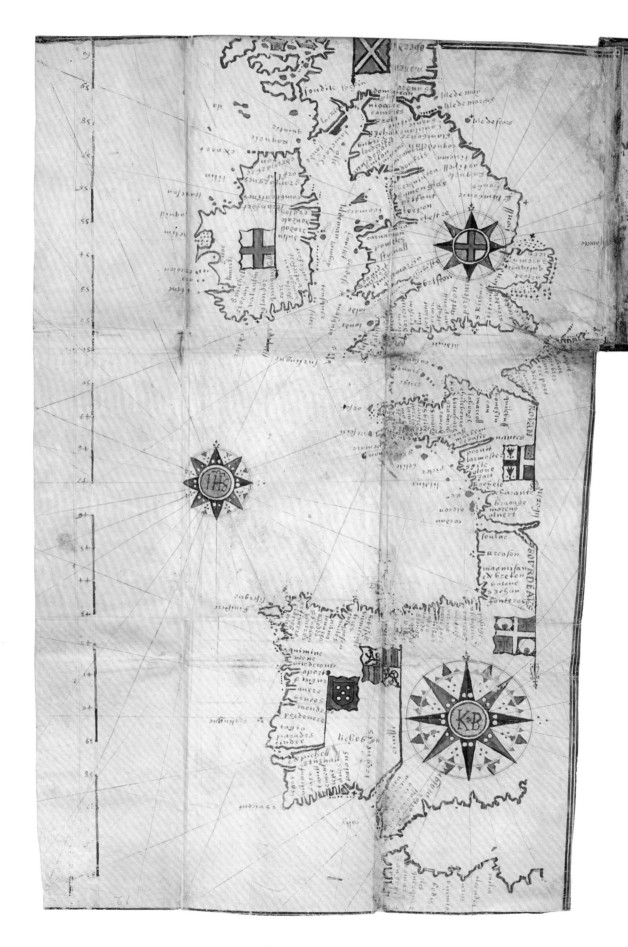

154

....

Xylographic nautical almanac

....

*c.*1546
Guillaume Brouscon (*fl.* 1543–48)
Ink on vellum
National Maritime Museum, NVT/40

Devised and produced in the Breton port
of Le Conquet, this almanac was partly
printed using woodblocks (xylography)
and partly hand-written, the symbols
highlighted with colour. It gave Breton
seamen practical information for their
daily lives and, in particular, the time of
the tides and dates of church festivals
and feasts. Compiled using signs and
symbols, it provided essential data
to illiterate mariners in an innovative
way, regardless of nationality. Pepys
collected it for his library and an
annotation indicates that he thought it
once belonged to Henry VIII. As he had
multiple copies, he later passed it on. MB

LITERATURE: Howse.

155

Rites of Funeral Ancient and Modern, in use Through the Known World

....

By Pierre Muret, trans. Paul Lorrain
(London, 1683)
National Maritime Museum, PBE4685

Pepys's bibliomania occupied much of
his time in later life. This copy of Muret's
work on funeral rites bears the inscription
'Samuelle Pepys' and is followed by
a playful verse. It also contains the
bookplate of his friend and colleague,
William Hewer, in whose house at
Clapham he spent his final years. Paul
Lorrain, Pepys's secretary, translator and
copyist, from 1678, translated Muret from
the original French and presented copies
to his employer. This was not the volume
that Pepys chose to retain in his library,
and it seems likely that he passed it to
Hewer. RB

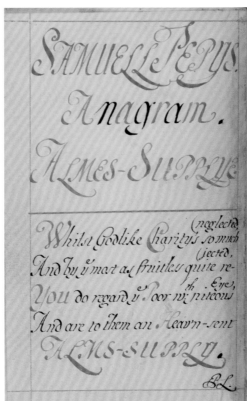

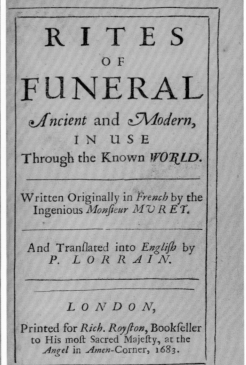

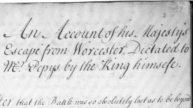

156

....

'An Account of His Majesty's Escape
from Worcester, dictated to Mr Pepys
by the King himselfe', 1680

....

Transcription of 1734
Ink on paper
British Library, Add. MS 31955, f. 2

Pepys first heard Charles II's account of
his escape after the Battle of Worcester
on board the *Royal Charles* in 1660. He
recorded in his diary that 'it made me
ready to weep to hear the stories that
he told of his difficulties'. Pepys heard
the narrative again, taking it down in
shorthand, during an audience with
the king at Newmarket, in Suffolk, on
3 and 5 October 1680. Pepys reworked
his notes into a longhand narrative,
which remains at Magdalene College,
Cambridge. This early eighteenth-century
transcription formed part of the library of
the Lord Chancellor, Philip Yorke, Earl of
Hardwicke. RB

LITERATURE: *Diary*, I, 155; Bryant, *Pepys: Years
of Peril*, pp. 338, 356.

157

....

Memoirs of Samuel Pepys, Esq. F.R.S ...
Comprising His Diary from 1659 to 1669

....

Edited by Richard Griffin, Lord
Braybrooke, (London, 1825),
2 vols re-bound
National Maritime Museum, PBE9953/1

Richard Griffin, Lord Braybrooke,
published the first edition of Pepys's
diary, together with selected
correspondence, in two volumes in
1825. It failed to do the diary justice,
Braybrooke later admitting he had
'used the pruning-knife with too much
freedom'. This copy was presented by
him and his brother, George, Master of

Magdalene College, Cambridge, to their
sister, Caroline, Lady Wenlock (d. 1868).
In 1865, she inserted extensive additional
illustrations, taken from the print
collection of her deceased husband, and
had the expanded work rebound in seven
folio volumes. RB

158

....

Will of Samuel Pepys

....

2 August 1701, with two codicils dated
12 and 13 May 1703
The National Archives, PROB 1/9/1-3

Pepys's final years were blighted by ill
health, but he remained mentally active
to the end. In 1701, he wrote his will,
dividing his estate between his nephews,
friends and servants. In May 1703, with
no hope of recovery, Pepys dictated two
lengthy codicils. These resolved the
matter of his library, which was held in
trust and eventually given to his *alma
mater*, Magdalene College, Cambridge.
Pepys died, aged seventy, on 26 May
that year. RB

LITERATURE: Tomalin, pp. 371–77.

The Scheame referred to in my foregoing Coddicil relating to the Completion & Settlement of my Library. viz.t

For the Completion of my Library

I will and require that the following particulars be carefully punctually and with all possible diligence and dispatch performed and executed by my Nephew John Jackson after my decease viz.t

1.st That a Generall Review be taken of my said Library compared with its Catalogue and all out lying Books immediately lookt up and put into their places

2.dly That my Collection of Stamps or any others which shall then be depending be finisht bound placed and properly entred in my Catalogue and Alphabet

3.dly That all setts of Books contained in my said Library under the name of Growing Facts be compleated to the time of my death and roome provided for the further Volumes of my Lord Clarendon's History now under the Presse

4.ly That Gronovius's sett of Greek antiquitys lately publisht be forthwith bought and added thereto and any other Kenderable Kenderata supposed at the discretion of my said Nephew with the advice of his learned friends

5.ly That this being done my said Library be closed and from thenceforward noe Additions made thereto

6. That the whole number and bulk of my Books being soe asertained one or more new Presses be provided for the convenient containing them soe as to be neither too much crowded nor stand too loose

7.ly That my Arms or Crest or Cypher be stampt in Gold on the outsides of the Covers of every Book admitting thereof

8.ly That their placing as to heighth be strictly Review'd and where found requiring it more nicely adjusted

9.ly That noe roome as their order stand be their fixt the whole be now Numbred a-new from the lowest to the highest

10.ly That this new Number be stampt on a peece of Red Leather fixt at the head of the Back of every Book where now the gilt paper is

11.ly That all the Additaments with their new Numbers be then properly inserted in the Bodys of the Catalogue and Alphabet and there elegantly and finally transcribed to remaine unalterable and forever accompany the said Library

12. Lastly that as farr as any roome shall be left for further improvements or Embellishments to my Books by Ruling Elegant Writing or Indexing the same be done at the discretion and conveniency of my said Nephew

For the further Settlement & Preservation of my said Library after the Death of my Nephew John Jackson. I doe hereby Declare.

That could I be sure of a Constant Succession of Heires from my said Nephew Qualified like himselfe for the Use of such a Library I should not entertaine a thought of its ever being alienated from them. But this uncertainty rendered with the infinite Paines and time and Cost employed in my Collecting Methodizing and reducing the same to the State wherein it now is I cannot but be greatly Sollicitous that all possible provision should be made for its unalterable preservation and perpetuall Security against the ordinary ffate of such Collections falling into the hands of an incompetent Heire and thereof of being said dissipated or imbezelled. And since it has pleased God to visit me in a manner that leaves little appearance of being my selfe restored to a condition of concerting the necessary measures for attaining these ends I must and doe with great Confidence rely upon the sincerity and discretion of my Executor and of Nephew for putting in execution the powers given them by my forementioned Coddicil relating thereto requiring that the same be brought to a determination in twelve Months time after my decease and that speciall regard be had therein to the following particulars which I declare to be my present thoughts and presuming Authorities in this matter viz.t

1.st That after the death of my said Nephew my said Library be placed and forever setled in one of our Universities and rather in that of Cambridge than Oxford.

2.dly Onis setled in a private Colledge there than the Publick Library.

3.ly And of the Colledges of Trinity or Magdalen preferably to all others

4.ly And of these two, theirs precious, rather in the later, for the sake of my owne and Nephew's Education therein

5.ly That in which soever of the two it is a faire Roome be provided therein on purpose for it and wholly and solely appropriated thereto

6.ly And if in Trinity that the said Roome be contiguous to and have communication with the New Library there

7.ly And if in Magdalen that it be in the New Building there and any part thereof at my Nephew's Election

8.ly That the said Library be continued in it's present forme and noe other Books mixt therewith save what my Nephew may add to them of his owne

9.ly That the said Roome and Books soe placed and adjusted be called by the name of Bibliotheca Pepysiana.

10.ly That this Bibliotheca Pepysiana be under the sole power and custody of the Master of the Colledge for the time being, who shall neither himselfe convey nor suffer to be conveyed by others any of the said Books from thence to any other place except to his owne Lodge in the said Colledge nor have more than ten of them at a time and that of there also a strict Entry be made and account kept and of the time of their being soe taken out and returned in a book to be provided and remaine in the said Library for that only purpose

11.ly That before my said Library be put into the possession of either of the said Colledges that Colledge for which it shall be designed first enter into Covenants for performing

12.ly And that for asort further security therein this two Colledges of Trinity Magdalen have a temporall Check upon one another And that the Colledge which shall be in present possession of the said Library be subject to an Annuall Visitation from the other and to the forfeiture thereof to the like possession and Use of the other upon Conviction of any breach of these said Covenants

M. E. J. Hughes

The Diary and its
Later Life

John Jackson Esqr.
Nephew of Samuel Pepys
Engraving, by Robert Cooper (d. 1828)
after Sir Godfrey Kneller, 1825.
Pepys's library came to Magdalene
only after the death of Jackson, who
completed it according to Pepys's
instructions.

National Maritime Museum, PBE9953/6.

When Pepys died in Will Hewer's Clapham home in May 1703, he left his collection of books to his old Cambridge college, Magdalene. It took twenty-one years for the bequest to be fulfilled. The 3,000 volumes finally arrived in 1724 to be housed in a smart first-floor gallery, behind the elegant neoclassical façade and stylish dormers of the college's most recently completed building. Superb though this collection was, there can be little doubt that the books he valued most in his extensive library were the six Morocco leather-bound volumes which contained his diary. He had written these 3,102 pages often by candlelight, late at night, in a small, carefully spaced hand across a period of nine-and-a-half years from the restoration of Charles II, through national disasters and triumphs, through the ups and downs of married life, the scientific discoveries of the Royal Society, and the meals, drinks and conversations of myriad taverns and coffeehouses. He had rescued them from the Great Fire as it terrifyingly advanced on his home in Seething Lane and sent them to Bethnal Green for safekeeping. He had carefully preserved them and kept them with him for the thirty-four years after he discontinued recording his daily life in them.

Magdalene College gratefully received the magnificent library, but was perhaps not equally appreciative of the uniqueness of the diary volumes it contained. These lay virtually unexamined for eighty years – a visiting tutor with an expertise in shorthand took an interest in 1728, but recorded in a letter that he was precluded from making progress by the ignorance of his unnamed host, who did not know his way around the collection, and his own reluctance to be a burden on the librarian. In the end, it was the publication of another such diary almost a hundred years later which resulted in the fame that Samuel Pepys's journal (as he called it) now enjoys. In 1818, the diary of the scholar and collector, John Evelyn, was published. A friend of Pepys, and someone who had advised him on his library, Evelyn, in precise and more formal prose, offered early nineteenth-century readers an astute, evocative and analytical view of the great events of the seventeenth century. The book was a huge success.

The discovery and publication of Evelyn's diary got the Fellows of Magdalene thinking: surely they, too, had an old diary from that period? The Master's uncle, Lord Grenville (who had been Foreign Secretary under William Pitt, the Younger), took a look, and advised that it might be worth commissioning someone to transcribe the diary. A harassed and impecunious scholar, who had come up to St John's College with a wife and young family, was identified: John Smith was to be paid the relatively handsome sum of £200 for the few months' work. It is clear that Grenville realized that the diary was not in a secret cipher but in a known shorthand and provided a key of sorts; but Smith did not receive all the information he needed: having drawn a blank in his enquiries with various experts in stenography, he set about decoding the writing more or less from first principles. It was towards the end of the painstaking process that Smith realized that the pamphlet from which Pepys learned his shorthand, Shelton's *Tachygraphy*, was on the shelf above the diary. Smith's transcription, in fifty-four volumes of longhand, concludes with a double page. On the right were Pepys's own final words on 31 May 1669: he will give up the diary as he fears he is losing his sight. On the left was Smith's signing off on 6 April 1822: Pepys's volumes have been put into 9,325 pages, '*deciphered ... by me, John Smith*'.

The transcription was edited and published by the Master of Magdalene's brother, Lord Braybrooke, in 1825. It included only about a quarter of what Pepys had written. Soon, a new edition was planned, this time edited by the mathematician and former President of Magdalene, Mynors Bright, who had retired through ill-health. It appeared between 1875 and 1879. This too was heavily bowdlerized: passages of sexual fantasy, descriptions of erotic experimentation and accounts of fumbles and gropes in the backs of carriages were all silently omitted. At least Mynors Bright immediately recognized the shorthand as Shelton's and went to the trouble of learning it in order to produce an independent transcription. When Henry Wheatley, a genuine expert on Pepys and an antiquarian of some note, produced a third version, published from 1893 to 1896, based on Bright's work but expanded, squeamishness persisted, though less rigorously applied and with ellipses (...) to hint at the omissions. Wheatley, who also replaced offensive words with terms more acceptable to Victorian readers, defended his approach in his preface, requesting the reader to 'have faith in the editor'. In some ways, drawing attention to the excisions

The Revd John Smith
Oil on canvas, English school, *c.*1840.

Magdalene College, Cambridge,
College portrait no. 119.

The last pages of John Smith's
transcription of Pepys's diary
1822.

Magdalene College, Cambridge,
Smith Transcription/54.

perpetuated a myth that the diary was much more sexy, explicit and lurid than it really was.

As Pepys's reputation continued to grow in the early decades of the twentieth century, the Fellows of Magdalene occasionally gave thought to another new edition. The grand announcement of a project to edit the diary in its entirety appeared in *The Times Literary Supplement* in 1933. But the Second World War intervened: the project's editor, the Pepys Librarian Francis Turner, was a legendary flying ace of the Great War who promptly re-enlisted, and there was no further progress. And always the old question as to whether to translate the naughty bits of the diary lurked behind discussions in the college. The Obscene Publications Act of 1959 changed the way these matters were considered: Fellows and scholars who commanded the respect of the wider public, as well as the college, now supported a complete version. C. S. Lewis, a professorial Fellow at Magdalene and a household name, could see no reason for censorship in a new edition. The final impetus was given by the *Lady Chatterley* trial in 1960, when Penguin Books were prosecuted under the Obscene Publications Act for publication of D. H. Lawrence's *Lady Chatterley's Lover*. The trial once and for all associated the desire to keep the erotic from the public gaze with arrogance and class: the mocking public response to the prosecution's earnest question, 'Is it a book that you would even wish your wife or your servants to read?' put an end to autocratic bowdlerization.

Eventually, a fine and energetic scholar was appointed to the project by the College: Robert Latham, who had careful and informed editions of seventeenth-century political papers already to his name, was commissioned to work with the famous American Pepysian William Matthews. The appointment of Latham was a game-changer. The Latham–Matthews edition began publication in 1970 and was completed (with Companion and Index) by Latham alone in 1983, after the death of Matthews in 1975. The project enjoyed the support of a number of other seventeenth-century experts, not least Richard Luckett, who would himself become Pepys Librarian after Latham's retirement and who knew about music, the theatre, architecture, shipbuilding, book buying – all those areas of life which Pepys himself so valued. They helped to compile the twelve volumes of the Diary including the Companion and Index volumes, which concluded the edition – an invaluable resource for scholars and for the general reader.

Yet the diary never seems to stand still: there are now numerous ways of getting a fix of Pepys. Recordings of the diary being read aloud are popular, as are BBC radio dramatizations and online versions. What would Pepys have made of this? I think he would not have been much surprised by the importance of his words for everyday readers and for scholars alike. He knew the value of his diary. He relished, as we do, its vivid detail, its care, and its carelessness.

Clerkenwell

Ely

Charter House

Holborne

Holborne

LINCOLNS INN FEILDS

Lincolnes Inn Feilds

St Gyles's Feilds

Fleete Street

Serjeants Inn

Pall-mall

Military Yard

Couent Garden

Padle Wharf

Blackfriers

THE

Durham house

Exchange

Temple Staire

Chal: Cross

Yorke house

Whitefall house

Salisbury house

Worster house

Scotland Yd

Durham house

Yorke house

Bun hill

Dese Paßer begrypt
een halve Engelsche Myle,
is een quartier ure gaens synde
ses van dese mate een gemene
Duytsche Myle van 15 in een graedt
synde 1½ Vre gaens.

Artillery
Yard

Bedlem

GRENT TOE

VERSI

Cheap

St. Paulus

TOWRSRAT

Tower hill

Dou gate

Billings Gate

Custom house

DE TOUWR

The   Tower

MESIS   F L U.

Bears garden   Winchester house   Batel bridge

Dead
mans
place

Horse Downe

Artillery
Yard

Notes

Samuel Pepys, Renaissance Man
Claire Tomalin
1 Pepys to Evelyn, 7 August 1700, in de la Bédoyère, p. 274.
2 *Diary*, III, 221.
3 Kate Loveman has checked the baptismal record of Jane Edwards (b. Birch), which is for June 1641. Jane's age is often miscalculated from her marriage licence of 1669, which states she was 'about twenty-four' and her husband twenty-five. But Jane lied about her age when she married a younger man.
4 *Diary*, I, 317.

Samuel Pepys: A Scholar and a Gentleman
M. E. J. Hughes
1 The National Archives, PROB 11/132. Will proven 26 September 1618.
2 The 200-year-old religious institution for the support of the poor was transformed into a school on the suppression of chantries and hospitals in 1547.
3 Tomalin, p. 21.
4 Huntingdonshire Archives KHAC4/4554/1/2.
5 PL941(2).
6 Oxford, Bodleian Library, MS Rawlinson, A. 194: 262–63.
7 PL2981–83.
8 PL1236.
9 My thanks to Cambridge University Library for access to their copy of the catalogue. The volume donated by Pepys was a famous Greek text from around the first decade AD (in Isaac Casaubon's standard Latin edition).
10 Milton, p. 8.
11 Hoole, p. 217.
12 PL2948–53.
13 Casaubon, p. 179.
14 *Diary*, III, 131.
15 McDonnell, *Registers*, p. xxiv. A 'fellmonger' dealt in hides or skins.
16 Hoole, p. 310.
17 A Sizar was an undergraduate who received financial support from the college and had menial duties.
18 Heywood and Wright, II, 402–03. The queen mentioned was Henrietta Maria, and a Catholic.
19 Morgan, pp. 464–65.
20 See David Hoyle's account in Cunich et al., p. 126.
21 By Pepys's day, the curriculum at Magdalene had already inspired a recent alumnus to establish a university halfway across the world. Henry Dunster graduated BA c.1630. After a brief teaching career, he became the first President of Harvard College.
22 Duport instructed his students to read 'the best and of the best note'. See Costello, p. 63.
23 Barrow, IX, xxvi.

24 For an account of Winstanley, see Wheale, p. 135.
25 PL293(1).
26 *Diary*, I, 221.
27 Tomalin, p. 45.
28 *The Young Clerk's Tutor* by J. H. [i.e., John Hawkins], 1682, offers aid to the novice secretary.
29 *Diary*, I, 222.
30 Rowse, p. 16.

Pepys and the Worlds of Medicine
Mark Jenner
1 Pepys, *Private Correspondence*, II, 311–12.

The Dissolute Court and Retribution
Tim Harris
1 *Diary*, VII, 267–68.
2 Malcolm, IV, 74.
3 Porter, pp. 70–72.
4 *Diary*, VII, 276.
5 Hall, p. xxiii.
6 Hanson, pp. 326–28.
7 Vincent, pp. 30–31.
8 *Diary*, VI, 208; Keeble, pp. 159–60; http://www.nationalarchives.gov.uk/education/resources/great-plague/.
9 Evelyn, *Diary*, III, 462; Malcolm, IV, 79.
10 Clarendon, II, 291.
11 *By the King. A Proclamation For a General Fast through England and Wales, and the Town of Barwick upon Tweed, on Wednesday the Tenth of October Next* (London, 1666).
12 *Diary*, II, 167, 170.
13 Cited in Spurr, 'Perjury, Profanity and Politics', p. 37.
14 *Diary*, VI, 210.
15 'Fourth Advice to a Painter', in Lord et al., I, 146.
16 *Diary*, VIII, 378.
17 *Diary*, I, 122.
18 Harris, *London Crowds*, pp. 38–39; Harris, *Restoration*, pp. 1–4, 44.
19 Raine, p. 83.
20 Cited in Harris, *London Crowds*, p. 61.
21 'Eleanor Gwyn', *ODNB*.
22 Spurr, *England in the 1670s*, p. 204.
23 Wilson, p. 63.
24 Lord et al., I, 424.
25 Clarendon, I, 591.
26 Bayley, pp. 3–4.
27 The National Archives, SP 29/180, f. 63.
28 Parke, p. 6.
29 Vincent, pp. 47, 62, 63, 67, 78–79, 198; 'Thomas Vincent', *ODNB*.
30 *Diary*, III, 292–93.
31 Allestree, p. 243.
32 Burnet, I, 453.
33 Sancroft, pp. 19, 21–23.
34 Evelyn, *Diary*, III, 421.
35 Hardy, pp. 27–29.
36 Killigrew, pp. 23–27, 29, 31.

Pepys and the Restoration Theatre
Warren Chernaik
1 *Diary*, IX, 13.
2 *Diary*, III, 209.
3 *Diary*, III, 294.
4 Nicoll, p. 293.
5 *Diary*, II, 58.
6 Thomson, p. 10.
7 Cited in Langhans, p. 1; Nicoll, p. 293.
8 *Diary*, VIII, 55–56.
9 *Diary*, IV, 182; V, 2.
10 Van Lennep, p. xxxviii; Langhans, p. 11.
11 Davenant, pp. 2–3, 9. The drawings, by John Webb, illustrate the opera's first production, before an invited audience at Rutland House in London in 1656.
12 Thomas, pp. 94–99; Loftis et al., pp. 95–108.
13 Dobson, p. 41.
14 *Diary*, V, 230; IX, 395.
15 *Diary*, II, 161; IV, 162.
16 Downes, pp. 51–52.
17 Sorelius, pp. 176–77.
18 *Diary*, VIII, 171; cf. VII, 423.
19 *Diary*, VIII, 7.
20 Spencer, pp. 112, 116, 117.
21 *Diary*, VIII, 521–22; IX, 48.
22 *Diary*, IV, 6; III, 20.
23 Downes, p. 53.
24 *Diary*, III, 39.
25 *Diary*, IV, p. 8; VIII, 387.
26 *Diary*, IX, 54.
27 *Diary*, I, 224; cf. II, 7.
28 Howe, pp. 30–36, 37–65; Dryden, p. 117.
29 *Diary*, VIII, 463.
30 *Diary*, IX, 189.
31 *Diary*, IX, 20.
32 Behn, II, 210.
33 *Diary*, VIII, 91.
34 *Diary*, VIII, 594.
35 Etherege, II, 288. Sir Car Scroope's prologue to Etherege's play makes a similar point: 'For Heav'n be thankt, 'tis not so wise an Age / But your own Follies may supply the Stage' (II, 185).
36 *Diary*, III, 295–96.
37 *Diary*, IX, 2.

Stuart Portraiture
Catharine MacLeod
1 *Diary*, VII, 44.
2 *Diary*, III, 230; VI, 359.

'... and so to the office': Pepys at Work
James Davey

1 *Diary*, VI, 285.
2 *Diary*, X, 295; Rodger, p. 97; Tanner, vol. 12, 17–29; Knighton, *Pepys and the Navy*, pp. 27–31
3 *Diary*, III, 171.
4 Rodger, pp. 33–49, 95.
5 *Diary*, IV, 304; Knighton, *Pepys and the Navy*, pp. 51–53; Rodger, p. 98.
6 Tanner, vol. 12, 31–32; Rodger, p. 99.
7 *Diary*, VI, 255.
8 Tanner, vol. 12, 64–65.
9 Rodger, pp. 106–7.
10 *Diary*, V, 137.
11 *Diary*, VII, 102.
12 *Diary*, VII, 122.
13 Lambert, pp. 64–71; *Diary*, VIII, 262.
14 *Diary*, VIII, 262.
15 *Diary*, IX, 102–04; Rodger, p. 101.
16 Rodger, p. 103; Tanner, vol. 12, 39–48.
17 Cited Ranft, p. 373.
18 Ranft, pp. 268–375.
19 Tanner, vol. 12, 679–702.
20 Davies, 'Pepys and the Admiralty Commission', p. 51; Tanner, vol. 12, 679–702; Ranft, p. 373.
21 Tanner, vol. 13, 26–54.
22 Davies, 'Navy, Parliament and Political Crisis'.
23 Cited in Pepys, *Memoires*, 'Introduction' by Davies, p. xiii.
24 Tanner, vol. 14, 47–61, 261–63.
25 Knighton, *Pepys and the Navy*, pp. 160–61.
26 Pepys, *Memoires*, 'Introduction' by Davies, pp. v–viii.
27 Hattendorf.
28 Rodger, p. 110; Hattendorf, p. 10.
29 *Cobbett's Annual Register*, 12 March 1803, p. 393.

Pepys, Tangier and Islam
Margarette Lincoln

1 *Diary*, II, 33.
2 *Diary*, VIII, 585.
3 *Diary*, IV, 319.
4 Lincoln, pp. 420–22.
5 *Diary*, IV, 349.
6 Pepys, *Tangier Papers*, p. 46.
7 Pepys, *Tangier Papers*, p. 21.
8 Pepys, *Tangier Papers*, p. 30.
9 *Diary*, IX, 298.
10 Macaulay, III, 64.
11 Bryant, *Pepys: Saviour of the Navy*, p. 216.

Pepys in Greenwich
Pieter van der Merwe

1 *Diary*, III, 111. The yacht was probably the *Catherine*: in Pepys, the 'King's house' or 'Greenwich-house' usually signifies 'the palace' but (given its increasing dereliction at this point), might here mean Inigo Jones's Queen's House.
2 *Diary*, VII, 141. The King's Head was in Stableyard Street, roughly across the south side of modern Cutty Sark Gardens.
3 *Diary*, III, 63; IV, 99. The Royal Observatory stands on the foundations of the then ruinous 'Castle', a largely Tudor residential lodge that preceded it.
4 Pepys to Evelyn, 7 November 1694, in de la Bedoyère, pp. 253–54. Pepys, though supportive, rightly thought that only Parliamentary funding would achieve the project, as later proved the case.
5 *Diary*, V, 75.
6 *Diary*, IX, 485.
7 *Diary*, II, 12.
8 *Diary*, VI, 338. Anne Hooker had married John Lethieullier, a wealthy merchant.
9 Now Heathgate House, no. 66 Crooms Hill.
10 *Diary*, VI, 339.
11 Now The Grange, no. 52 Crooms Hill, but much rebuilt.

Samuel Pepys, 'The Right Hand of the Navy'

1 *Diary*, VI, 89.

Trade and a Consumer Culture

1 Pepys to Evelyn, 13 November 1690, in de la Bédoyère, p. 226.
2 *Diary*, I, 129.
3 Cited in Boyer, p. 36.

Pepys and the New Science
Robert Iliffe

1 Amusingly, Pepys's short entry for the same day was dominated by his criticism of Povey's alleged incompetence as an accountant.
2 Tomalin, p. 361.
3 *Diary*, VIII, 236.
4 See Tomalin, p. 56.
5 Tomalin, pp. 340–41.
6 See Nicolson, *Pepys' Diary and the New Science*.
7 Pepys, *Naval Minutes*, p. 390.

A New Visible World
Richard Dunn

1 Dunn, pp. 21–54.
2 Dunn, pp. 55–58.
3 Nicolson, *Science and Imagination*, pp. 161–69.
4 Hooke, p. 4.
5 Hooke, p. 8.
6 *Diary*, V, 240.
7 *Diary*, VI, 18.
8 Power, Preface, sig. 1.
9 Hooke, Preface, sig. 4.
10 Dunn, pp. 50–54; Haynes, pp. 35–49.
11 Shadwell, p. 22.
12 Lloyd; Haynes, pp. 45–47.
13 Nicolson, *Science and Imagination*, p. 169.

Pepys and Religion
Clare Jackson

1 *Diary*, I, 280.
2 *Diary*, I, 76.
3 *Diary*, V, 235.
4 *Diary*, I, 295; III, 47.
5 *Diary*, III, 235.
6 *Diary*, III, 178.
7 *Diary*, VIII, 51.
8 *Diary*, VI, 87.
9 *Diary*, IX, 211.
10 *Diary*, III, 43.
11 *Diary*, IV, 92–93.
12 *Diary*, V, 97.
13 *Diary*, VIII, 362.
14 *Diary*, III, 72.
15 *Diary*, IV, 259.
16 *Diary*, IV, 11–12, 96, 190.
17 *Diary*, IX, 300.
18 Wright, sig. A3v.
19 *Diary*, IX, 554.
20 *Diary*, III, 134–35.
21 *Diary*, III, 292–93.
22 *Diary*, IV, 372.
23 *Diary*, IX, 379.
24 *Diary*, II, 12.
25 *Diary*, IV, 369.
26 *Diary*, VII, 164.
27 *Diary*, VII, 215.
28 *Diary*, VIII, 338.
29 Pepys, *Letters*, 1656–1703, pp. 104–05.
30 Grey, II, 426.
31 Pepys, *Letters*, 1656–1703, p. 127.
32 Pepys, *Letters*, 1656–1703, p. 129.
33 Pepys, *Letters*, 1656–1703, p. 135.
34 Grey, II, 426.
35 *Diary*, III, 54 n. 1. Mills also evidently supplied similar confirmation regarding regular communion when Pepys had sought to become a Parliamentary candidate in the early 1670s.
36 *Diary*, VII, 99.
37 *Diary*, IX, 126.
38 *Diary*, VIII, 588.
39 *Diary*, IX, 338; and see V, 92 n. 2.
40 Loveman, 'Pepys and "Discourses touching Religion"', p. 81.
41 Cited in Tomalin, pp. 379–80.

Pepys's 'Retirement'
Kate Loveman

1 *Second Discovery*, p. 2.
2 British Library, Add. MS 78680, item 17, f. 2r; Pepys, *Private Correspondence*, II, 248.
3 Pepys, *Letters and Second Diary*, p. 244.
4 Pepys, *Letters and Second Diary*, p. 329.
5 British Library, Add. MS 78462, f. 12v; Pepys, *Private Correspondence*, I, 177, 261.
6 Evelyn to Pepys, 26 August 1689, in de la Bédoyère, p. 188.
7 Pepys, *Memoires*, p. 6.
8 Pepys, *Memoires*, 'Introduction' by Davies, pp. ix–xiv.
9 *Paper IV, Mr. Pepys to the President, and Governors of Christ-Hospital* [1699], f. B1r–B1v, reproduced in Pepys, *Mr. Pepys*.
10 *Paper II, Mr. Pepys to the Lord Mayor* [1698], f. A1r, A1v, reproduced in Pepys, *Mr. Pepys*.
11 Pepys, *Private Correspondence*, I, 176.
12 *Memoranda ... Relating to the Royal Hospitals*, p. 46.
13 McKitterick, VII, part ii.
14 The National Archives, PROB 1/9, Will of Samuel Pepys, 'The Scheame referred to in my foregoing Codicil relating to the Completion & Settlement of my Library'.

Regime Change and Pepys's Legacy

1 British Library, RP 694/1.

Sources and Further Reading

The place of publication is London, unless otherwise stated.

Abbreviations

Diary *The Diary of Samuel Pepys: A New and Complete Transcription*, ed. by Robert Latham and William Matthews, 11 vols (1970–83)

Letters [Samuel Pepys], *Letters and the Second Diary of Samuel Pepys*, ed. by R. G. Howarth (1932)

ODNB Matthew, H. C. G., and Brian Harrison (eds), *The Oxford Dictionary of National Biography*, www.oxforddnb.com

PL Pepys Library, Magdalene College, Cambridge

Private Correspondence [Samuel Pepys], *Private Correspondence and Miscellaneous Papers of Samuel Pepys 1679–1703*, ed. by J. R. Tanner, 2 vols (New York, [1926])

Ackroyd, Peter, *London: The Biography* (2000)

Allestree, Richard, *Eighteen Sermons, Whereof Fifteen Preached before the King. The rest Upon Publick Occasions...* (1669)

Andrade, E. N. da C., 'Samuel Pepys and the Royal Society', *Notes and Records of the Royal Society of London*, 18 (1963), 82–93

Archer, M., *English Delftware / Engels Delfts aardewerk* (Amsterdam, 1973)

Barber, Richard, *Samuel Pepys Esquire* (1970)

Barrow, Isaac, *Theological Works*, ed. by A. Napier, 9 vols (Cambridge, 1859)

Bayley, Charles, *The Causes of God's Wrath Against England; And a Faithfull Warning From the Lord to Speedy Repentance; Fore-told by, and Delivered in a Letter to the King, Date the 4th of the 7th Month, 1663* (1665)

Behn, Aphra, *The Works of Aphra Behn*, ed. by Montague Summers, 6 vols (New York, 1967)

Birchwood, Matthew, *Staging Islam in England: Drama and Culture, 1640–1685* (Cambridge, 2007)

Blankert, Albert, *Ferdinand Bol (1616–1680): Rembrandt's Pupil* (Doornspijk, 1982)

Bowen, H. V., J. McAleer and R. J. Blyth, *Monsoon Traders: The Maritime World of the East India Company* (2011)

Boyer, M., *Japanese Export Lacquer from the Seventeenth Century in the National Museum of Denmark* (Copenhagen, 1959)

Bryant, Arthur, *Samuel Pepys: The Man in the Making*, 2nd edn (1947)

———, *Samuel Pepys: The Saviour of the Navy*, 2nd edn (1949)

———, *Samuel Pepys: The Years of Peril*, 2nd edn (1949)

Burnet, Gilbert, *The History of My Own Time*, ed. by Osmund Airy, 2 vols (Oxford, 1897–1900)

Bussey, David, *John Colet's Children: The Boys of St Paul's School in Later Life, 1509–2009* (Oxford, 2009)

Casaubon, Meric, *Generall Learning: A Seventeenth-Century Treatise on the Formation of the General Scholar by Meric Casaubon*, ed. by Richard Serjeantson (Cambridge, 1999)

Clarendon, Edward Hyde, Earl of, *The Life of Edward Earl of Clarendon ... in Which Is Included, A Continuation of His History of the Grand Rebellion ...*, 2 vols (Oxford, 1857)

Clifton, G., *Directory of British Scientific Instrument Makers, 1550–1851* (1995)

Colley, Linda, *Captives: Britain, Empire and the World, 1600–1850* (2002)

Collinge, J. M., *Office-Holders in Modern Britain, vol. 7, Navy Board Officials, 1660–1832* (1978)

Costello, W. T., *The Scholastic Curriculum at Early Seventeenth-Century Cambridge* (Cambridge, MA, 1958)

Coury, Ralph M., and R. Kevin Lacey (eds), *Writing Tangier* (New York, 2009)

Cunich, Peter, David Hoyle, Eamon Duffy and Ronald Hyam, *A History of Magdalene College Cambridge, 1428–1988* (Cambridge, 1994)

Darley, Gillian, *John Evelyn: Living for Ingenuity* (New Haven, CT, and London, 2006)

Davenant, Sir William, *The Siege of Rhodes: The First and Second Part...* (1663)

Davies, J. D., 'The Navy, Parliament and Political Crisis in the Reign of Charles II', *The Historical Journal*, 36:2 (1993), 271–88

———, 'Pepys and the Admiralty Commission of 1679–84', *Historical Research*, 62 (1989), 34–53

Dawson, A., *English and Irish Delftware, 1570–1840* (2010)

Dekker, E., *Globes at Greenwich: A Catalogue of the Globes and Armillary Spheres in the National Maritime Museum, Greenwich* (Oxford, 1999)

de la Bédoyère, Guy (ed.), *Particular Friends: The Correspondence of Samuel Pepys and John Evelyn* (Woodbridge, 2005)

Dickinson, Philip G. M., and A. Jamieson, *The History of Huntingdon Grammar School, Written on the 400th Anniversary of the Founding of the School* (Huntingdon, 1965)

Dicks, S., *The King's Blood: Relics of King Charles I* (2010)

Dobson, Michael, 'Adaptations and Revivals', in Deborah Payne Fisk (ed.), *The Cambridge Companion to English Restoration Theatre* (Cambridge, 2003), 40–51

Downes, John, *Roscius Anglicanus*, ed. by Judith Milhous and Robert D. Hume (Bath, 1987)

Dryden, John, *The Poems and Fables of John Dryden*, ed. by James Kinsley (Oxford, 1962)

Dunn, Richard, *The Telescope: A Short History* (2009)

Etherege, George, *The Dramatic Works of Sir George Etherege*, ed. by H. F. B. Brett-Smith, 2 vols (Oxford, 1927)

Evelyn, John, *The Diary of John Evelyn*, ed. by E. S. Beer, 6 vols (Oxford, 1955)

———, *A Discourse of Medals, Ancient and Modern...* (1697)

Gaschke, Jenny (ed.), *Turmoil and Tranquillity: The Sea through the Eyes of Dutch and Flemish Masters, 1550–1700* (2008)

Grey, Anchitell (ed.), *Debates of the House of Commons, from the Year 1667 to the Year 1694*, 10 vols (1763)

Griffiths, A., *The Print in Stuart Britain, 1603–1689* (1998)

Hall, A. Rupert, and A. D. C. Simpson, 'An Account of the Royal Society's Newton Telescope', *Notes and Records of the Royal Society of London*, 50:1 (1996), 1–11

Hall, George, *A Fast-Sermon, Preached to the Lords in the High-Court of Parliament ... Octob. 3, 1666...* (1666)

Hanson, Neil, *The Dreadful Judgement: The True Story of the Great Fire of London, 1666* (2001)

Hardy, Nathaniel, *Lamentation, Mourning, and Woe, Sighed Forth in a Sermon Preached...the Next Lords-Day after the Dismal Fire in the City of London* (1666)

Harris, Tim, *London Crowds in the Reign of Charles II: Politics and Propaganda from the Restoration to the Exclusion Crisis* (Cambridge, 1987)

———, *Restoration: Charles II and His Kingdoms, 1660–1685* (2005)

Hattendorf, John, 'Introduction' to Josiah Burchett, *A Complete History of the Most Remarkable Transactions at Sea* (Delmar, NY, 1995), 9–24

Haynes, Roslynn D., *From Faust to Strangelove: Representations of the Scientist in Western Literature* (Baltimore, MD, and London, 1994)

Heywood, James, and Thomas Wright (eds), *Cambridge University Transactions during the Puritan Controversies of the 16th and 17th Centuries*, 2 vols (1854)

Higton, H. K., *Sundials at Greenwich: A Catalogue of the Sundials, Nocturnals and Horary Quadrants in the National Maritime Museum, Greenwich* (Oxford, 2002)

Homer, R. F., 'Pewter in the British Museum', *The Journal of the Pewter Society*, 6:4 (1988), 118–28

Hooke, Robert, *Micrographia: or Some Physiological Descriptions of Minute Bodies Made by Magnifying Glasses with Observations and Inquiries thereupon* (1665)

Hoole, Charles, *A New Discovery of the Old Art of Teaching Schoole* (London, 1660)

Hornstein, Sari R., *The Restoration Navy and English Foreign Trade, 1674–1688* (Aldershot, 1991)

Howe, Elizabeth, *The First English Actresses: Woman and Drama, 1660–1700* (Cambridge, 1992)

Howse, Derek, 'Some Early Tidal Diagrams', *Mariner's Mirror*, 79 (1993), 27–43

Howse, Derek, Norman J. W. Thrower and David B. Quinn (eds), *A Buccaneer's Atlas: Basil Ringrose's South Sea Waggoner, a Sea Atlas and Sailing Directions of the Pacific Coast of the Americas, 1682* (Berkeley, CA, 1992)

Ingamells, John, *Later Stuart Portraits, 1685–1714* (2009)

Jaffer, Amin, *Luxury Goods from India: The Art of the Indian Cabinet-Maker* (2002)

Keeble, N. H., *The Restoration: England in the 1660s* (Oxford, 2002)

Killigrew, Henry, *A Sermon Preach'd Before the King The first Sunday of Advent, 1666* (1666)

Knighton, C. S., *Pepys and the Navy* (Stroud, 2003)

——— (ed.), *Catalogue of the Pepys Library at Magdalene College Cambridge, Supplementary Series, vol. 1, Census of Printed Books* (Cambridge, 2004)

Knights, Mark, *Representation and Misrepresentation in later Stuart Britain: Partisanship and Political Culture* (2005)

Kusukawa, Sachiko, 'The Historia Piscium (1686)', *Notes and Records of the Royal Society of London*, 54 (2000), 179–97

Lambert, Andrew, *Warfare at Sea in the Age of Sail* (2000)

Langhans, Edward, 'The Theatre', in Deborah Payne Fisk (ed.), *The Cambridge Companion to English Restoration Theatre* (Cambridge, 2003), 1–18

Latham, Robert (general ed.), *Catalogue of the Pepys Library at Magdalene College Cambridge*, 7 vols (Woodbridge and Cambridge, 1978–94)

Lincoln, Margarette, 'Samuel Pepys and Tangier, 1662–1684', *Huntington Library Quarterly*, 77:4 (2014), 417–34

Lloyd, Claude, 'Shadwell and the Virtuosi', *Proceedings of the Modern Language Association*, 44 (1929), 472–94

Loftis, John, Richard Southern, Marion Jones and A. H. Scouten, *The Revels History of Drama in English*, vol. 5, 1660–1750 (1976)

Lord, George deForest, et al. (eds), *Poems on Affairs of State: Augustan Satirical Verse, 1660–1714*, 7 vols (New Haven, CT, 1963–75)

Loveman, Kate, 'Pepys in Print, 1660–1703', in *Oxford Handbooks Online* (New York)

———, 'Samuel Pepys and "Discourses touching Religion" under James II', *English Historical Review*, 127 (2012), 46–82

———, *Samuel Pepys and His Books: Reading, Newsgathering, and Sociability, 1660–1703* (Oxford, 2015)

Macaulay, Thomas Babington, *The History of England from the Accession of James II*, 5 vols (1863)

McDonnell, Michael, *The Annals of St Paul's School* (1959)

———, *The Registers of St Paul's School, 1509–1784* (1977)

McKitterick, David (ed.), *Catalogue of the Pepys Library at Magdalene College Cambridge*, vol. 7, parts i and ii: *Facsimile of Pepys's Catalogue* (Cambridge, 1991)

MacLeod, Catharine, and Julia Marciari Alexander (eds), *Painted Ladies: Women at the Court of Charles II* (New Haven, CT, and London, 2001)

Malcolm, James Peller, *Londinium Redivivum; or, An Antient History and Modern Description of London...*, 4 vols (1802–07)

Matar, Nabil I., *Islam in Britain, 1558–1685* (Cambridge, 1998)

———, *Turks, Moors, and Englishmen in the Age of Discovery* (New York, 1999)

Memoranda, References, and Documents Relating to the Royal Hospitals of the City of London ... (1836)

Millar, Oliver, *Sir Peter Lely, 1618–80* (1978)

———, *The Tudor, Stuart and Early Georgian Pictures in the Collection of Her Majesty the Queen*, 2 vols (1963)

Miller, Kathleen, 'Illustrations from the Wellcome Library: William Winstanley's Pestilential Poesies in *The Christians Refuge...*', *Medical History*, 55 (2011), 241–50

Milton, John, *Milton's Tractate on Education: A Facsimile Reprint from the Edition of 1673*, ed. by Oliver Browning (Cambridge, 1883)

Morgan, Victor, *A History of the University of Cambridge*, vol. 2, 1546–1750 (Cambridge, 2004)

Mörzer Bruyns, Willem, *Sextants at Greenwich: A Catalogue of the Mariner's Quadrants, Mariner's Astrolabes, Cross-staffs, Backstaffs, Octants, Sextants, Quintants, Reflecting Circles, and Artificial Horizons in the National Maritime Museum, Greenwich* (Oxford, 2009)

Nicoll, Allardyce, *A History of English Drama, 1660–1900*, vol. 1, *Restoration Drama 1660–1700* (Cambridge, 1952)

Nicolson, Marjorie, *Pepys' Diary and the New Science* (Charlottesville, VA, 1965)

———, *Science and Imagination* (Ithaca, NY, 1956)

Oates, J. C. T., and D. McKitterick, *Cambridge University Library: A History*, 2 vols (Cambridge, 1986)

Ollard, Richard, *Character Sketches: Samuel Pepys and His Circle* (2000)

Parke, James, *Another Trumpet Sounded In the Ears of the Inhabitants of England, Rulers, Priests and People That They Might Be Awakened...* (1667)

Pepys, Samuel, *Letters and the Second Diary of Samuel Pepys*, ed. by R. G. Howarth (1932)

———, *The Letters of Samuel Pepys, 1656–1703*, ed. by Guy de la Bédoyère (Woodbridge, 2006)

———, *Memoires of the Royal Navy, 1690*, ed. by J. D. Davies (Barnsley, 2010)

———, *Mr Pepys upon the State of Christ-Hospital*, ed. by Rudolf Kirk (Philadelphia, PA, 1935)

———, *Pepys's Later Diaries*, ed. by C. S. Knighton (Stroud, 2004)

———, *Private Correspondence and Miscellaneous Papers of Samuel Pepys, 1679–1703*, ed. by J. R. Tanner, 2 vols (1926)

———, *Samuel Pepys and the Second Dutch War: Pepys's Navy White Book and the Brooke House Papers*, ed. by Robert Latham (1995)

———, *Samuel Pepys's Naval Minutes*, ed. by J. R. Tanner (1926)

———, *The Tangier Papers of Samuel Pepys*, ed. by Edwin Chappell (1935)

Piacenti, Kirsten Aschengreen, and John Boardman, *Ancient and Modern Gems and Jewels in the Collection of Her Majesty The Queen* (2008)

Pincus, Steve, *1688: The First Modern Revolution* (New Haven, CT, and London, 2009)

Porter, Stephen, *The Great Fire of London* (Stroud, 1996)

Power, Henry, *Experimental Philosophy, In Three Books: Containing New Experiments Microscopical, Mercurial, Magnetical...* (1664)

Raine, James Jnr (ed.), *Depositions from the Castle of York Related to Offences Committed in the Northern Counties in the Seventeenth Century*, Surtees Society, 40 (Durham, 1861)

Ranft, B. McL., 'The Significance of the Political Career of Samuel Pepys', *Journal of Modern History*, 24:4 (1952), 366–75

Ratcliff, J. R., 'Samuel Morland and His Calculating Machines c. 1666: The Early Career of a Courtier-Inventor in Restoration London', *British Journal for the History of Science*, 40:2 (2007), 159–79

Reynolds, Graham, *The Sixteenth and Seventeenth-Century Miniatures in the Collection of Her Majesty the Queen* (1999)

Roberts, J. (ed.), *Royal Treasures: A Golden Jubilee Celebration* (2002)

Rodger, N. A. M., *The Command of the Ocean: A Naval History of Britain, 1649–1815* (2004)

Routh, E. M. G., *Tangier: England's Lost Atlantic Outpost, 1661–1684* (1912)

Rowse, A. L., 'Pepys, the Complete Gentleman', *Spectator*, 13 Sept. 1974, 16

Sancroft, William, *Lex Ignea: or The School of Righteousness* (1666)

Scarisbrick, D., *Jewellery in Britain 1066–1837: A Documentary, Social, Literary and Artistic Survey* (Wilby, 1994)

The Second Discovery of the Jacobite Plot: Shewing the Intreagues That Was Carrying on against the Government at the Cock-Match at Bathe... (1690)

Shadwell, Thomas, *The Virtuoso*, ed. by Marjorie Hope Nicolson and David Stuart Rhodes (1966)

Sharpe, Kevin, *Rebranding Rule: Images of Restoration and Revolution Monarchy, 1660–1714* (New Haven, CT, and London, 2013)

Slight, H. and J., *Chronicles of Portsmouth* (Oxford, 1828)

Smith, Eric J. G., 'Jacob Bodendeich', *Silver Society Journal*, 13 (2001), 66–80, and 14 (2002), 109–22

Smith, Thomas R., 'Manuscript and Printed Sea Charts in Seventeenth-Century London: The Case of the Thames School', in Norman J. W. Thrower (ed.), *The Compleat Plattmaker: Essays on Chart, Map, and Globe Making in England in the Seventeenth and Eighteenth Centuries* (Berkeley, CA, 1978), 45–100

Sorelius, Gunnar, 'The Rights of the Restoration Theatrical Companies in the Older Drama', *Studia Neophilologica*, 37 (1965), 176–77

Sotheby & Co., *Catalogue of the Well-Known Collection of Relics of Samuel Pepys* (1931)

Spencer, Christopher (ed.), *Five Restoration Adaptations of Shakespeare* (Urbana, IL, 1965)

Spurr, John, *England in the 1670s: 'This Masquerading Age'* (Oxford, 2000)

———, 'Perjury, Profanity and Politics', *The Seventeenth Century*, 8 (1993), 29–50

Tanner, J. R., 'The Administration of the Navy from the Restoration to the Revolution', in *English Historical Review*, 12 (1897), 17–66 and 679–710; 13 (1898), 26–54; 14 (1899), 47–70 and 261–89

Thomas, David (ed.), *Theatre in Europe: A Documentary History. Restoration and Georgian England, 1660–1780* (Cambridge, 1989)

Thomson, P., *The Cambridge Introduction to English Theatre 1600–1900* (Cambridge, 2006)

Tomalin, Claire, *Samuel Pepys: The Unequalled Self* (2002)

Turner, A., *Early Scientific Instruments: Europe, 1400–1800* (1987)

Tuttell, Thomas, *The Description and Uses of a New Contriv'd Eliptical Double Dial...* (1698)

Twigg, John, *The University of Cambridge and the English Revolution, 1625–1688* (Woodbridge, 1990)

van Beneden, B., and N. de Pooter (eds), *Royalist Refugees: William and Margaret Cavendish at the Rubenshuis* (Schoten, 2006)

van der Merwe, Pieter, *The Queen's House, Greenwich* (2012)

Van Lennep, William (ed.), *The London Stage, 1660–1800*, part 1, 1660–1700 (Carbondale, IL, 1965)

Vincent, Thomas, *God's Terrible Voice in the City...*, 5th edn (1667)

Vitkus, Daniel, *Turning Turk: English Theater and the Multicultural Mediterranean, 1530–1630* (New York and Basingstoke, 2003)

Waterhouse, E., *Painting in Britain, 1530–1790* (New Haven, CT, and London, 1994)

Weld, Charles Richard, 'History of the Mace Given to the Royal Society by King Charles the Second', *Proceedings of the Royal Society*, 5:64 (1846), 611–19

Wheale, Nigel, *Writing and Society: Literacy, Print and Politics in Britain, 1590–1660* (London and New York, 2000)

Wilson, John Harold, *Court Satires of the Restoration* (Columbus, OH, 1986)

Wright, Abraham, *Five Sermons, in Five several Styles; or Waies of Preaching* (1656)

Picture Credits

List of Contributors

Essay authors

Warren Chernaik is visiting Professor of English at King's College London, Emeritus Professor of English at the University of London and a Senior Research Fellow at the Institute of English Studies. He has written widely on Renaissance literature and poetry.

James Davey is Curator of Naval History at the National Maritime Museum. He co-curated, with Quintin Colville, the Museum's *Nelson, Navy, Nation* gallery (2012). His latest book is *In Nelson's Wake: The Navy and the Napoleonic Wars* (2015).

Richard Dunn is Senior Curator of the History of Science at the National Maritime Museum. He was lead curator for the Museum's *Ships, Clocks & Stars* exhibition (2014) and author, with Rebekah Higgitt, of the accompanying book, *Finding Longitude*.

Laura Gowing is Professor of Early Modern English History at King's College, London. Her work is concerned with the lives of women and, more broadly, social and cultural history. Her latest book is *Gender Relations in Early Modern England* (2012).

Tim Harris is Munro, Goodwin, Wilkinson Professor of European History at Brown University, Providence, Rhode Island. His latest book is *Rebellion: Britain's First Stuart Kings, 1567–1642* (2014).

M. E. J. Hughes is a Fellow at Magdalene College, where she directs studies in English works in the field of medieval satiric and political writings. She is also the Pepys Fellow Librarian, responsible for the college's two historic libraries.

Robert Iliffe is Professor of Intellectual History and History of Science at the University of Sussex. He is an expert on relations between science and religion, and on material culture and science. His latest book is *High Priest of Nature: The Heretical Life of Isaac Newton* (2013).

Clare Jackson is Senior Tutor of Trinity Hall, Cambridge and specializes in seventeenth-century Britain. In 2014 she presented a landmark series on 'The Stuarts' for BBC2. Her latest book is *Charles II* ('Penguin Monarchs' series, 2015).

Mark Jenner is Reader in Early Modern History at the University of York. He works on the social and cultural history of early modern England and is the author, with P. Wallis, of *Medicine and the Market in England and its Colonies, c.1450–1850* (2007).

Mark Knights is Professor of History at the University of Warwick and specializes in later Stuart Britain. His latest book is *The Devil in Disguise: Delusion, Deception and Fanaticism in the Early English Enlightenment* (2011).

Margarette Lincoln was Deputy Director at Royal Museums Greenwich, 2007–15. Her latest book is *British Pirates and Society, 1680–1730* (2014).

Kate Loveman is Senior Lecturer in English Literature 1600–1789 at the University of Leicester. She is the author of *Reading Fictions 1660–1740: Deception in English Literary and Political Culture* (2008) and numerous articles on Samuel Pepys.

Catharine MacLeod is Curator of Seventeenth-Century Portraits at the National Portrait Gallery. Her most recent publication is *The Lost Prince: The Life and Death of Henry Stuart*, with Timothy Wilks, Malcolm Smuts and Rab MacGibbon (2012).

Claire Tomalin, author and journalist, is known for her acclaimed biography of Samuel Pepys, among others. Her biography of Charles Dickens was adapted for the film *The Invisible Woman* in 2013. In 2014, she chaired the judges for the Samuel Johnson Prize for non-fiction.

Pieter van der Merwe, MBE, is the National Maritime Museum's General Editor and Greenwich Curator. He also writes on maritime art, portraiture, and theatre history.

Catalogue contributors

Joshua Newton, University of Cambridge and St Paul's Girls' School [JN]

From the National Maritime Museum

Katy Barrett, Curator of Art [KB]
Mike Bevan, Archivist [MB]
Robert Blyth, Senior Curator of World and Maritime History [RB]
James Davey, Curator of Naval History [JD]
Louise Devoy, Curator of the Royal Observatory Greenwich [LD]
Richard Dunn, Senior Curator of the History of Science [RD]
Gillian Hutchinson, Curator of the History of Cartography [GH]
Margarette Lincoln, Deputy Director [ML]
Kristian Martin, Exhibitions Curator [KM]
Amy Miller, Curator Emeritus [AM]
Barbara Tomlinson, Curator of Antiquities [BT]
Pieter van der Merwe, General Editor and Greenwich Curator [PvdM]

Index

Published to accompany the exhibition
Samuel Pepys: Plague, Fire, Revolution

National Maritime Museum,
Greenwich, London
20 November 2015–28 March 2016

Samuel Pepys: Plague, Fire, Revolution
© 2015 National Maritime Museum,
Greenwich, London

Designed by Adam Brown_01.02

First published in 2015 in hardcover
in the United States of America by
Thames & Hudson Inc., 500 Fifth Avenue,
New York, New York 10110

In association with Royal Museums
Greenwich, the group name for
the National Maritime Museum,
Royal Observatory Greenwich,
Queen's House and *Cutty Sark*
www.rmg.co.uk

thamesandhudsonusa.com

Library of Congress Catalog Card
Number 2015941269

ISBN 978-0-500-51814-4

Printed and bound in China by
C & C Offset Printing Ltd